THE ROYAL N
AND THE PALESTINE PATROL

NAVAL STAFF HISTORIES
Series Editor: Capt. Christopher Page
ISSN 1471-0757

Naval Staff Histories were produced after the Second World War in order to provide as a full an account of the various actions and operations as was possible at the time. In some cases the Histories were based on earlier Battle Summaries written much sooner after the event, and designed to provide more immediate assessments. The target audience for these Naval Staff Histories was largely serving officers; some of the volumes were originally classified, not to restrict their distribution but to allow the writers to be as candid as possible.

The Evacuation from Dunkirk: Operation 'Dynamo', 26 May–4 June 1940
With a preface by W. J. R. Gardner.

Naval Operations of the Campaign in Norway, April–June 1940
With a preface by David Brown

The Royal Navy and the Mediterranean, Vol. I: September 1939–October 1940
With an introduction by David Brown

The Royal Navy and the Mediterranean, Vol. II: November 1940–December 1941
With an introduction by David Brown

German Capital Ships and Raiders in World War II:
  Vol I. From Graf Spee to Bismarck, 1939–1941
  Vol. II. From Scharnhorst to Tirpitz, 1942–1944
With an introduction by Eric Grove

The Royal Navy and the Palestine Patrol
Ninian Stewart

THE ROYAL NAVY
AND THE
PALESTINE PATROL

NINIAN STEWART

With a Foreword by the
FIRST SEA LORD

FRANK CASS
LONDON • PORTLAND, OR

First published in 2002 in Great Britain by
FRANK CASS PUBLISHERS
Crown House, 47 Chase Side, Southgate
London, N14 5BP

and in the United States of America by
FRANK CASS PUBLISHERS
c/o ISBS, 5824 N.E. Hassalo Street
Portland, Oregon, 97213-3644

Website: www.frankcass.com

British Library Cataloguing in Publication Data

The Royal Navy and the Palestine patrol. – (Naval staff
histories)
1. Great Britain. Royal Navy – Foreign service – Israel
2. Coastal surveillance – Israel 3. Palestine – History –
1929–1948
I. Page, C. L. W.
359.4'0941'09045

ISBN 0-7146-5210-5 (cloth)
ISBN 0-7146-8254-3 (paper)
ISSN 1471-0757

Library of Congress Cataloging-in-Publication Data

The Royal Navy and the Palestine Patrol / preface by Ninian Stewart; with a
foreword by the First Sea Lord.
p. cm. (Whitehall histories: Naval Staff histories, ISSN 1471-0757)
Includes bibliographical references and index.
ISBN 0-7146-5210-5 (cloth: alk. paper) – ISBN 0-7146-8254-3 (paper)
1. Great Britain. Royal Navy. Palestine Patrol – History. 2.
Palestine – History – 1917–1948. I. Stewart, Ninian. II. Series.

VA454 .R675 2002
956.94'04–dc21   2002018818

Typeset in 10.25/12 Sabon by Cambridge Photosetting Services
Printed in Great Britain by MPG Books Ltd, Bodmin, Cornwall

Contents

Illustrations

Foreword

by Admiral Sir Nigel Essenhigh KCB ADC
Chief of the Naval Staff and First Sea Lord

In the aftermath of the Second World War, no task that fell to the Royal Navy was more demanding than the interception of sea-borne illegal immigration into Palestine 1945–48. The Royal Navy's Palestine Patrol undertook this operation in close co-operation with the Royal Air Force. Other civilian and military authorities played important parts by watching out for vessels likely to attempt clandestine voyages and by attempting to prevail on foreign governments to impede their departure.

Naval forces, mainly destroyers operating from Haifa in Palestine, allocated to the Patrol were sizeable. The international diplomatic environment at the time, peacetime legal constraints and the need to avoid inflicting casualties imposed considerable difficulties on when, where and how arrests could be made. Skilled ship handling was essential and boarding parties faced considerable hazards. After interception and arrest, immigrants were, except on one occasion, detained by the Palestine civil authority, but only until they could be released within the lawful immigrant quota. They were not returned whence they came. Thus, from the Royal Navy's perspective, it seemed that there could be no conclusion to the operation, as their implementation of the political policy only ensured that illegal immigration was bound to continue.

The human factor was, as ever, vital to the success of the patrol; many of those involved onboard the Navy's ships were wartime personnel, looking forward to speedy demobilisation. In these circumstances, the efficiency and determination that were shown are all the more praiseworthy. Nelson prayed for humanity in his Fleet and this same quality was well demonstrated time and again. Notwithstanding the troubles that have continued to afflict the region since the end of the Patrol, the efforts of all those involved should not be dismissed as wasted. Their well-executed and successful contribution helped towards the best solution that could be found at the time, and maintained the Navy's high standing and unique reputation.

I welcome this account which records the naval view of events for the first time, and covers the higher direction of the operation as well as dramatic events at sea. This new Naval Staff History provides a candid analysis of the Palestine Patrol, its many successes and its occasional failures. This account illustrates a further classic example of the inherent flexibility of maritime forces through the successful deployment on especially testing constabulary operations of Royal Navy vessels designed primarily for major open ocean warfare. My hope is that it will serve as a tribute to those who served with such professionalism and restraint in the Patrol during those taxing times.

Ministry of Defence
London, 2002

Preface

The League of Nation's mandate system placed on the mandated government for Palestine the task of preparing the territory for self-rule and remedying the shortcomings and after effects of Ottoman misrule. To the difficulties of reconciling Jews and Arabs between the two World Wars was added the consequences of Adolf Hitler's persecution of Jews. Although Allied victory in 1945 put a stop to that terrible activity, the Zionist movement organised travel to Palestine by numbers far in excess of the legal limit. The Royal Navy's success in intercepting this illegal seaborne immigration has been greatly overshadowed by events on land, which led to Britain giving up the mandate in 1948. Interest in events at sea has also tended to focus on the events that followed the interception and arrest of *President Warfield* (*Exodus*) and the decision to send its illegal immigrants back to Europe.

Accounts of illegal immigration activities from the Jewish standpoint have appeared regularly. Hitherto, the only official Royal Navy account has been a classified document containing details of the early days and issued as a guide in 1947. In 1996 the approaching 50th anniversary of the creation of the State of Israel revitalised interest in the Navy's activities. Thus this Naval Staff monograph was prepared as an historical record, and as a source on which the Royal Navy and others could draw. The narrative was completed with considerable assistance from those who had served in the patrol. Also, in 1997, the author was invited by Commander S. Yanay formerly of the Israeli Navy, to speak at two reunions of the crews of illegal immigrant vessels in Haifa and Tel-Aviv. He was accompanied by Lieutenant-Commander A.J.L. Tyler RN and Mr E.J.P. Barrett, who also spoke. Both had served in the patrol, the former having the unique viewpoint of being Jewish, and the latter then a member of a destroyer's boarding party. The British speakers were made most welcome and additional information came to light through other presentations and very friendly discussions. As the researched material became more comprehensive there seemed a likelihood of interesting a wider readership, and the decision was taken to publish this account as a new Naval Staff History.

Whilst in preparation, a view was found to exist in certain interested parties too young to have taken part in the Patrol that this was something that the Navy would not wish either to recall or commemorate. This perception is certainly not that of the many who have helped provide recollections for their time in the Patrol, particularly if serving at the more junior levels. Nor is it the view of their army opposite numbers who in 1999 placed a memorial at Eden Camp, Yorkshire to all servicemen who lost their lives in Palestine 1945–48.

At the 1997 reunion in Israel of the crews of the ships that carried the immigrants, Israeli veterans went out of their way to speak in appreciative tones of the Navy's ability and the restraint shown. In retrospect it can be seen that the Patrol has left little lasting hatred or animosity on either side.

The intention has been to make the account a comprehensive record and to facilitate use by Staff College students and others requiring information on this neglected naval operation. Also, this fairly detailed study serves the important purpose that those who took part in any of the incidents do not feel their part has been overlooked.

The spellings of place names in this part of the world have been many and varied, as far as possible those employed have followed the naval usage of the time. Also, the illegal vessels were known by several different names, starting with that under which they sailed under previous owners. Sometimes the spelling of a name varied. Efforts have been made to name these ships correctly but complete success is unlikely. No two authorities are likely to agree completely on numbers embarked in immigrant ships since, once arrested, crew members concealed their identity amongst passengers or hid until the coast was clear.

No peacetime operation has been more testing for the Royal Navy than the interception of illegal immigrants to Palestine between 1945 and 1948. Success was achieved through the seamanship and professionalism of the sailors in the warships boarding parties. It was required to support the British government's efforts to control the conflict between Arabs and Jews. Over 50 years later that underlying conflict continues.

Today, navies around the globe, including that of Israel, are having to cope with escalating flows of would-be immigrants, as well as with the smuggling of drugs and arms. In dealing with these issues they face situations which have many features similar to the Royal Navy's earlier experience in Palestine and where useful parallels can be drawn. That is what this Naval Staff History, the first ever to be made immediately available for open publication, provides.

ACKNOWLEDGEMENTS

Amongst those who served in the Patrol to whom the author is grateful for their advice, recollections, photographs and other assistance are: the late Admiral of the Fleet Sir William Staveley GCB, Rear Admiral J.R.D. Gerard-Pearse CB, Rear-Admiral E.F. Gueritz CB OBE DSC, the late Captain D.H.R. Bromley DSC RN, the late Captain P.S. Hicks-Beach OBE RN, Captain J.A.F. Lawson RN, Captain M.N. Tufnell DSC RN, Commander A.D. Casswell RN, the late Commander J.S. Kerans DSO RN, the late Lieutenant-Commander E. Ravenscroft RN, Lieutenant-Commander A.J.L. Tyler RN, Lieutenant-Commander C.P.N. Wells-Cole RN, Mr E.J.P. Barrett, Mr J.B. Goodliffe, Mr I. MacLean and Mr G. Mortar. Also Mr F. Liebreich, himself a pre-war illegal immigrant, whose study of the operation was conducted at the same time as this work was being undertaken and as a dissertation for a Doctorate of Philosophy. He also helped greatly with the arrangements for the British speakers in Israel in 1997.

The advice, assistance and encouragement given the author by the Foreign and Commonwealth Office, in particular Mr Keith Hamilton, and the Staff of the Public Record Office have been invaluable. Also, the staff of the Imperial War Museum, and Mr Hodge of the National Maritime Museum, were most helpful with unearthing photographs. Through the good offices of Mr I. MacLean the photographs, all of them elderly, have been reproduced to a higher standard than was possible in earlier times.

Cover Note:
Under the supervision of the late Mr J.D. Brown OBE and later Captain C.L.W. Page RN, this document was prepared in the Naval Historical Branch, a Branch of the Naval Staff Directorate within the Ministry of Defence, Whitehall.

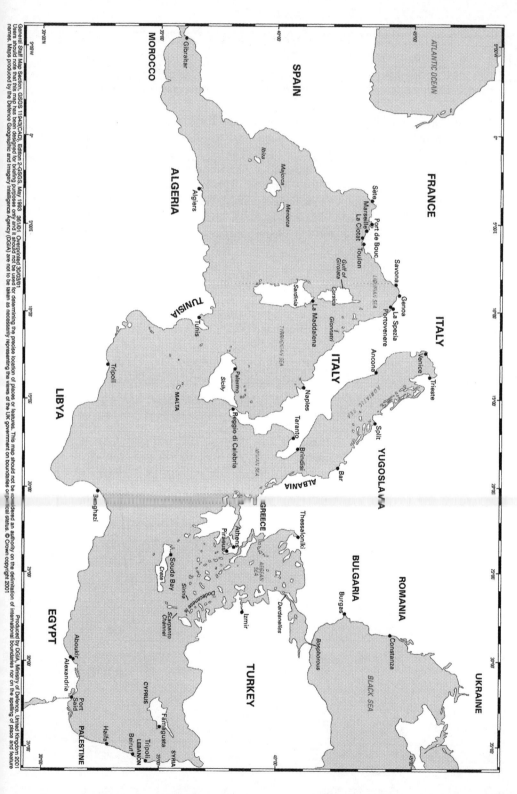

Map 1: THE MEDITERRANEAN

Map 2: PALESTINE

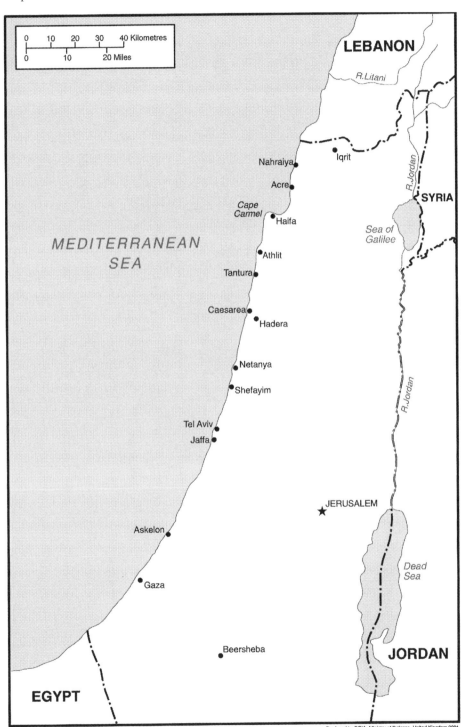

PART I:

THE BRITISH AND PALESTINE

1

Zionism and the Beginnings of Jewish Immigration

Following the destruction of the Temple by Nebuchadnezzar at the beginning of the sixth century BC the majority of the Jewish communities of the *Diaspora* (the *Dispersed*) spread over Asia, Africa and Europe, and later even more widely. Apart from a period of eighty years in the first and second centuries AD, the area of the former Jewish biblical kingdoms of Israel and Judah passed from empire to empire. By the seventh century AD the population was predominantly Muslim 'Arab' in language and culture and it remained so for the next thousand years. From the 1400s the Ottomans administered the area as part of other regions. Meanwhile, the Jews continued to regard Jerusalem as the home of their religion. During the eighteenth century a religious movement saw limited Jewish immigration into Palestine and the Jewish population increased between 1770 and 1820 from 5,000 to 12,000.[1] By 1880 their numbers had doubled again to 24,000, part of a population of about half a million Palestinians. Then vicious persecutions led to major emigration of Jews from Russia and Romania, mainly to the United States, but some to Palestine, whose Jewish population reached almost 50,000 by the beginning of the twentieth century. The decade before the First World War saw over 30,000 more Jews reach Palestine from Eastern Europe. Many of these new immigrants were imbued with a fervour to colonise the land and in 1887 at a Jewish Congress in Basle a Zionist organisation was founded to create an officially recognised Jewish national home. The organisation adopted a national flag and anthem and a Jewish national fund was created.[2] Attempts to divert the Zionists to other areas, notably East Africa, failed and the movement remained determined to create its 'national home' in Palestine.

THE BRITISH MANDATE

During the First World War British Government policy in assisting and encouraging Zionists was based on a combination of realism and idealism.

3

There was a perceived need to enlist in the Allied cause Jewish financial interests described by one member of the Cabinet as the 'powerful and cosmopolitan community which, not from New York alone, controls the loan markets of the world'.[3] There was also a longer-term desire to strengthen the British position in the Near and Middle East. But genuine sympathy existed for the principle of a 'Jewish Homeland'. In 1917 the Balfour Declaration (see Annex D for text), undertook to provide practical support for the establishment of a national home for Jews in Palestine. The reservation that their rights had still to be respected satisfied neither the Arab population nor the Arab nations, which Britain had encouraged to revolt against the Turks on the condition that areas freed from the Sultan would be under Arab rule. The two undertakings were to prove incompatible.

In the late autumn of 1917 British Imperial forces under General Allenby began an offensive that culminated in the capture of Jerusalem on 9 December. A naval force assisted on the seaward flank. Britain could now, if it wished, proceed with Balfour's promise. However, the Arabs foresaw themselves becoming a minority and objected strongly to Jewish immigration. The British were torn between the desire to use Jews as dependent colonists to develop the area and assure British control of a vital strategic area and the need not to alienate the Arabs and the rest of the 90 million Muslims in the British Empire. In 1920 a limit on Jewish immigration was introduced of 1,000 each month, increased later in the year to an annual quota of 16,500. Nevertheless, Arab unrest led to immigration being suspended altogether the following year. In 1922 British rule of Palestine under a League of Nations mandate was approved by the League. A White Paper prepared by Mr Winston Churchill, Secretary of State for the Colonies, called for Jewish immigration based on the 'economic absorptive capacity' of the area.[4] Not being a member of the League, the United States did not share in the responsibility for supervising the mandate.

By 1923 the population of Palestine consisted of 83,000 Jews, 589,000 Muslims and 71,000 Christians. The territory did not form part of the British Empire, the mandate required not only measures to overcome the effects of previous mis-rule but also preparations for self-rule. As an early step, an attempt was made to set up a Legislative Council under the Officer Administering the Government, otherwise known as the High Commissioner, with the Muslim Arabs, the Christian Arabs and the Jews all providing elected members. Unfortunately the Arabs boycotted elections, the Council was not instituted and further progress never proved possible. The mandate document required (Article 4) recognition of 'an appropriate Jewish agency for the purpose of advising and cooperating with the administration on economic, social and other matters affecting establishment of a Jewish national home and the interests of the Jewish nation'. In 1929, the Jewish Agency was formed from the Zionist organisation in Palestine and recognised as the central representative organisation for Jews in Palestine as regards family and health matters, education and immigration. When eventually the mandate ended the Agency became the government of Israel.

Article 6 of the mandate required the 'facilitation' of Jewish immigration 'whilst ensuring the rights and position of other sections of the population are not prejudiced'. At first post-war Jewish immigration was sizeable and the population doubled, but many found that Palestine was not a land of milk and honey and this, combined with Arab hostility, led to figures falling. Comparative tranquillity set in until 1929, by which time Jews formed nearly a fifth of the population. At this point the problem of Jewish access to the Wailing Wall in Jerusalem and utterances at a Zionist Congress in Zurich led to serious Arab riots and attacks on Jews.[5] A British Parliamentary Commission of Inquiry confirmed that Jewish immigration and the consequences it was having for Arab peasants and tenants was the fundamental causes of such instability. The British Government accepted a recommendation that there be tighter control of immigration.[6] However, the Zionist organisation objected violently and this led once again to an about-turn. Nothing more was done for the time being to restrict or control immigration, the rate of which soon greatly increased.

As the 1930s progressed Jews, not only in Germany but elsewhere in Central and Eastern Europe, suffered increasingly and a large scale movement out of Europe was set in train, many seeking and being granted entry to Palestine. The Greek schooner *Velos* was the first vessel to bring a significant number of seaborne illegal immigrants when, in June 1935, she put 300 Jews ashore near Tel Aviv. This landing took the Jewish Agency by surprise, being an initiative organised by an underground movement in Greece where Zionism was not favoured by Jews. The Agency's policy was to placate the British, but it chose not to intervene. The *Velos*, which set the pattern for unseaworthiness and squalor characteristic of illegal immigrant vessels, made another attempt later but was intercepted after 50 out of 300 immigrants reached the shore.

2

Naval Operations: The Arab Revolt and Refugees

THE ROYAL NAVY AND FACILITIES ON THE PALESTINE COAST

In 1934 the Admiralty laid down that ships of the Mediterranean Fleet were not to be detached from other duties to intercept craft carrying illegal immigrants.[7] They were to do no more than keep a lookout for suspects and report them to the Palestine authorities, only short detours for this purpose being permitted. A year later the Abyssinian crisis necessitated the main body of the Mediterranean Fleet being stationed in the Eastern Mediterranean and three cruisers and seven destroyers arrived at Haifa in September. Lying at the southern end of the bay of Acre, inside Cape Carmel and on the lower slopes of Mount Carmel, where Elijah spent much of his life, Haifa had, following the arrival of the British in 1918, developed into the only significant port on the Palestine coast. Although in winter continual gales meant no alongside berth was safe or secure, the approaches provided an excellent anchorage.

Visible north across the bay from Mount Carmel lies Acre, captured by Richard 'Coeur de Lion' in 1291. There Commodore Sir Sydney Smith repulsed General Bonaparte in 1800 and Vice-Admiral Sir Robert Stopford achieved a great victory with an allied force over invading Egyptian forces in 1840. Acre lacked a deep anchorage and in the 1930s possessed nothing more than a small harbour for coasting vessels, a jetty for small craft up to 10 tons and an 8–9 fathom anchorage. The exposed coast to the south of Haifa had even less to offer. King Herod made Caesarea a great port but it had suffered destruction as a consequence of the Crusades and decayed into an insignificant coastal town and a landing place for small boats. Further South, both Jaffa and Tel Aviv (a city created by Jewish settlers out of a Jaffa suburb) shared a jetty and a lighter basin exposed to bad weather. The coast beyond Jaffa was populated mainly by Arabs who did not welcome descents by illegal Jewish immigrants into their midst, nor were the roads suitable for spiriting them away quickly. The

6

great Phoenician port of Askelon had long since been destroyed. Gaza, 40 miles south of Jaffa and two miles inland, had an open roadstead nearby but, at the time of the mandate, the few landing places were useable only in good conditions between April and October.

THE ARAB REVOLT

By 1936 the Jews numbered some 400,000, 30 per cent of the total population. and the Arabs rose in revolt. At the outbreak there were only two British Army battalions in Palestine and this lack of troops was long lasting, greatly hindering attempts to suppress the rebellion during the next two years and necessitating naval assistance on several occasions. When rioting began two cruisers formed the nucleus for the Haifa Naval Force, which between April and September 1936 carried out many tasks ashore. These included fighting fires in timber yards caused by arson and manning two naval howitzers stationed at a military camp to disperse bands of Arab snipers. From June onwards the howitzers were augmented with naval manned lorries carrying 2-Pdr Pom-Poms and searchlights. This counter-measure was so successful that within three months their strength was increased to a total of seven lorries. To prevent gun running a patrol of the whole coast by destroyers was instituted on 26 June and as many as 150 vessels a week were searched for arms. This proved an effective preventive measure although no culprits were found. At the request of the Army additional naval platoons were landed in July to operate in Haifa and also undertake the protection of Jewish settlements (*Kibbutz*) in the surrounding countryside. When a general strike broke out in August 1936, the Navy freed army troops for mobile duties elsewhere by taking over control of Haifa using nine naval platoons formed into the *Haifa Town Force* under the command of the Squadron Royal Marine Officer, 3rd Cruiser Squadron. The Navy was also called on to help the railway. Thirteen naval train crews, each consisting of a driver and a fireman, underwent training by the railway authorities and within three weeks were passed fit to take charge of a railway train. Intimidation by Arab extremists soon forced Arab employees to abandon their work and the Navy manned signal boxes and maintained a service for ten days, which avoided a serious dislocation and caused the railwaymen to return to work. Naval armoured trains did much to counteract attempts at sabotage on the railways until troops were available to picket the lines.

In August sloops relieved the destroyer patrol and at the end of the month the task of the Haifa Town Force ceased.[8] But disturbances continued and later three Royal Marine platoons had again to be landed at the request of the police. In September a full Army division arrived, which greatly lessened the calls on the Navy. Events had once again demonstrated the versatile and speedy response which the Navy could provide and, on this occasion, at a time when very extensive naval operations were being undertaken in other parts of the Mediterranean. This capability was called on again in each of the two following years.

GREY EMINENCE: THE NAVAL PRESENCE AT HAIFA, 1937

When in July 1937 publication of a Royal Commission's report on the future of Palestine became imminent, the battle cruiser HMS *Repulse* (Captain J.H. Godfrey RN) was sailed at short notice to Haifa. The aim was for her to send landing parties ashore as a deterrent to disturbances and to maintain calm. *Repulse* arrived ready to put ashore two platoons of Royal Marines, a seaman company with a machine gun section, a fire and salvage party and customs guards but as the populace remained quiet, they remained onboard. The Royal Commission concluded that the Arab and Jewish positions were irreconcilable and recommended that Palestine be partitioned and the mandate ended, except for a small area around the Holy City. The recommendations were accepted by the British Government and by the Jews. But the Arabs would not agree to partition and continued their revolt until by the end of 1938 Jaffa, Hebron, the old city of Jerusalem and most of the country outside the main cities were under their control.

Whilst *Repulse* was at Haifa a rather different requirement arose. The High Commissioner needed a ship ready to deport the leader of the Muslims in Palestine, Haj Amin El-Husseini, the President of the Supreme Muslim Council, otherwise known as the Grand Mufti of Jerusalem, the highest Muslim religious figure and as such the authority on Muslim law. He was to be arrested at 1500 on 17 July and flown to the RAF airfield at Haifa. Then after a night onboard *Repulse* one of her picket boats would transfer him to a destroyer, aptly named *Hasty,* newly arrived from Malta and stationed out of sight of land. *Hasty* was then to take him to exile in the Seychelle Islands. However, the Grand Mufti evidently became aware of what was afoot, evaded capture and escaped from Palestine. *Repulse* remained at Haifa another ten days and then turned over the task of Senior Naval Officer Haifa to *Hasty* and departed.

Three months later the arrangements planned for the Grand Mufti were put into effect when five of his associates were arrested. After bed and breakfast in the County-class cruiser HMS *Sussex* (Captain H.E.C. Blagrove RN) they were put onboard a destroyer HMS *Active* (Lieutenant-Commander B.G. Scurfield RN) for a voyage to the Seychelles. The presence of such notables onboard so small a warship for a thirteen-day passage via the Suez Canal cannot have been very easy or pleasant for their hosts. They themselves were mainly lent from HMS *Hunter,* mined off

Spain during operations connected with the Spanish Civil War and currently under repair at Malta.

HMS *REPULSE* RETURNS – 1938

Almost twelve months after *Repulse*'s first arrival, on the afternoon of 6 July 1938 a large bomb, probably placed by a Jewish faction, exploded in the Arab market at Haifa. There had been other incidents and grave disturbances were foreseen, possibly even a full-scale civil war. The High Commissioner at once signalled the CinC Mediterranean Fleet requesting assistance by a naval vessel with sufficient men to provide landing parties. Shortly after midnight his telegram reached Admiral Sir Dudley Pound who was with the main body of the fleet off Navarin, at the end of the Mediterranean Fleet summer cruise. He detached *Repulse* to sail at 25½ knots and diverted the cruiser HMS *Emerald* (Captain A.W.S. Agar VC DSO RN) to Haifa. *Emerald* arrived the same day and landed five platoons, one to each Police District.

Repulse relieved *Emerald* 24 hours later and her arrival helped calm the situation. Her platoons included sailors as well as Royal Marines and since the sailors were older men than the soldiers to whom the locals had been accustomed, they were regarded as a pleasant change. For its part, the Army welcomed the presence of a large and impressive warship. Nevertheless, more bombs exploded on 10 July and five platoons were kept very busy dispersing mobs and patrolling. Provision of three additional platoons on 11 July enabled the Royal West Kent Regiment to undertake a punitive expedition against Arabs who had attacked a Jewish colony outside Haifa. By 17 July *Repulse*'s contribution ashore was established as a Company Headquarters, three Seaman and two RM platoons and her 3.7-inch howitzer crew. Two sailors or Royal Marines accompanied each foot patrol being undertaken by British Palestine Policemen. Some soldiers from the Suffolk Regiment had been embarked in the *Repulse* for the Fleet cruise and these now found themselves working temporarily on the same tasks.

The future of Palestine was at this time being considered by a fresh Commission and considerable political uncertainty reigned. In addition to the activities of the Arabs, extremist Jewish elements were now causing trouble. A quota system of permitted immigration had recently been introduced and illegal immigration was in progress but not at such a level that Naval assistance was necessary. The High Commissioner preferred to strengthen the Coast Watching Organisation and to rely on diplomatic approaches to governments in countries from which the illegal immigrants sailed, particularly Greece. But Naval assistance was not disdained when on 18 July intelligence warned that a vessel named *Artimisia* intended to land 160 Polish Jews. HM Tug *Brigand* patrolled the coast for eight daylight hours, without result, and searched again when an arrival time of about 2359 on 21 July was forecast. *Brigand*'s instructions were to follow the Admiralty policy outlined earlier and simply report suspicious vessels via *Repulse*. Although the *Artemissa*, to use her correct name, did not appear on the scene until December, Captain Godfrey was in no doubt that seaborne illegal immigration was in progress. He described this quota-beating practice as 'Gate crashing'.[9]

Repulse was also called on to assist with measures against gun running overland from Syria and the Lebanon into Jewish settlements, but this was in her captain's view something for which a seaman's training did not provide adequate preparation. Seamen were however employed as lorry guards and thus were able to see something of the country, which otherwise they had no chance of doing. When howitzers provided by HMS *Hood* and HMS *Warspite* arrived on 20 July, these went to Iqrit, close to the border with Palestine's Arab neighbour Lebanon. *Repulse*'s howitzer was already attached to the Royal Ulster Rifles and in action there, helping counter gun running. Emplacements were also constructed in several other places, using detained Arabs, and the guns were moved rapidly between them by day and by night. This mode of operation kept bandits in a state of uncertainty as to the particular area which fire could reach promptly. A few rounds were also fired periodically in the close vicinity of villages whose inhabitants were credited with pro-bandit tendencies. The Army provided ammunition, but whether this should be paid for by the Admiralty or the War Office became the subject of inter-Departmental debate.

COMMAND ORGANISATION AND RELATIONSHIPS

Naval assistance continued with two RM platoons helping the West Kent Regiment cordon and search a small town and a further platoon, composed of Stokers, being landed as search parties and guards for the Railway workshops. Things did not improve and on 25 July 45 Arabs died when a bomb exploded in the melon market and fires broke out in Haifa, causing *Repulse* to reinforce her shore parties with two Emergency platoons. The rebels held the initiative largely due to the civil authority, the District Commissioner, refusing to acknowledge that civil authority was in any way failing to cope. This attitude meant he declined 'each and every measure' recommended as a precaution by the local military commander, a Brigadier of very considerable experience of Palestine. Government rules laid down that once military assistance had been called upon, a District Commissioner had to follow the advice of the Military Commander. The local incumbent was evading this requirement on the grounds of his own responsibilities for maintaining law and order. For the local Naval and military commanders this was very embarrassing, since after each fresh incident they were taxed by General Officer Commanding Palestine asking what they were doing to prevent further outrages.

One consequence of the District Commissioner's attitude was that too much of the soldiers' time was taken up guarding of their own barracks. With great difficulty his agreement was obtained for the establishment of a combined military Chairman of the Town Security Committee and Town Commander. This post was then created, endowed with quite sweeping powers and filled by *Repulse*'s Executive Officer (promoted to Acting Captain). The Navy thereby gained authority to control activities in Haifa and the soldiers were freed for operations in the countryside. One immediate benefit was a successful operation which rounded up bandits south-west of Carmel on 26 July.

Repulse was relieved by the battleship HMS *Malaya* (Captain F.A. Buckley RN) on 22 August. Incidents recorded during her stay were as follows: 67 fires, 36 bombs, 24 stonings or stabbings and 8 shootings. *Malaya* was able to leave in September, having been relieved by the light cruiser HMS *Penelope* and later the Netlayer HMS *Protector*, which remained until shortly before Christmas. Thereafter strong Army reinforcements brought out from England enabled the Palestine Government to gain the upper hand over the Arabs, who were never again able to cause the British significant trouble. Henceforward, Jewish organisations were responsible for the most serious disruptions of order.

Events between 1936 and 1938 demonstrated, not for the last time in this record, some roles ashore for which large naval vessels were then well suited. An average of 21 officers and 251 Ratings/Other Ranks were stationed ashore by *Repulse* in 1938. On 25 July totals reached 29 officers and 431 Ratings/Other Ranks, which represented about half the battle-cruiser's total ship's company.

JEWISH UNOFFICIAL ORGANISATIONS

The troubles with the Arabs and the situation with immigration encouraged the growth and development of Jewish organisations of a military nature. Rudimentary Jewish settlement defence units had been formed at the start of the century on the lines of armed Jewish self-protection groups customary in Russia. When, after the First World War, the Jews became increasingly attacked by Arabs, a secret workers' self defence force was founded and this became the Hebrew Defence Organisation (*Irgun Hahaganach ha'ivrith* or *Haganah*). Later the most militant members of Haganah, 'the Revisionists',[10] broke away and in 1931 formed the National Military Organisation (*Irgun Zvai Leumi*), also known as ETZEL or IZL,

11

which advocated activism and seized arms. It was in the Jews' own interests that Arab risings should be suppressed and for this reason Haganah actively assisted the British after 1938. Thereby they improved their own military capabilities and, since they operated to some extent under British command, achieved tacit recognition. Following 'Crystal Night' (*Kristallnacht*, 9 November 1938) in Germany, an independent Illegal Immigration Bureau (*Ha-Mossad le'aliya Bet*) (*Institute for Immigration B*) (i.e. Unofficial Immigration and generally known as *Mossad*)[11] was also set up. In 1940 Abraham Stern, a senior member of the IZL, refused to observe the wartime truce with the British and set up the *Locahme Herut Israel (Fighters for the Freedom of Israel)*, colloquially known as the *Stern Gang*, which continued attacks on the British and Jews opposed to its activities.

The German threat to the Near East in mid-1941 caused the Haganah to form Striking Companies (*Pulgoth Hamachatz* or *Palmach*). A naval arm (*Palyam*) followed in 1943, some members being from illegal immigrant vessel crews, and swimmers were trained in underwater sabotage. An air element also formed and an intelligence/counter-intelligence service (*And Shai*). As will be seen Haganah developed quickly into a very capable organisation and by the end of the Second World War was operating from the Middle East across Europe to the United States, with a strength in 1944 of 36,871 men including 1,517 *Palmach*. In 1946 the Haganah took over the staffing of Mossad, which was by then subject to directions by the Jewish Agency.

THE REFUGEE PROBLEM

In contrast with 1935, when the total of Jewish immigrants reached 55,407, restrictions on immigration led to only 9,441 legal immigrants arriving in 1937 and 11,222 in 1938. By that time the politically disturbed state of Europe was causing immense numbers, not only Jews, to leave their homelands and become refugees, greatly increasing the problem over entry into Palestine. Between 1933 and 1938 350,000 people are thought to have departed from Germany and Austria and provision was needed for the departure of the remaining 390,000 Jews. Following the 1938 Munich Agreement and, six months later, the German occupation of Bohemia and Moravia, large numbers of Jews left former Czechoslovakia. In the autumn of 1938 Italy expelled all Jews who had entered the country after 1919. Whilst many countries, including Great Britain, helped absorb refugees amongst their own populations, opposition from Arabs and Arab nations still meant Britain could not readily allow greater numbers of Jews into Palestine. The *Times* correspondent in Jerusalem, writing in May 1939, estimated that in the previous year 7,000 immigrants had gained admission illegally and, he believed another one thousand were arriving each month.

Indeed, the Haganah, encouraged by the German Government, was shepherding refugees from Central Europe down the Danube to Romanian and
Bulgarian ports, where they embarked in craft obtained by Mossad.

Since both sides in Palestine continued to refuse any form of reconcili-
ation, early in 1939 the British Government issued a White Paper aban-
doning partition. As the creation of a Jewish state would be contrary to
British obligations to the Arabs an independent Palestinian State would be
created instead. This was to be achieved within ten years, there were to
be measures to protect the Holy Places and the different communities and
the Jewish population would be permitted to increase to one-third of the
total population of the country. On that basis 75,000 Jews would be
admitted in the next five years, with the first 25,000 being allowed to enter
as soon as accommodation could be provided for them. At the end of the
five years there was to be no further Jewish immigration without the agreement of the Arabs. The White Paper was not well received by the House
of Commons; when debated there the Government's majority fell from 248
to 89. It also caused intense and universal Jewish resentment and animosity
towards the British. Nevertheless, the White Paper went some way towards
meeting the case put forward by the Arabs and played a part in their rebellion dying away.

The British had to account regularly to the Permanent Mandates
Commission of the League of Nations for their stewardship. In mid-1939
the Commissioners, by a majority of four to three, ruled that:

a. the way ahead planned in the 1939 White Paper was not in con-
formity with the terms of the mandate;

b. the provision of a national home for the Jews had to remain a
prime objective.

This outcome begged the question of Arab rights and could only prolong
or worsen the revolt and so Britain placed the issue before the full League
of Nations Assembly. It had not been discussed by the time the Second
World War broke out and the League ceased to function. The lack of a
final decision was most unfortunate, as the leaders of the Jews were able
to enlist the Commission's ruling to gain support against British restrictions
on immigration.

THE *LAS PERLAS*

At the end of April 1939, two days after one vessel put ashore 218 refugees
and the Greek steamer *Assimi* with 270 refugees had been intercepted and
sent back, the Colonial Secretary in London announced fresh measures.
Both the coastguard system and the Marine Police were to be strengthened and reorganised to counter seaborne illegal immigration. Until these

arrangements were completed ships of the Mediterranean Fleet would intercept vessels bringing in illegal immigrants. At the same time the Greek Government brought in a law prohibiting transport to Palestine of people not in possession of valid passports with visas for that destination.

Destroyers undertook the first patrols. On 1 July 1939 HMS *Icarus* (Lieutenant-Commander C.D. Maud RN) took a captured schooner inshore whilst HMS *Ivanhoe* (Lieutenant-Commander B.G. Scurfield RN) searched for a suspicious vessel, named SS *Las Perlas*, reported by a reconnaissance aircraft. After nightfall a darkened steamship was sighted 27 miles south-west of Carmel Light House steering south at 8 knots. There now began a sequence of events of a kind frequently repeated when interceptions took place after the Second World War.

On *Ivanhoe* approaching, the *Las Perlas*, as she turned out to be, signalled SOS twice on her siren and flashed by light the International two letter signal for 'Mutiny – require assistance'. Lieutenant D.J.B. Jewitt RN (the Boarding Officer) and Lieutenant A. Phipps RN (as Witnessing Officer) went over with an armed whaler's crew and a Palestine policeman, to establish if the SOS was genuine and whether a mutiny had indeed taken place. The Master explained that his ship was bound for Beirut with 370 male and female passengers but he and the crew had been taken prisoners by the passengers five nights previously. He requested that *Ivanhoe* provide protection to take him into a port but could not decide which port it was to be. When pressed for a decision he sought to resign his command. The leaders of the passengers explained that there were no provisions, water or medical comforts, forty of their number were sick and the Captain was making no attempt to land them at the destination which they had paid to travel to, namely the Palestine coast. The crew confirmed their Captain's story, they were clearly in fear of the passengers and two complained of their hands being tied and being made to work at pistol point.

Lieutenant Jewitt concluded that despite a disagreement between Captain and passengers there was insufficient proof of mutiny. *Ivanhoe* had no authority to accept the Master's resignation and he was warned that if he chose to enter Palestine territorial waters his vessel would be arrested. The Boarding Officer later reported 'I considered that the sequence of events in the *Las Perlas* might be an illicit method of obtaining permission to enter Palestine ports under the protection of the Royal Navy.' His surmise was fully justified. Since the ship was entirely seaworthy and capable of making port the Boarding Party then withdrew.

The *Las Perlas* steamed slowly and erratically eastwards for the rest of the night. When eventually the vessel crossed the 3-mile limit and entered Palestine's territorial waters she was boarded again. The Captain was found locked in his cabin, and again this was explained by a refusal to take the ship anywhere but Beirut. Although only one of the two engines functioned at first and some of the crew would not work, the Boarding

14

Party set course for Haifa. A smouldering fire in a coal bunker had to put out with salt water using passenger labour, but the majority of those onboard were in a bad way, listless and hysterical, others fainting. Their leader, supported by a doctor present onboard, explained that this was due to no water being fit to drink and to lack of food. Water was issued from a supply brought by the boarders, bread found in the Captain's cabin was distributed and *Ivanhoe* sent over more supplies. Unfortunately, during this process an Able Seaman of the boarding party accidentally shot himself in the leg and died after reaching Haifa. Before arrival in port a Police Launch came out and took over control. Lieutenant Jewitt commented that the leaders of the passengers were 'of very great assistance' during both the two periods he was onboard.

3

The Wartime Years

By September 1939 the naval patrols had been diverted to matters of higher priority and on 2 September Mossad brought in a ship, the *Tiger Hill*. Although intercepted by Marine Police, who opened fire, she reached the beach at Tel Aviv. 1,417 illegal immigrants, refugees from Poland, Romania, Bulgaria and Czechoslovakia were embarked. Some escaped and some were detained by the Army. (A list of the known major illegal immigrant vessels up until 3 September 1939 can be seen at Annex A.) At the start of the war the British and French instituted contraband control patrols to prevent supplies vital for the Nazi war effort reaching Germany from the Black Sea via Italian ports. Contraband Control vessels patrolled between Greece and Crete with instructions that ships found in the normal course of contraband control examination to be carrying illegal immigrants were to be detained and sent to Haifa.

Since there were no Naval patrol craft available for the Palestine coast arrangements were made for the Port and Marine Division of the Palestine Police to come under the operational control of the Navy. The crews were given temporary unpaid posts in the Royal Naval Volunteer Reserve and the launches were commissioned as HM Ships, under the heading of Palestine Coast Patrol. Administration remained the responsibility of the Inspector-General Palestine Police and the police continued to be paid by the Palestine Government. This arrangement, which ran from early 1940 until the autumn of 1945, proved an unqualified success. One consequence was that for the first, and probably only time, the White Ensign was to be seen flying on two launches on the Sea of Galilee.

At the start of the war, the Jews in Palestine supported the British side against their persecutors in Germany but attempts at illegal immigration continued. (Service in British forces also provided a back door route to military training and equipment.) In the first 18 months of the 1939 White Paper quota period about 37,000 immigrants arrived and must have come mainly by sea. A limit of 1,500 immigrants a month was then set and illegal entries were turned back or transported to other places, such as

Mauritius. As the war continued and its extent spread, both sides instituted control of shipping over large areas and, wartime hazards apart, this increasingly ruled out efforts at infiltration in small trading craft.

There were two particularly untoward maritime incidents, but in neither was the Royal Navy concerned. In November 1940 the 11,885-ton liner *Patria* embarked 3,600 illegal immigrants at Haifa for deportation to Mauritius. Haganah sabotaged *Patria* with explosives, she sank and 260 passengers died. This tragic and unnecessary loss of life was exceeded after the Panamanian-registered *Struma*, which had set out from Romania, was turned back by the Turkish authorities. She was attacked in the Black Sea and sunk on 24 February 1942 by the Soviet submarine SC-213 (Lieutenant DM Denezhko);[12] 768 out of the total of 769 immigrants crowded on board this 170-ton former yacht were drowned. This tragedy caused Haganah to forbid any more sailings from Romania and for 18 months seaborne immigration ceased. Between May 1939 and August 1944 six ships sailed from Balkan ports with 16,797 immigrants.

THE WAR OFF THE LEVANT COAST, 1941 AND 1942

The entry of Italy into the War in 1940 posed a threat to the Levant from the Italian held Dodecanese Islands nearby. In June 1941 the increasing use being made by German aircraft of airfields in Syria necessitated British troops seizing control of the two Levant territories governed by the Vichy French under League of Nations mandate – Lebanon and Syria (*Operation Exporter*). To encourage the cooperation of the inhabitants of Syria and the Lebanon to cooperate they were promised independence once the war was over. This undertaking and other British wartime actions against France (albeit Vichy) caused much resentment. It became inevitable that in the immediate post-war period many Frenchmen would be disinclined to take the side of the British in any controversy concerning Palestine.

At the end of 1941 the CinC sought Admiralty approval to recruit skilled mechanics in Palestine, even if not English speaking. The question of race was not raised but in practice only Jews were likely to be adequately qualified. The request was approved and by June 1942 a total of 46 had been entered as Engine Room Artificers together with 20 less well qualified as Motor Mechanics for motor torpedo boats and landing craft. Twice that number had been sought. Although the CinC's staff had great difficulty in securing fair pay, recruiting started for Telegraphists, Signalmen, Writers, Sick Berth Attendants, Stewards and also Seamen for mine watching, boats crews and harbour defence. Unfortunately a considerable number of volunteers could not pass the medical examination for entry. Also the Palestine Government was anxious to retain sufficient numbers of adequately qualified residents to meet the needs of the country's economy.

In theory Palestinian ratings could serve anywhere, but in practice the CinC planned they be stationed in the Mediterranean. This enabled active service ratings to be relieved and sent back to the United Kingdom to man new construction vessels and bring them into service. By January 1943 the numbers entered locally had risen to over 400, including two officers. Manpower in Palestine was running short and the Naval Officer-in-Charge (Captain G.O. Lydekker OBE DSC RN) reported that the Navy's demands exceeded the numbers available to be recruited. At first, security screening was necessary only for officers, but the deterioration of the security situation caused increasing difficulties from June 1943 onwards and the Admiralty ended recruiting of Telegraphists, Writers and Stewards.

THE IMMIGRATION QUESTION

In late 1943 the British Cabinet decided that, in the light of the persecution suffered by the Jews throughout Germany and German-occupied territory, illegal immigrants would be allowed to remain and admitted through the quota. At much the same time a tour of the USA by the Chairman of the Jewish Agency, Mr David Ben-Gurion, roused considerable sympathy and American public opinion henceforward became very vocal. But whilst Ben-Gurion wished immigration to be controlled by the Jewish Agency, and was very successful in securing the active support which was to come later, he did nevertheless emphasise the necessity to cooperate with the Arabs. Indeed the principles of self-determination embodied in the 1941 Atlantic Charter, Prime Minister Churchill's and President Roosevelt's joint statement of war aims, legitimised the Arab attitude to the continuing influx of Jews. It was however the President's belief that Palestine should be partitioned.

In 1944, with the situation for Jews in Europe steadily worsening, the Colonial Secretary authorised admission of up to 30,000 Jews from Nazi-occupied nations and the Haganah set about extracting them from Nazi-held ports. A considerable number of authorities, including the Foreign Office and other organisations, were involved in all the complications of finding ships and securing safe conduct. By the end of the year some 8,000 had been rescued in eight 400-ton craft but not without further tragedies. At much the same time the Special Operations Executive (SOE) branch at Cairo arranged for some 35 Jews to be parachuted into South-Eastern Europe. Although the aim was that they should conduct and organise sabotage, SOE was in little doubt that those concerned had additional tasks given them by the Agency or Haganah. SOE also considered diverting small craft taken up for clandestine operations to the task of bringing in Jewish immigrants.

More fundamentally, the British Cabinet agreed in January 1944 that, whether the Arabs liked it or not, Palestine would be partitioned, but no announcement was to be made until after the American presidential elections in November. The long delay proved fatal; despite Mr Churchill's long history of support for the Zionist cause, in February Jewish extremists started to turn against the British. The post of Minister of State in the Middle East had been created to represent the British Government and relieve Commanders-in-Chief of political tasks and it was at this time filled by Lord Moyne. With 24 hours to go before President Roosevelt was elected to a fourth term, the Stern Gang, acting entirely on its own initiative, attacked and killed Moyne. As Secretary of State for the Colonies, his previous post, Lord Moyne had opposed the voyage of *Struma* to Palestine and his murder was largely revenge for the tragedy that had occurred. He had also had the task of rejecting a proposal put forward by the Agency for the formation of a Jewish Division, which the Chiefs of Staff considered likely to be resented by the Arabs. The Moyne assassination resulted in a substantial set back for Zionists in contact with the British. Mr Churchill, was at the time fully occupied with other Mediterranean events, in particular civil strife in Greece, and he did not proceed any further with plans for Palestine.[13]

In the meantime police patrols under naval control continued and by the start of 1945 most Port and Marine Division Patrol Launches were showing considerable signs of wear and tear. Since this was largely due to hard service as part of the Navy, provision of two Royal Navy Harbour 72-foot Harbour Defence Motor Launches (HDMLs) as replacements was requested. Both Captain Lydekker and the Palestine Government regarded the patrols undertaken by launches as of very great importance but all available were fully occupied, the Admiralty had to be involved and long delays ensued.

4

The Displaced Persons

The closing stages of the Allied advance into Germany exposed the full horror of the Nazi concentration camps and the end of the war saw tens of thousands of Jews amongst the many homeless people in Europe. Mr Churchill saw no advantages in retaining the Mandate, which he considered a thankless task, and suggested handing Palestine over to the United States, if they would have it. But the Chiefs of Staff expected adverse Muslim reaction, which would damage Britain's interests in the Middle East, in particular access to oil. They also foresaw that Egypt would soon call for the removal of the British Strategic Reserve in the Near and Middle East and that the next best base would be Palestine.

Roosevelt's successor, President Truman, was far more swayed by electoral considerations and he wasted no time in broaching the subject of Jewish immigration. In July 1945 he urged the new Labour Prime Minister, Mr Attlee, to admit greatly increased numbers to Palestine.[14] The subject was discussed between the two leaders. Since the League of Nations had been suspended and the United Nations Organisation had not yet formed they agreed that an Anglo-American Commission should investigate Palestine's post-war situation and report within four months. Nevertheless in a speech at the end of August Truman called for the immediate admission of 100,000 immigrants. His utterances incensed Palestine's Arab neighbours, and Egypt, Iraq, Syria and Lebanon all warned Truman that the creation of a Jewish State would be opposed by force of arms.

The work of the Anglo-American Commission started in the late autumn, but neither the fact that it was in progress nor indeed the eventual outcome had any effect on either illegal immigration or American sentiment. In the meantime the British proposed to continue immigration at the existing figure of 1,500 a month. The Arabs agreed this policy but the Zionists demanded the admission of the 100,000 called for by President Truman and individual Americans increasingly supported their activities.

Mossad, with an overt arm named *Vaad Hatzalah* (Rescue Committee), had by now established 25 emissaries in 13 countries. The total number of emissaries, including those under cover of other activities, increased to some 200 by 1947. A European Headquarters was set up in Paris, where relations with the French government were said to become excellent, and offices opened in Milan, Prague, Bratislava, Budapest and Vienna. A wireless network connected Europe with Palestine. A major transportation route was established from Eastern Europe into France and Italy, frequently via the US Zone of Germany. Others ran from North Germany to Sweden and to Belgium, and from Romania and Hungary to Yugoslavia. In France large villas near Marseilles served as final collection points and a total of eight camps with a capacity for over 5,000 were opened, with such supporting facilities as forgers preparing travel documents. A little later, by June 1946, the Minister of the Interior (Monsieur E. Depreux) arranged contact whereby the French Counter-Intelligence Service (the DST) provided Mossad with information on British information gathering activities.

Mossad was well able to exploit the disturbed, disorganised, ill-fed and poverty-stricken conditions which existed in mainland Europe in the immediate post-war period. Recently liberated nations had yet to restore fully their own authority, some had fallen under Soviet domination, whilst the defeated nations were not their own masters but forced to respond to external directions, exercised by many different authorities. Nor were internal communications in good shape for controlling government agencies, such as immigration authorities or the police. These in their turn were not sufficiently strongly established to withstand strong-arm tactics by Jewish zealots, ably organised by leaders hardened by persecution and who were assisted by two well-established relief organisations – UNRRA and the AJDC.

The United Nations Relief and Rehabilitation Authority (UNRRA) had been set up as a supply organisation for relief and rehabilitation purposes, largely as an American initiative, and by now was providing personnel for the administration of the majority of displaced persons camps in Western Germany. The Americans installed Senator Lehmann of New York, a Jew, as the Director-General of UNRRA and subsequently Mr Fiorello LaGuardia, former Mayor of New York, himself half-Jewish and currently seeking the Jewish vote in competition against a full New York Jew. The Jewish Agency seconded personnel to work with, but not under the control of, UNRRA and the extent of their activities was thus concealed. Numbers of displaced persons were overwhelming and the Jews were able to take every advantage of UNRRA, which was soon an active (though not always witting) participant in illegal immigration to Palestine. Palestinian Jews formerly serving in the British Army reappeared in UNRRA camps, as did their American opposite numbers, and undertook military training for prospective immigrants. UNRRA's chief of operations for the three Western-occupied zones in Germany wrote of UNRRA that it was:

a convenient agency for the promotion and sustenance of armed aggression by the forces of Zionism against the British mandate in Palestine in fulfilment of the UN mandate.

The American Joint Distribution Committee (AJDC), known as *The Joint*, had been formed in the USA at the end of the First World War to assist indigent Jews. Although having no international authority or standing, the work done by the AJDC in Europe duplicated that of UNRRA. By this means it shared UNRRA facilities, whilst blossoming out and behaving as a separate entity within the framework, and under cover, of UNRRA. Unlike the latter, the AJDC's employees were extremely able and the greater proportion of a very large revenue, collected mainly in the USA, was thought to be expended not on food, clothing or other necessities but transporting and maintaining migrants on their way through Europe to the Mediterranean coast. In May 1947 the Joint Intelligence Committee concluded that:

(a) The AJDC is directly involved in promoting illegal immigration to Palestine, and

(b) without AJDC assistance the movement of Jews to Palestine on the present large scale would be impossible.

Another organisation suspected of participating in illegal immigration was the Canadian Organisation for Rehabilitation through Training (CORT), which, like the AJDC, had a large vehicle organisation.[15]

At an early stage after the German surrender, Mossad discovered that, following an incident with the press, President Truman had given instructions permitting Jewish refugees from Eastern Europe to enter the American zone of occupation in Germany and in Austria. Mossad was able to move Jews through Poland and Czechoslovakia to reach those two zones. There they were housed in Displaced Persons camps, which thus became staging camps for illegal immigrants. Some 250,000 Jews went through the camps by 1948 and Mossad gave preference for onward transportation to individuals most able to help build a state of Israel. Some 30 per cent of those chosen were of military age (16–35), older children and women in the early stages of pregnancy came next in order of priority and men and women over the age of 40 filled the remaining places. A contingent of Palyam acted as *'marines'* in illegal immigrant craft and by this means a Palyam commander afloat kept in touch with the Haganah national command in Palestine. The Palyam also trained and organised the immigrants and arranged stocks of weapons. Methods of passive and active resistance were rehearsed, and not the least of its aims was the creation of favourable propaganda.

Support for illegal immigration was not restricted to former allies. From late 1945 until demobilisation in June 1946, after the Foreign Office had taken the matter up with the War Office, the Jewish Brigade Group of the

British Army assisted Jews to travel across France to Marseilles. Another route crossed from Bavaria and Austria to La Spezia and Venice where travellers were helped by the Jewish Brigade Group and later by a fictitious British Army Unit *412 General Transport Company*, which operated for nearly 12 months. Two secondary routes existed, one to Romania's Black Sea port Constantza and another to the Yugoslav coast. President Tito's acquiescence to transits is said to have been won by Mr LaGuardia promising UNRRA supplies essential to the survival of the Yugoslav population.

DISPOSAL OF SURPLUS HM SHIPS

Shortly after the end of the war in Europe, Admiralty Military Branch (M Branch)[16] received an enquiry from Colonel Frank Bustard OBE, senior partner of the shipping agency Bustard and Sons. The Colonel had recently returned from wartime service which had acquainted him with the possibilities which lay with landing ships and craft brought into service during the war for amphibious operations. His firm now wished to acquire Tank Landing Ships and Craft (LSTs and LCTs) for commercial use and in due course sloops, frigates and corvettes on behalf of the Palestine League. Fortunately Director Naval Intelligence (DNI) got wind of what was in train and pointed out that the Palestine Maritime League (PML) was linked with the Haganah and possibly terrorist organisations as well. He requested that no sales should be made available 'to this or any other Jewish organisation, particularly at the present time when serious trouble in Palestine may be imminent'. With that proviso dealings with Bustards went ahead and later the firm chartered a large number of Landing Ships (Tank) for a long period. Other nations were warned of the possibility of approaches seeking craft for illegal immigration, particularly Canada and America, although in the latter case this was thought unlikely to achieve much.

Despite such precautions, HMS *Cutty Sark* was later sold to the Jewish Maritime League (JML), led by an active supporter of the New Zionist Organisation. This vessel was eminently suitable for immigrant running, she had been built on the Clyde as a steam yacht[17] from the plans of a small destroyer. In 1939 she was requisitioned by the Admiralty and became a warship. The sale only came to light when Naval Officer-in-Charge at Lowestoft signalled in early November 1945 seeking instructions concerning stores onboard including Wireless Telegraphy, modern radar and other navigational equipment which the JML wished to take over. Since the vessel was reported as not being in a fit state to go to sea, needing £20,000 worth of repairs, and it was possible that Lord Strabolgi[18] or Lord Nathan, supporters of JML, might raise objections in Parliament, the

Admiralty's Military Branch decided not to cancel the sale. There was reason to believe that use as a hostel or sea training vessel for boys was intended and if contractors made application for a licence for work then no facilities would be allowed. A contemporary note in *The Times* reported that she had been renamed '*Joseph Hertz*' and would be moored on the Victoria Embankment, but the front pages of other newspapers predicted a more likely use.

The Security Service, via DNI, now confirmed that Colonel Bustard could be expected to engage in further efforts on behalf of Palestinian shipping agencies and that he was closely connected with the Palestine Maritime League (PML), which was known to be involved in illegal immigration. Instructions were therefore given that no sales to Bustard and Sons or Jewish interests, especially the PML or the JML, were to be allowed without specific Admiralty authority. Eventually, in April 1947, a temporary embargo was placed on sales to foreign nations of British commercial cargo ships, passenger-carrying ships, or ships which could be converted for those purposes, of over 100 gross tons, other than for the express purpose of being broken up. Nine months later suspicion fell on a firm purchasing the former Royal Navy sloops HMS *Lowestoft* and HMS *Shoreham* on behalf of a Panamanian Company, to be registered in Panama and refitted at Genoa. As they were lying at Cardiff in an unfit state to go to sea arrangements could be made for registration to be withdrawn and to prevent repairs or departure. Nevertheless, these ships continued to cause concern and the legal obstacles to detaining any vessel in a British port were soon to become apparent.

PART II:

PALESTINE PATROL, 1945–46:
UNOPPOSED ARRESTS

5

Naval Assistance for the Palestine Government

By early September 1945, the Chiefs of Staff (CoS) Committee in London were in no doubt that seaborne illegal immigration was under way and instructions went to Supreme Allied Commander Mediterranean (SACMED) that:

> With the end of the war, it is expected that illegal Jewish immigration to Palestine will be intensified and the bulk of the illegal immigration will undoubtedly be by sea. You should, therefore, take all steps to prevent ships engaged in this trade from leaving ports in your command. It will be appreciated that although the coast of Palestine is regularly patrolled, it is desirable that such ships should be stopped before they leave port, rather than off the coast of Palestine.[19]

The signal added that, based on intelligence, large numbers of small craft were likely to be employed, rather than old steamers, and that Landing Craft would be included. The statement that the 'coast of Palestine' was being 'regularly patrolled' was misleading, since there was nothing there other than worn-out police launches. As yet the Navy had not been called in. But more importantly, no warning was given to take precaution against activities by sympathisers in SACMED's own forces, in particular the Jewish units that still existed there.

THE ROYAL NAVY'S ORGANISATION AND ARRANGEMENTS FOR PALESTINE

Command of the Mediterranean Fleet and naval establishments ashore in the Mediterranean area was exercised by Admiral Sir John Cunningham,[20] to whom the Levant command, Flag Officer Levant and Eastern Mediterranean (FOLEM) at Alexandria, was subordinated. FOLEM was a Vice-Admiral's post, currently filled by Vice-Admiral W.G. Tennant, and his responsibilities covered the area extending from the Aegean to Egypt. They included keeping a careful eye on naval aspects of the closing down of the French mandates in Syria and the Lebanon and the final departure of the French administration in fulfilment of the earlier promise to that effect. Ashore in the Levant, naval matters were under the superintendence of Senior Naval Officer Levant Administrations (Cyprus, Haifa and Beirut) (SNOLA(H)) functioning on FOLEM's behalf from HMS *Moreta*, the naval shore establishment at Haifa. There, the Navy's comprehensive wartime support and repair facilities were being closed.

In September 1945 Tennant proposed that his post should cease at the end of the year.[21] Their Lordships decided that FOLEM should remain until revision of the Anglo-Egyptian Treaty, then at a very delicate stage, was complete. SNOLA(H) was not a suitable authority to run the patrol and the Admiralty agreed a need for an operational commander provided with a command staff and sited in a cruiser with full command, control and communications capabilities. This task could be undertaken by a Mediterranean Fleet seagoing Admiral. Thus once naval forces became committed to operations in Palestine waters *Tactical Control*[22] was exercised by a Flag Officer acting locally. FOLEM continued to hold *Operational Control* and *Administrative Control* of the Eastern Mediterranean.

The RAF was commanded from Jerusalem where there was an Army and Royal Air Force Joint Headquarters (JHQ) with intelligence staffs. At this stage the JHQ lacked any Naval representative. To ensure coordination of surface and air operations in Home Waters, Naval CsinC held Operational Control of Royal Air Force maritime aircraft through *Maritime Headquarters* at which naval and air staffs worked closely together and on an equal footing. Although the Admiralty indicated the Palestine Force's operational commander should have facilities for coordinating searches with the RAF, an MHQ was not set up there. This shortcoming was soon to cause difficulties. Liaison with Army forces in Northern Palestine did not present any difficulties since the Army commander at hand in Haifa held sufficient delegated authority to work direct with the Naval commander.

'OWN FORCES'

The disturbed state of Palestine already necessitated the presence of a part of the Mediterranean Fleet in the Eastern Mediterranean area – the Palestine Force. The major units of the Fleet which were being drawn upon were:

1. **The Fifteenth Cruiser Squadron** (CS.15-Commodore M.J. Mansergh CB CBE): five light cruisers.

2a. **The Third Destroyer Flotilla** (D.3 – Captain M. Richmond DSO OBE RN): five large Fleet destroyers of the 'M-class' and four much smaller 'Hunt'-class escort destroyers, organised as the 5th and 6th Destroyer Divisions respectively.

2b. **The Fourteenth Destroyer Flotilla** (D.14 – Captain J.H. Ruck-Keene DSO OBE DSC RN): in the process of replacing two 'J'-class ships (HMS Jervis and HMS Javelin) with more modern and economical 'Ch'-class ships.

3. **Four Minesweeping Flotillas** (MSFs) under Senior Officers: the 5th MSF, which in late 1946 combined with the 8th MSF to form 2nd MSF; 12th MSF (until March 1946); and 19th MSF (until June 1946). Each flotilla included between six and eight robust Fleet Minesweepers of the modern 'Algerine' class, suitable for patrol duties. Other, smaller, minesweepers were engaged only in extensive post-war clearance operations.

4. **Anti-Aircraft Sloops and Frigates,** not allocated to flotillas or divisions: four frigates and four ' Black Swan'-class sloops, organised under the heading of Mediterranean Fleet Escorts. Three other 'Black Swan'-class sloops were on the station but formed a separate Trooping Division moving British troops and allied servicemen between ports and harbours in the Mediterranean.

Manpower was in short supply throughout the Navy at this stage of demobilisation. Although the Navy was being put on a peacetime footing as quickly as possible, ships of the Mediterranean Fleet still relied on a strong element of Reservists and '*Hostilities Only*' personnel. The ships' companies of the 3rd DF were most affected, for they had not been home since the end of the war. and when the CinC visited Haifa on 11 November he was able to break the news that the 'M's would return home in the New Year. They were to be replaced by the more modern 'V'-class Fleet destroyers, carrying fewer guns and manned by smaller ships' companies. Discontent had recently caused a mutiny in HMS *Javelin* and this news from the CinC not unnaturally improved the outlook of the 3rd DF. But the CinC gave a warning that some of their people might have to be retained on the station to make up shortages in other ships.

For surface search and detection purposes the warships of the types described were fitted with centimetric surface warning radar sets dating from the later war years and capable of detecting surface vessels out to the horizon. These sets needed very careful manual tuning and could not be counted on to detect small targets to their maximum range, particularly in high sea states when Plan Position Indicator (PPI) display screens became cluttered by returns from waves. They lacked stabilisation to keep the picture 'North up' and when the ship altered course contacts on the screen moved in azimuth. The range and bearings of contacts was read off the PPI and plotted manually on an Admiralty Research Laboratory Plotting Table (ARL Table). This compensated automatically for 'Own Ship's Movement' and thus enabled the course and speed of a contact to be established. Details of new detections and movements of contacts were reported verbally to the Officer of the Watch on the bridge and some ships had arrangements whereby he could view the plot from the bridge (View Plots). Off the Palestine coast at night as many as six contacts at a time could be showing on patrol vessel radar scans; and things were made no easier by many coastal trading vessels seldom showing navigation lights until aware of the approach of another vessel.

THE PLOT THICKENS

In August 1945 Admiral Tennant reported an uneasy quiet in Palestine. The Jewish community were waiting for an indication of the newly elected British Labour government's attitude to Zionist claims in the hope that their homeless and destitute relatives in Europe would be allowed to find refuge there. FOLEM forecast that all sections of the Jewish community were likely to provide support for a campaign against immigration restrictions. In the meantime, the Arabs awaited signs of a move either by the British or the Jews. Warning of what was to come was timely since the CinC, when laying down policy for the transition from war to peace conditions, foresaw the interruption of gun- and slave-running as a secondary role for his fleet but made no mention of illegal seaborne immigration. This started to get under way when at the end of the month two Jewish fishing boats went out to meet the first post-war illegal immigrant vessel, the *Dalin* and after two days searching a Kibbutz fishing boat brought ashore 35 immigrants on 2 September.

Dalin was followed by another five vessels, bringing increasing numbers, all of which landed their passengers successfully. *Nettuno A* from Italy, landed 70 immigrants on 4 September and *Gabriella*, from Greece, landed 40 on 9 September, both at Caesarea. Reports of up to 400 hundred illegal immigrants landing on the night 15/16 September reached the British authorities. A Sergeant in a Jewish Royal Army Service Corps company already known to be engaged in illegal immigration activity organised the embarkation of 168 illegal immigrants onboard the *Pietro A* in Italy and fitted a radio. The passengers were landed at Shefayim on 19 September. *Pietro* then returned to Italy carrying Mossad emissaries, radio operators ('*Gideons*') and Palyam members. Also embarked were 50 representatives from the Jewish Agency and another Jewish organisation, they were to work in Displaced Persons camps and Jewish communities. On 25 September the Port and Marine Division of the Palestine Police stopped a Syrian fishing vessel and arrested 10 illegal immigrants. Immigrants from the *Nettuno B* landed at Shefayim on 1 October and nine days later an armed attack on the Atlit transit camp near Haifa freed 200 illegal immigrants held there. In early September, approximately 150 illegals succeeded in disembarking in Haifa from SS *Ville D'Oran* concealed amongst legitimate immigrants.

Illegal immigration was becoming very troublesome and the Palestine Government was well aware that large numbers of Jewish refugees in Greece and Germany were awaiting their chance, not to mention others in Central Europe. Three vessels, including one named the *Asya*, were said to be available in Greece to embark illegal immigrants. Armed members of Palmach were providing security at landing places and other sections of Haganah moved the arrivals on to their destinations. Haganah was also actively gathering intelligence on coastal security measures, enabling situation reports to be passed from the Mossad centre by radio to approaching ships, all of which were, post-war, equipped with wireless. But finding sites suitable for landings was not proving easy as they needed to be close to Jewish settlements and away from police or Army posts.

The situation led FOLEM to give warning that the Palestine Administration was about to request naval assistance. He foresaw very large increases in the numbers likely to arrive – the Navy's 'Monthly Intelligence Report' (MIR) quoted for September a figure of 500 brought in by caïques.[23] FOLEM's requirement was for three or four destroyers or sloops with which to institute patrols. He accepted that for legal reasons vessels could only be arrested inside territorial waters, suspect vessels would thus be free to remain outside the 3-mile territorial limit until nightfall and then slip in during dark hours. This raised for the first, but by no means the last, time the question of whether search and arrest outside the limit of territorial waters could be allowed. Discussions in Whitehall included brief consideration of a precedent, 'anti-hovering' laws allowing the arrest of ships outside territorial waters. In the nineteenth century, Parliament had passed an Act permitting the arrest of suspected smugglers up to 100 leagues from the British coast. This proved unsatisfactory and in 1876 the Act was repealed. Similarly, at the time of Prohibition the United States allowed coastguard vessels to arrest bootlegger supply ships rendezvousing with customers outside territorial waters. But a seizure under these provisions had led to the United States Government having to pay heavy damages. The Navy was therefore instructed, and the Palestine Government was informed, that peacetime international law did not permit visiting or searching a vessel on the high seas unless she was suspected of having committed, or being about to commit, a breach of international law. Exceptions were only to be allowed if a suspect vessel flew an ex-enemy flag, i.e. those of Germany, Italy, Hungary, Romania or Bulgaria; then she could stopped and searched, but only until peace treaties came into effect. Other ships could also be stopped and boarded only and solely if it was necessary to ensure they were not ex-enemy vessels under false colours. Thus until a vessel transporting illegal immigrants entered Palestine Territorial waters and thereby broke the 'municipal law' of Palestine she was not to be stopped or arrested. As will be seen later, the Navy were in consequence soon presented with some very awkward problems.

Tension in Palestine continued to mount with Zionist leaders and notables in the Arab world publicly demonstrating little or no readiness to compromise on the immigration issue stirred up by President Truman. Both Palestine's northern neighbours, Syria and the Lebanon, took special measures to prevent Jews entering their territory. That the sea route was the easier option was demonstrated in October when Palestine's Arab neighbour Syria turned back 105 Bulgarian Jews who arrived from Turkey with valid visas. By that time, Naval Intelligence was reporting evidence of detailed plans and organisations active in Egypt, Greece, Turkey and Italy. FOLEM requested a second cruiser be kept in the Eastern Mediterranean basin from about 9 October and Naval ('Tableland') and RAF ('Sunbeam') operation orders were prepared in the Combined Services Operations Room at Alexandria in expectation of calls for assistance. Whilst provision was made to run the port of Haifa and keep Haifa Oil Refinery in operation, unlike the 1936–39 period other forms of assistance ashore were not to be provided. Intelligence received from Cairo and northern Mediterranean ports and collated by Staff Officer (Intelligence) Levant and Middle East (SO(I)LEM) at Alexandria was to form the basis for the number of vessels on patrol. Shipping intelligence provided by local port authorities could seldom give much of a guide as to times or names of expected arrivals or departures. Patrol lines were planned a few miles out from the shore and covering some 60 miles of the Palestine coast where Jews might be expected to land and be received by Jews, rather than Arabs; all vessels approaching that area were to be investigated. Initially the period of duty for ships undertaking sea patrols was to be three months, with the two destroyer flotillas alternating on station.

A further attempt at mingling illegal immigrants with legal passengers was forecast by the press in Istanbul who reported that the Soviet–Romanian Transport Company intended to sail the *Transylvania* on 22 October with 1054 Jewish emigrants onboard. Britain requested the governments of Belgium, Czechoslovakia, Holland, France, Italy, Romania and the USSR stop illegal immigrants departing for Palestine. Possession of an entry permit or visa for one country was in some cases necessary for leaving another, so Mexican and Panamanian authorities were requested not to issue entry permits to immigrants who clearly had no intention of travelling to their territory. Recently the Palestine Government had sent three Immigration Officers to attend embarkation of legal immigrants at Taranto and their efforts in preventing 'intermingling' had been successful. This led Lord Gort, the High Commissioner of Palestine,[24] to favour preventive measures at the ports of embarkation as likely to be the only effective means of preventing seaborne illegal immigration. Often criticised for concentrating too much on minor matters, on this occasion Gort showed wider vision in suggesting that the problem would eventually be one for the successor organisation to the League of Nations. The High Commissioner also broached the possibility of illegal immigration vessels being diverted to Cyprus or, as an alternative, the passengers deported to Cyprus. The events concerning *Patria* and *Struma* led him to rule out that course of action. Lord Gort agreed the view suggested by Secretary of State for the Colonies that whilst every effort should be made to capture the vessels and prosecute the crews, illegal immigrants reaching Palestine should be permitted to go free with their number being deducted from the legal quota – in other words that 'gate crashing' should be treated leniently and allowed to continue.

THE START OF PATROL OPERATIONS

The activities of the illegal immigrant runners led, much later, to 27 September 1945 being identified as the effective date from which naval personnel in ships of the Palestine Force were entitled to the award of the Naval General Service Medal with the clasp 'Palestine'. During October the Mediterranean Fleet's detached Palestine Force grew to include a cruiser, five destroyers of the 3rd Flotilla and the sloop HMS *Peacock*. On 16 October the 1st Guards Brigade arrived at Haifa to augment the Middle East strategic reserve and join 1st Division in the northern half of Palestine whilst 6th Airborne Division was on its way to the Gaza area in the south. Haifa's facilities, and the fact that Jews comprised a far smaller proportion of the population than at Tel Aviv, meant it was best suited for landing or trans-shipping illegal immigrants who had been detained. Nevertheless the plight of the latter was in plain view and Jewish elements, in a town where immigration had doubled the population in a little over ten years, took every advantage of this situation. As early as the night of 19/20 October an attempt was made to sabotage police launches but failed.

Anti-immigration patrols were activated on the evening of 20 October when the Senior Naval Officer (Afloat) (SNO(A)) in HMS *Orion* (Captain R. Heathcote DSO RN) ordered the 'Hunt'-class destroyers HMS *Haydon* (Commander J.M. Rowland RN) and HMS *Stevenstone* (Lieutenant-Commander C.A.H. Owen DSC RN) to sail from Haifa and HMS *Brissenden* (Lieutenant L.R.P. Lawford DSC RN) to sail from Beirut. Intelligence indicated the approach of an illegal vessel, but despite the usual host of small Levantine trading vessels and auxiliary trading schooners plying a peaceful trade along the coast nothing suspicious was seen. The principal difficulties proved to be scarcity of firm intelligence and the perennial post-war problem of shortage of communications ratings to man ships' radio circuits: for example, three circuits needed to be manned whenever air searches were in progress.

On 26 October SS *Transylvania*, under a Romanian master, arrived as anticipated with forty-two illegal immigrants amongst legal immigrants and the illegal contingent was removed to the Atlit Transit Camp. A response soon came when the Palyam damaged two Palestine Police Launches at Haifa and sank another at Jaffa, causing the High Commissioner to request the Colonial Office do all they could to expedite the arrival of the HDMLs originally requested in January. The Stern Gang also attempted to blow up the refinery.

THE FIRST ARREST

By the beginning of November the 'Dido'-class cruiser HMS *Sirius* (Captain R.I.M. Edwards CBE RN) was moored stern on to the main jetty at Haifa with Commodore Mansergh (CS.15) embarked and serving as Senior Naval Officer Levant (Haifa)(Afloat) (SNOLA(Haifa)). This cumbersome original title very soon became shortened to 'SNO (Afloat) Haifa' (SNO(A)) and thereafter if CS.15 was not embarked, the commanding officer of the resident cruiser took charge as SNO(A). The force was reinforced on 2 November by HMS *Marne* (Lieutenant-Commander P.A.R. Withers DSO DSC RN), HMS *Musketeer* (Lieutenant-Commander R.H. Aubrey DSC RN) and one 'Hunt'-class ship of the 3rd Flotilla. Secure 'Scrambler' telephonic communication was established with the joint Army–RAF operations room at the King David Hotel in Jerusalem. This link, though liable to sabotage and breakdown, proved vital to the rapid passing of intelligence and the control of searches.

When CinC Mediterranean Fleet visited Haifa between 9 and 11 November in HMS *Aurora* the RAF was already undertaking air searches whilst a reinforced marine section of the Palestine Police conducted offshore patrols. By 14 November FOLEM had instituted patrols although the direct involvement of the Navy had not yet been approved and was still being considered in Whitehall. Thereafter two ships at a time were at sea on patrol, with stand-offs being taken at Beirut. On 21 November FOLEM signalled that, at the request of the High Commissioner and with the concurrence of CinC Middle East, he had instructed CS.15 to use destroyers to intercept an approaching schooner. If ex-enemy she would be boarded on the high seas and, if found to be carrying illegal immigrants, arrested; if not ex-enemy then she would be shadowed and arrested on entering Palestine's territorial waters.

FOLEM's signal reached the Admiralty at 1655 the same day. Action of this kind had been agreed already between departments in Whitehall but

Ministers had not yet been asked for approval. This was not a welcome task at any level of the Navy but their agreement was obtained on 23 November, by then the first interception of an illegal immigrant vessel had been completed. Late the previous evening, when investigating flares inshore north of Jaffa Light, the sloop HMS *Peacock* (Lieutenant-Commander F.M. Osborne DSC RN) sighted the small Greek steamer Dimitrios lying very close to the beach with four or five small boats ferrying immigrants ashore. No resistance was offered to Peacock's boarding party of an officer and five men, who found 20 dirty but fit and well clothed illegal immigrants onboard.

Three hours after the *Peacock*'s suspicions were first aroused, HMS *Haydon* on an adjacent patrol line sighted another flare and pursued two small sailing boats making for the shore. These were rounded up with some difficulty, the final arrest taking the destroyer drawing 17 feet, into only 30 feet of water. Similar craft were seen on the beach, as were people on the low sand cliff tops, and since these events took place between 0300 and 0500 they were thought to be a reception party. Indeed, a Palmach security team had seized a group of Arab fisherman, but one escaped and informed the Police of what was afoot. The Boarding Officer found large quantities of food and clothing in both boats, a telltale tube of Greek toothpaste added to his suspicions and he concluded that, although in possession of fishing licences, and in view of attempts to escape, these were not genuine fishermen. This was entirely correct. Four sailing boats, similar to those used by the Arabs, had in fact been employed. One contained a Palyam member who rose later to be the commander of the Israeli Navy. Both the captured boats were towed by the *Haydon*'s motorboat to Jaffa and handed over to the Police with their crews, who spent six months in prison.

Mossad had chartered the *Dimitrios* in Greece and her master willingly admitted he had embarked 50 passengers from Athens, the 20 still onboard were dirty but fit and well clothed. One of the passengers stated that it was common knowledge among Jews in Poland that regular shipments of illegal immigrants were departing from Greece for Palestine. He added that the Russian authorities assisted the crossing of frontiers to reach Greece for that purpose and a Jewish contact in Greece arranged the remainder of their journey. The Haifa District Court later acquitted the Master and crew of all charges, probably on the grounds that as the ship was intercepted inside territorial waters they could not be charged with aiding illegal immigrants. However, on subsequent appeal the Master was convicted and sentenced to two years in prison. The *Dimitrios* was the forerunner of many unseaworthy vessels carrying masses of unwelcome humanity in overcrowded and filthy conditions to a land which the organisers of these human cargoes led them to believe was theirs by right.

The riposte to the arrest came on the night of 24/25 November when two coast guard stations, one near Hadera and the other near Tel-Aviv, were attacked with explosives in a carefully planned operation for which the Palyam claimed credit. The subsequent search for the terrorists engaged in this attack resulted in the first open clash between Haganah and British troops for several years.

Captain (D.3) assumed local control and administration of both destroyers and sloops when he returned to Haifa 28 November in the Flotilla Leader HMS *Milne* accompanied by the cruiser HMS *Aurora*. From 3 December SNO(A) instituted a routine of a single-ship patrol, with a second ship at anchor in Haifa Bay at two hours' notice. The remainder of his force berthed at Haifa except for one ship stood down at Beirut. Standard patrol sectors 20 miles long were established along the 117-mile coast and named after alcoholic drinks, for example 'Scotch Whisky'. Patrolling ships carried a Palestine Policeman whose presence made arrests legal. From 19 December a nightly curfew was imposed on the coast between Attra and Tantura.

The opening phase of the operation saw the boarding and search of many caïques in order to prevent attempts to land immigrants over open beaches when weather conditions were suitable. The warships gained valuable experience in effecting interceptions by homing onto contacts detected by the air patrols, shadowing to the 3-mile limit, stopping vessels, when necessary by firing across their bow, and finally directing Marine Police launches, reinforced by naval personnel, in to board a vessel. Good cooperation between all three services concerned – Royal Navy, Royal Air Force and the Marine Section of the Palestine Police – could not be taken for granted, they had to learn to work together and at first the task was not regarded as of the first importance. At an early stage the General Officer Commanding (GOC) at Jerusalem requested the provision of a Naval Liaison Officer at JHQ. Captain (D), Third Destroyer Flotilla sent his Flotilla Signals Officer Lieutenant G.A. Millward RN on a temporary basis to undertake a task which the first incumbents found not to be particularly clearly defined. After five weeks he was relieved by the Flotilla Gunnery Officer, Lieutenant C.P.N. Wells-Cole RN. Later, following considerable questioning of the need for additional manpower, a permanent post was established.

Arrangements were found still to be less than perfect following a police intelligence forecast of a night landing north of Acre, near the Jewish settlement at Nahariya, on 22 December. Two ships were sent out on patrol and found nothing. Two days later Royal Air Force Levant was given the scent and launched an air search, which sighted the 'target' and reported her movement. By then it was late on Christmas Eve and staff were dispersing for the night. The information did not reach CS.15 and 24 hours later there was news of a successful landing by the 200-ton schooner *Marie*, given by the organisers the Hebrew name or alias *Hannah Szenesh*. After being sighted by the reconnaissance aircraft, the *Marie* had prudently diverted away from the landing beach to which she had been seen heading, evaded the patrolling destroyer and beached herself on Christmas Day in the area originally predicted. She put ashore 250 immigrants, mainly Polish Jews who for the last 36 hours of the voyage were said to be without water. Something of the bitterness with which the British were regarded as a result of their well-meant efforts to hold the balance of fair play between Arab and Jew could be judged from the inscription on a flag found in the vessel:

> This is the boat *Hanna Szenesh* [*sic*] which disembarked immigrants on Naharia sea shore with assistance of the Jewish Defence Organisation and in memory of six million Jews killed in Europe and as a certificate of shame to the British Government.

Thereafter for quite a lengthy period no other illegal immigrant vessels were encountered. The many vessels intercepted, although reluctant in some cases to obey the Navy's orders to stop outside territorial waters, all submitted without opposition to boarding after crossing the 3-mile limit. CS.15 departed on 27 December and bad weather meant the patrol did not have to be maintained for the period over the end of December. Although the resident cruiser provided 40 sailors a night to guard Navy House in Haifa, there was a lull in terrorist activity ashore and there were no restrictions on leave or travel. In response to the request made twelve months earlier, two 72-foot Harbour Defence Motor Launches (MLs 1145 and 1246) at last arrived and were turned over to the Palestine Police on 4 January. ML 1277 followed, delayed by breakdowns, and she had been sent all this way in too poor a mechanical state to be accepted by the intended owners. Another six months passed before ML 1126 arrived as a substitute.

PRECAUTIONS AGAINST SABOTAGE

Police coast-watching and radar stations were again attacked on 21 January and 20 February, whilst Police launches and other vessels were again sabotaged. Conditions for ships when off patrol at Haifa were never easy; considerable precautions had to be taken whether in harbour or at anchor outside, and similar measures were necessary when in Cypriot ports. An Officer of the Watch was maintained on deck round the clock, gangway staffs were armed with revolvers and at least two or three upper deck sentries were posted armed with 9mm Lanchester sub-machine guns. Their tasks were made no easier by the understanding that the trade of the port should not be interrupted and thus many small craft came and went close to the warships. At night each warship illuminated the water in its vicinity using yardarm groups, backed up by illumination circuits, and turned propellers every ten minutes or so to wash underwater swimmers away. Precautions included the dropping into the water of one-and-a-quarter-pound (½kg) explosive charges to deter swimmers. Expenditure became so heavy, with individual ships dropping as many as forty charges a night, that to economise Operation 'Clock' was instituted, whereby some or all ships dropped charges at predetermined but constantly varied times. Later a further economy was achieved by using a boat to drop charges ahead of a line of ships (Operation 'Watch'). The extent of precautions necessary placed severe demands on ships' companies, who even off watch were constantly disturbed by the explosions.

In addition to Operation 'Clock', each morning ships' bottoms needed to be searched for limpet mines as an additional precaution (Operation 'Frog'). In those days the Navy's Gunnery branch was responsible for diving matters. Thus besides his activities as the Navy's man in Jerusalem, Lieutenant Wells-Cole[25] undertook this task of swimming under ships each morning. Initially the Davis submarine escape breathing apparatus was employed and later the very expert Temporary Acting Lieutenant-Commander L.K. Crabb OBE GC RNVR was brought from Venice as a diving instructor. CS.15 (now Rear-Admiral H.R.C. Kinahan) praised his enthusiasm and hard work under difficult material and weather conditions. There was never any lack of volunteers for his courses: it was found that an individual could be trained in between seven and 14 days and by this means each ship acquired a team of about one officer and four men trained as Ship's Shallow Water Divers. Water conditions, in particular the underwater visibility, in the area were such that two divers with the right equipment could complete a thorough search of a ship's bottom in three to four minutes. But if there was a possibility the saboteurs had used Cordtex explosive a more thorough search was needed taking ten times longer. Whether due to effective precautions or, as some of the opposition say, a decision not to attack warships, none was ever damaged in this way. 'Buster' Crabb's services were called on several times and he conducted training at Malta besides taking charge of diving parties at Haifa.

THE POLICY BACKGROUND

In December 1945 the limit set for Jewish immigrants in the 1939 White Paper was reached. At this point immigration should have continued only if agreed by the Arabs, but the British Government decided that, in the circumstances, admission of 1,500 immigrants per month would continue. The High Commissioner, by now Lieutenant-General Sir Alan Cunningham, had then to perform the unpleasant task of informing representatives of the Arabs and the Jews. The former protested furiously against the break-ing of the promise that there would be no further immigration without their consent. The latter were equally annoyed because the figure set did not meet their demands. Illegal immigrants continued to be admitted against the quota and this meant that until November 1946 the available places were entirely taken up by 'gatecrashers'. Since illegal arrivals were not sent back whence they came, the High Commissioner was also faced with the problem of custody of ever increasing numbers. He foresaw being forced to introduce deportation, increase the quota or, as a deterrent, simply cease releases until HMG announced a decision regarding future immigration. Any of these courses of action were bound to be bitterly resented by one or other element of the community and so nothing more was done for the time being. General Cunningham did request patrols, either British or Greek, off the coast of Greece as an additional measure. But the CinC considered patrols off Palestine more effective and lacked sufficient ships for both areas. In any case the problem of sailings from Greek ports was being dealt with through the Greek government.

THE *RONDINA*

Early in 1946 Mossad experienced difficulty in finding vessels for more than 1,500 Jews each month and sought larger ships. The first of these was the 500-ton *Rondina*, described by a Jewish source as 'modern, strong, pleasant and spacious and the property of a Jew, Mr Pinter'. Mr Pinter regularly engaged in this form of trade and on this occasion the vessel cost the Jewish 'authorities' £25,000, the overall cost of the venture being £35,000. Her fuel was apparently obtained in exchange for whisky, whilst food came from Army installations. Nine hundred would-be passengers made the final stages of their journey to the coast near Savona in Italy concealed in 40 Army lorries led by a jeep in which sat a Jew disguised in a Lieutenant's uniform.

The first warning of the *Rondina*'s approach came on the morning of 16 January 1946, when Palestine Military Intelligence staff reported that two days previously an illegal immigrant vessel had been seen in the Scarpanto Channel heading for Palestine at a maximum speed of six knots. Senior Naval Officer Afloat (SNO (A)), currently in HMS *Sirius* sent two destroyers out on a patrol. This catered for the risk of a slightly higher speed of advance and his prudence appeared to be justified later when JHQ forecast a landing before midnight in the Tel-Aviv or Caesarea area. Both places were catered for and a third destroyer was sailed to patrol to the northward. Air Officer Commanding RAF Levant was unable to arrange an afternoon air search; he lacked sufficient aircraft for searches on two days and an attempt at a landing the following day seemed more likely.

Later JHQ came to the same conclusion but since the intelligence reports were inconsistent, SNO(A) felt it prudent not to relax his precautions.

Nothing was found during the night and at daylight two of the destroyers were recalled. Then at 1000 an aircraft located a 500-ton motor vessel which caused suspicion and the destroyer HMS *Talybont* (Lieutenant-Commander J.A. Holdsworth RN) was dispatched to intercept her. The initial position proved to be 20 miles in error, not unusual for a single-seat fighter rather than a maritime aircraft with a navigator. However, a Mustang fighter provided further reports and an interception was successfully made in 33° 25'N 34° 51'E at 1415. The suspect flew an unidentifiable flag, there were rafts and wooden ladders on deck and a canvas screen failed to conceal the presence of a considerable number of people. A boarding party was sent to establish the vessel's nationality and as it approached three or four heavy cases, resembling those used for transporting rifles and ammunition, were seen being put over the side. The master claimed to be Portuguese and tried to enlist sympathy by a tale of having been in a German concentration camp and seen many Jews exterminated. Nevertheless, he could not produce his vessel's papers and documents of ex-enemy and Hebrew origin recovered from the water showed connections with Jewish soldiers in Italy.

Although well outside territorial waters, the *Rondina* was directed to Haifa, on grounds of unidentifiable nationality. As soon as her fate was decided a large number of people appeared from below, hoisted the Zionist flag and began to sing. She carried 908 young immigrants (551 men, 357 women), who were almost immediately released by the Palestine Government as deductions against the quota. The original plan made by those organising her voyage had been that they should enter as legal immigrants, but the quota then closed, due probably to 'gatecrashers', and a decision was made to continue the voyage. Amongst them were some notable underground fighters against the Germans and a shortage of Jewish labour meant that immediate employment was available for all.

The *Rondina* was very well equipped, being amply provided with American and stolen British Army rations and blankets, as well as excellent navigational aids. Sanitary arrangements were of lesser priority, it seemed, for they were entirely lacking and with so many people onboard the smell was appalling, but the standard of cleanliness elsewhere was high. She had been carefully navigated and details of her voyage were reconstructed from her chart. Although positions and track had been erased from the last one, which *Talybont* recovered from the water, markings with a hard pencil had not been totally erased and these confirmed she had sailed from Italy. *Rondina*'s Master was unsuccessfully prosecuted under Palestine Emergency Regulations. The vessel herself was not liable to forfeiture for, although she was an ex-enemy vessel not carrying proper papers, she had been arrested on the high seas and she was later returned to her owners.

At this time post-war demobilisation was causing acute shortages of manpower throughout the Navy, particularly in some skilled trades. The 'Hunt'-class destroyer HMS *Stevenstone* rejoined the patrol in January with no Electrical Artificers or Electrical Mechanics of leading rate and only 50 per cent of her complement of Leading Stokers. This was not untypical. The 14th Destroyer Flotilla, with Captain Ruck-Keene in HMS *Chequers*, relieved the 3rd Flotilla on 2 February and the 'M'-class destroyers departed to pay off.

At the end of January the routine for patrols was again relaxed and all that was required was one destroyer anchored in Haifa Bay at two hours notice. On 7 February intelligence necessitated the routine of one destroyer on sea patrol and another at two hours notice being reinstituted. Three days later the RAF initiated a routine afternoon sweep by four fighter aircraft out to 30 miles from the coast. SNO(A) was concerned that these searches did not go out far enough and that a vessel could remain out of range and then reach the coast during the night. He sought the use of twin-engined Warwick maritime reconnaissance aircraft instead, but there were insufficient numbers of these aircraft for a daily patrol. The High Commissioner took a hand, believing that the RAF in Palestine needed major increases in key personnel and flying hours to meet his requirements and he raised through the Colonial Office the insufficiency of aircraft available to search for Mossad ships. Three weeks later the Air Staff responded that there was no question of reinforcing the RAF squadrons in Palestine; sufficient air support was held to be available. Then terrorist incidents ashore again increased in scale and tempo;[26] three RAF airfields were attacked and also, not for the first time, Mount Carmel radar station, where there was serious damage.

Whether or not Admiral Tennant was aware that Mossad in Paris had decided to increase operations, in March 1946, he forecast a likely large increase in scale of the illegal immigration traffic. FOLEM felt the existing force of destroyers assisted by two or three police launches would be inadequate to deal with such an invasion and he suggested that six additional HDMLs would be needed. The Admiralty refused however to commit any more forces, holding that whilst the Royal Navy had a part to play, the Palestine Government held the primary responsibility for prevention of illegal immigration. Six surplus Royal Navy HDMLs were offered to the Palestine Government but shortage of naval manpower meant that it would have to provide crews. The offer was declined as the Palestine Government also lacked the manpower. In the meantime, in April the American Joint Distribution Committee stopped funding Mossad on the grounds that its efforts were proving unsuccessful. As has been mentioned Mossad had concluded earlier that larger ships should be used. That decision made the task of the Patrol easier in one respect, for although a large vessel had a better capability for resisting arrest, she would be easier to identify and intercept than small craft mingled with coastal traffic.

41

THE 14TH DESTROYER FLOTILLA'S FIRST ARRESTS –
THE *WINGATE* AND THE *ASYA*

On the night 25/26 March the 14th DF made its first arrest, when HMS *Chevron* (Commander J.F.D. Bush RN) intercepted and took into Haifa a small motor vessel reported to be *Kismet Adalia*, alias *Charles Orde Wingate*, carrying 248 passengers. Although the attempt had been thwarted, supporters ashore had made very widespread reception arrangements. There were incidents when Jews, police or security guards opened fire, including a prolonged fire fight, with a party attempting to blow up an electric transformer. The District Court subsequently declared the *Wingate* forfeit.

The next interception, two days later, was a copybook example of good teamwork. Details passed by SO(I)LEM proved extremely accurate, enabling the approaching vessel to be located by a Warwick aircraft which homed in HMS *Chequers*. When intercepted, the *Asya*, known under the alias *Tel Hai*, was flying the Turkish flag and the presence of illegal immigrants concealed below decks was given away by a five-seater heads on either side of the ship's waist, an excessive number of life rafts and inquisitive faces peering out. The boarding party sent to establish identity met no resistance and, as soon as they arrived onboard, swarms of illegal immigrants came on deck and replaced the Turkish flag by several Zionist flags. The Master and crew of 12 (nine Turks and three Greeks) claimed that they had no control over the passengers and that the locked Wireless Room was in charge of a passenger who could not be identified. This explanation paralleled that given by the Master of the *Las Perlas* seven years previously and, in combination with concealment of crew amongst the passengers, came to be used by the sailing crews as a routine and reliable means of attempting to escape prosecution.

Although *Aysa*'s master claimed to have sailed from Corsica, the charts showed, and he then confessed, that he had embarked the passengers at La Ciotat, a Jewish community on the French coast near Marseilles, a 'smugglers' cove' sited at the foot of precipitous cliffs with no access by motor vehicles. Members of the crew reported that French police had supervised the embarkation and an UNRRA investigation later found that illegal immigrants there were being supplied with UNRRA victuals. The *Asya*'s intended destination appeared to be just north of Jaffa but the Master now quite willingly steered for Haifa at seven and a half knots. The immigrants numbered 733, about half being female, mainly pregnant, and were dressed in good quality hiking rig, many exhibiting tattoos showing concentration camp identification numbers. A German doctor appeared to be their leader, he had two nurses working in a sick bay and a dispensary provided with adequate quantities of drugs and dressings. The passengers sang continuously, had large quantities of food onboard –

much of it American rations – which they ate by messes. They appeared very content at being taken to Haifa. The District Court declared the vessel forfeit to the Government and appeals against this judgement were unsuccessful.

After the *Asya*'s arrival intelligence reports that no further illegal vessels were in the offing again enabled a temporary reduction in patrol activity. This was fortunate as a shortage of engine-room personnel and constant short notice for steam imposed considerable strain. Joint operations did not always match joint intelligence, it seems: *Sirius* reported when she left on 7 April that although the Lieutenant RN appointed as Naval Liaison Officer, Joint Operations Room Jerusalem, was bringing about improvements, arrangements for cooperation between aircraft and destroyer patrols had 'still not proved very satisfactory and were too dependent on personalities'. By now FOLEM's overall tasks had become much reduced, his post was replaced and the responsibilities for Operational and Administrative Command passed to the CinC.

LEGAL VESSELS: ILLEGAL PASSENGERS

Although not a matter for the navy, passengers arriving in legal vessels continued to include concealed illegal immigrants. In November 1945, 37 illegals had been found onboard SS *Mataroa* and in April 1946 76 illegal immigrants arrived over and above the 833 legal passengers onboard SS *Champollion*. The latter's owners, Messageries Maritimes, a French Government concern, were informed that a further event of this kind 'might' lead to criminal proceedings including forfeiture of the vessel. A special UNRRA officer in American Army uniform and two American Joint Distribution Committee representatives (one apparently a former Zionist infiltrator into UNRRA) were shepherding the illegal immigrants onboard the *Champollion* and an interpreter attached by the shipping line complained of their anti-British utterances. Colonial Office officials declined to take up with UNRRA the conduct of their employees and the matter had to be pursued again later, with more success.

Romania was by now again becoming an area where illegal immigrants could be expected to embark and a dummy run the previous year by a Soviet-Russian Transport Company vessel with 42 illegals embarked was thought to have been connived at by the Soviets. After pressure from the British Military Mission, the authorities at Constanza frustrated an attempt by a coastal steamer to take 1,500 illegal immigrants onboard.

SUSPICIOUS CRAFT

The small trading vessel *Dory* was reported to have left Ancona on 19 April and arrangements for an air search ceased when the Police at Jaffa saw the craft on 26 April. At the time she was thought to have successfully landed illegal immigrants but current Israeli records show this not to have been the case.

6

The Rising Tide of Seaborne Illegal Immigration

THE PALESTINE COMMISSION REPORT

On 1 May the Anglo-American Palestine Commission issued its report, including a recommendation that 100,000 entry permits should be authorised immediately. It also suggested that Palestine should be neither an Arab nor a Jewish state. The figure of 100,000 was set in acknowledgement that there were 500,000 Jews in Europe who had no hope in 'starting up again and will wish or be compelled to leave Europe'; the Committee evidently bore in mind that there were parts of the world other than Palestine to which the remaining 400,000 could emigrate.

In other respects, the Commission's solution was the same as that contained in the British 1939 White Paper. Not surprisingly, in view of the Arab attitude, the Prime Minister thought it prudent to establish whether the US Government would help face the consequences of admitting 100,000 Jews despite Arab objections, and share the inevitable increased military and financial responsibilities. He accompanied this enquiry with a blunt warning that the risk of Soviet penetration of the Middle East was the only decisive factor weighing Britain against giving up the Mandate. This approach proved fruitless, the US Government at first prevaricated and much later refused to be involved in these practicalities.

The Committee had also highlighted the existence of illegal Arab and Jewish armies and the Government decided that these must be disbanded before going any further. This view was totally unrealistic, indeed the lack of any such prospect was demonstrated by increased terrorist activity by both the Haganah and the IZL caused by lack of progress in admitting the 100,000. Eventually the British Government came round to agreeing that figure, but by then even that number did not satisfy Zionist aspirations. The report of the Anglo-American Commission simply worsened the problem with the Arabs, whilst leaving responsibility for maintaining peace and calm in an increasingly divided land with the power left holding the mandate when the League of Nations collapsed.

45

SMYRNA, FEDE AND FENICE, PART I: INTELLIGENCE SUCCESSES

Intelligence reported the Smyrna was preparing to leave Constanza on 7 April with 1,500 illegal immigrants embarked. This vessel, owned by Jean Pandelis, a Greek residing in Bucharest and one of two brothers who had owned Struma, had been intended to be employed evacuating Jews in 1944. The venture failed; she later came into the hands of the Revisionists and was transferred to the Central Committee of the Jewish Community in Bucharest who arranged her voyage to Palestine. Romania being an occupied former enemy nation the British Military Mission was requested to intervene with the Allied Control Commission and the Soviet authorities confirmed that those concerned held visas for entry to Mexico. There was no authority in Romania authorised to act in the name of the Mexican Government and the visas were forgeries issued by Jewish officials in the Ministry of the Interior. Air searches flown by Warwick aircraft and sea patrols started 9 April and a false alarm caused 18 fighter aircraft to conduct a dawn search on 13 April, with two Warwicks searching as well. Twenty-four hours later there were reports of the approach of the Hanna Fold with 930 immigrants, but nothing was seen and on 19 April Smyrna was reported still to be at Constanza.

Mossad also planned to sail two ships, Fede and Fenice, from La Spezia in Italy. Three groups of refugees were assembled in Italy at some distance from the port whilst the ships were stored, with food and provisions taken from British Army stores. Then 38 British Army trucks, diverted from their authorised route from Udine to Rome by members of 179 and 650 Palestinian General Transport Companies of the Royal Army Service Corps, embarked the immigrants and set out for La Spezia. They were led by a Jew disguised as a British Army major. However, the operation had become too well known and a local belief that it was an attempt by Nazis or Fascists to flee the country caused the police to stop the convoy, seize both ships and establish the truth. The local prefect subsequently volunteered that he would not have taken any action but for a warning of Fascists escaping.

Once halted the immigrants started a hunger strike, ever a good method of gaining public attention but seldom carried to great lengths. These events came to the notice of Professor Harold Laski, the current chairman of the Labour Party Executive Committee,[27] who chanced to be in the neighbourhood. He was known to back the admission of the 100,000 immigrants as recommended by the Anglo-American Commission and undertook, with the assistance of the Embassy Labour attaché, to represent the viewpoint of the would-be immigrants to the British Government. At much the same moment representatives of the Jewish Agency went to see General Cunningham, whilst leading supporters of the Jews in London visited the Foreign Office. These meetings led to agreement that Fede and

Fenice's passengers would be counted against the quota of legal immigrants and, on that basis, admitted to Palestine. The numbers involved were too many to include in the April quota and so the Agency undertook that the two ships would not arrive before 17 May. The British Ambassador reported that Professor Laski had handled a difficult task firmly yet tactfully, but this solution once again had unfortunate consequences for those who had a better case for going to Palestine and were applying to do so by the proper means.

In early May HMS *Chevron* brought a draft of Palestinian Royal Navy ratings from Alexandria to Haifa and when they disembarked a kit bag containing blocks of gun cotton fitted with a detonator, Bickford's fuse and safety lighter was found left onboard. The draft was immediately searched, detonators were also found in clothing, and Sick Berth Attendant Martosh (returning from the minesweeper HMS *Sphinx*) was later handed over to the Police to face serious charges concerning explosives.

SMYRNA, FEDE AND *FENICE*, PART II: INTERCEPTIONS

When discussing the fate of those onboard *Fede* and *Fenice*, the Agency representatives had chosen not to mention the matter of the *Smyrna*. Both the High Commissioner and Foreign Office were well aware this vessel was likely to reach Palestine with illegal immigrants before 17 May. Attempts to prevent her sailing proved unsuccessful and on 8 May she was reported to have departed from Constanza. An aircraft sighted her on 13 May, she was intercepted and shadowed by HMS *Jervis* (Commander D.H. Maitland-Makgill-Crichton DSO RN) until 2.6 miles from Carmel Point and then instructed to stop, a burst from a 20mm Oerlikon gun across her bows proving necessary. When the boarding party arrived onboard her Master explained that the passengers had raided his cabin and thrown away his personal papers, as well as destroying the wireless apparatus. The police then took over and the vessel with 1,760 refugees was taken into Haifa. By then there were no signs of the Mexican visas used to leave Romania.

Once again the Boarding Officer reported incredible overcrowding and very primitive sanitary arrangements. Water had run out some days previously and the immigrants were pathetically grateful for the little which the Boarding Party could provide. Food supplies had been exhausted 48 hours before the boarding. Release of the *Smyrna*'s passengers against the quota started on 28 May and the Master and her crew were not prosecuted, due to doubt whether they were in control of the ship when she entered territorial waters. Vigorous steps were taken through diplomatic representatives in both Bucharest and Moscow to prevent a further sailing, for which preparations at Constanza were well advanced; these were successful, the vessel, again owned by Mr Pandelis, eventually departing without embarking illegal immigrants. She was last heard of going ashore on the Yugoslav coast with passengers embarked and becoming a total wreck.

On 18 May, following another sighting by the RAF, *Fede* and *Fenice*, wearing Italian flags, were intercepted by HMS *Charity* (Lieutenant-Commander D.W. Austin RN), joined later by HMS *Chaplet* (Lieutenant-Commander R.H.C. Wyld DSC RN). The *Fede* was boarded and directed to Haifa whither the *Fenice* followed her. Both ships were very full of immigrants, many being young people of both sexes in high spirits. Police took over without difficulty on arrival at Haifa but, because of the circumstances already outlined, the vessels were not detained once their passengers had been removed and thus they were able to return to Italy.

COMMAND, CONTROL AND COMMUNICATIONS – PRACTICAL ASPECTS

HMS *Superb* (Captain W.G.A. Robson DSO DSC RN), arrived in June and although the most modern cruiser to undertake the SNO(A) Haifa task, soon found the volume of signal traffic almost more than a private cruiser with a diluted complement could cope with. A shortage of senior rates and Coder ratings was particularly felt and after the first period of wireless activity all visual signal traffic was transferred to voice radio, the signalmen transferred to coding duties and Radar Plot ratings were brought in to help man the TBS (Talk Between Ships) VHF radio. These changes, which increased the number of ratings employed on communication duties by about 50 per cent, improved the handling of signal traffic but inexperience led to many mistakes. Much of the cipher traffic was, as normal, handled by Supply Officers and this, combined with their routine duties, imposed a heavy strain. There were about twenty to forty signals a day to pass to authorities outside Haifa and poor daytime conditions for HF transmission caused considerable delays.

A different organisation was in any case being planned, largely because the use of a cruiser meant she was not available for other pressing tasks. Following a visit to Haifa in early May by the new Commander-in-Chief, Mediterranean Fleet, Admiral Sir Algernon Willis, there were two development. First, since the Admiral was a fervent teetotaller, the names of patrol sectors had to be changed from alcoholic drinks. A Naval Wireless Telegraph station was established (with able and swift assistance from Army Signals) on 17 June in the 1st Division Headquarters at the Mount Carmel Lighthouse. The post of Senior Naval Officer, Levant lapsed and Staff Officer Operations to SNO(A) Haifa became Naval Officer-in-Charge (NOIC) Haifa with responsibility for operating the patrols and passing intelligence, this post being held by Commander P.J. Knowling RN. These changes permitted the cruiser to be withdrawn from Palestine, leaving the resident Captain (D) as SNO(A) holding responsibility for issuing NOIC (Haifa) with general directions on Naval patrols. The standard of wireless operating was low to start with and a destroyer anchored off Haifa guarded the broadcast as a safeguard. But she lacked the invaluable telephone link to JHQ and the new arrangements did not turn out satisfactorily.

The presence of the cruiser had in any case become increasingly hazardous. Palestine Police CID reported a planned attempt to sabotage her on the night 10/11 June (this later turned out to have been abandoned at the last minute). The CinC expressed concern, signalling 'Bestir Thyself', and on 18 June SNO(A), then CS.1, moved all the warships out from Haifa to anchor berths. *Superb* had provided a Royal Marine section to patrol oil wharfs and an enlarged seaman section to patrol the remainder of the dock area, tasks which now passed to the destroyers. Plans had also existed for *Superb*'s engineering staff to take over the running of Haifa power station in the event of a strike and this task was transferred to 3 Infantry Brigade. Owing to terrorist activity, leave was being curtailed to 2000, with all Jewish premises out of bounds and men ashore remaining together in parties accompanied by armed escorts.

At the end of a four-month stint on 2 June, the 14th Destroyer Flotilla could claim 100 per cent success in intercepting attempts at seaborne illegal immigration and D.14 felt it was no longer necessary for eight destroyers to be allocated to the patrol. In the meantime the Arab press was taking the line that the activities of the destroyers encouraged illegal immigration, by seeing the vessels safely into Haifa. These thereby avoided the hazards of beaching and then putting passengers ashore through the surf, sometimes in winter weather! D.14 also reported that the absence of convenient repair facilities dangerously affected the operational efficiency of his destroyers after three months of deployment and he felt the normal period of duty should be no longer than that period.

The Third Flotilla's newly arrived 'V'-class destroyers and its 'Hunt'-class escort destroyers now took over under D.3 in HMS *Saumarez*[28] (Captain W.H. Selby DSC RN). At much the same time the Mediterranean Fleet re-established a Destroyer Command led by Rear Admiral, Mediterranean Fleet Destroyers (RA(D)) (Rear-Admiral E.D.B. McCarthy CB DSO) flying his flag in the 'Dido' Class cruiser HMS *Phoebe* (Captain J.A. McCoy DSO RN), an addition to the fleet. RA(D)'s command included the 3rd and 14th Destroyer Flotillas, the 33rd Escort Flotilla (previously 'Mediterranean Fleet Escorts'), the Trooping Division and the 5th and 8th MSFs. The 12th and 19th MSF left the station. When the task of boarding illegal immigrant vessels became increasingly demanding, RA(D) assumed the task of supplementing the natural resourcefulness of the warships by coordinating requirements for equipment, developing new suggestions and training. He also conducted regular meetings between Staff

Officers and Commanding Officers recently returned from the Palestine coast to examine and follow up fresh proposals. Sub-committees were appointed to deal with the more complex problems, enlisting the assistance of specialist supporting organisations such as the Senior Armament Supply Officer (SASO) Malta, Malta dockyard and, for matters concerning tear gas, the Armament Warfare School at Porton, Wiltshire.

THE PRESSURE INCREASES

Reports from military intelligence that two suspected immigrant ships had left Piraeus on 31 May led to five days of combined air and sea searches, for which sea patrols were reinforced and a Lancaster four-engined aircraft conducted a search out to 100 miles without success. A third vessel was later reported as having sailed from Italy. Reliable intelligence reported one of the vessels from Greece turning back on 6 June and another due to arrive the night of 6/7 June. HMS *Volage* (Commander R.F. Paul CBE RN) investigated a caïque which threw into the sea a drum of opium, but the real suspect was then reported also to have turned back and to be planning to try again on the night of 7/8 June.

Shortly before midday on 7 June, a Warwick sighted an unidentified caïque, with mast and bowsprit but proceeding under power. Although the aircraft's crew was new to the task, and there were many other small craft in the area, she was immediately identified as a suspect and intercepted by HMS *Saumarez* two hours later. All forms of identification had been painted out but when *Saumarez* approached the Egyptian flag was replaced by a Zionist flag and some 300–400 people were seen to be onboard the 100-ton vessel, thought to be the *Agios Ioannis*.

Despite 40mm Bofors gun shots across her bow, the caïque manoeuvred evasively and refused to stop and be boarded to establish her identity, which would have also given the Boarding Officer an opportunity to look round. After dark name boards showing 'Haviva Reik' were put up. *Saumarez*, assisted by a Police Launch, continued to shadow until the 3-mile limit was reached at 0145 on the following day. The suspect was then stopped, boarded from the Police Launch and towed to Haifa. No crew could be found. The passengers indicated that they had embarked off the Italian coast but evidence showed the voyage was a private enterprise by a local relief committee in Greece. Four hundred and fourteen of the 466 onboard claimed to be Greek but only seventy were affiliated to a Zionist party, probably due to Zionism's pre-war lack of popularity in Greece. Almost all the passengers claimed to have lived in German concentration camps. Unlike other vessels, the *Haviva Reik* was not well provisioned, nor was what she was carrying British Army or UNRRA stores.

THE GRAND MUFTI: PART II

The Navy now became involved in a renewed hunt for the Grand Mufti of Jerusalem, Haj Amin El-Husseini, whose activities during the 1936–39 Arab revolt had resulted in the attempt to detain him in 1937. During the war years, he had sided with the Germans against the Jews and there were calls by Jews for him to be prosecuted as a war criminal. A somewhat roundabout route found the Grand Mufti in France after the war, then he disappeared and was thought to be heading for Egypt. Intelligence suggested that, strange as it might seem, he had embarked at Toulon in HMT *Devonshire*, a troopship bound for Port Said carrying some 600 British soldiers. HMS *Virago* (Lieutenant-Commander D.G.D. Hall-Wright RN) inherited the role given HMS *Hasty* some eight years and a whole era earlier and lay in wait off Port Said until the *Devonshire* anchored there early on 14 June. A boarding party led by Sub-Lieutenant Lord Crofton RN, accompanied by two Palestine Police Officers acquainted with the Mufti, then inspected the passengers and searched the ship. *Virago* was under strict instructions not to reveal the identity of their quarry to anyone onboard or ashore. However, the word was out in Port Said before *Devonshire* arrived; the next day two army officers from GHQ Cairo let the cat out of the bag to both the Ship's Master and a female known to be sympathetic to the Mufti's activities. In the meantime the O.C. Troops in *Devonshire* caused a scene, lodging with the military authorities a complaint at the use of sailors, not his 600 'sworn men' to conduct searches. He left Lieutenant Commander Hall-Wright in no doubt that the *Virago* was, in his view, very suitably named.

Forty-eight hours later the BBC Overseas Service reported details and soon the *Middle East Mail* declared that had Amin El-Husseini been found then *Virago* would have set off in the wake of HMS *Active* ten years earlier. Eventually the *Devonshire* was permitted to berth alongside in Port Said, passengers were checked as they disembarked and the ship was searched for the second time, again without result. But the fact that only two out eighteen of the passengers due to embark at Toulon had arrived onboard may have meant that yet again the Mufti had been forewarned. He did in fact reach Egypt by air, was welcomed by the King and allowed to remain.

BIGGER SHIPS AND MORE PEOPLE

Larger scale problems were encountered for the first time when on 25 June an aircraft reported the *Colon*,[29] ex-HMCS *Beauharnois*, one of two 950-ton former Royal Canadian Navy 'Flower'-class corvettes. She had been bought by Zionist supporters for $US150,000, fitted out at the cost of the same amount and manned with a Jewish crew, some of whom had served in the US Navy, or in Zionist pioneer youth movements in the USA, and to whom their ship was known as '*Josiah Wedgwood*'. The passengers embarked in Italy, where Mossad was having little difficulty in obtaining cooperation from individuals at every level, shamed by the persecution of Jews in their country brought about by Germany. It did not help that the British were portrayed as leading the current demand, largely instigated by the USSR, that Italian warships be handed over to the victorious powers.

Colon was a faster and better-found vessel that any encountered hitherto. NOIC Haifa suspected that she might transfer crew or passengers to caïques, thus increasing the number of vessels to be intercepted, whilst she herself kept outside territorial waters and avoided arrest. As soon as *Colon* was sighted by RAF reconnaissance south-west of Cyprus three destroyers (HM Ships *Venus* (Lieutenant-Commander W.J. Munn DSO RN), *Talybont* and *Haydon*) were despatched to effect an interception. When met at 2105 on 25 June the vessel wished to go to Haifa: when reminded that the law of the land came into force at the 3-mile limit her movements became very uncertain, as though those in charge were seized by indecision and trying to decide on the best course of action. She stopped at 0040 on 26 June, remained stopped for nearly 14 hours and then signalled that stocks of food were exhausted and sick people were onboard. On being informed that there was nothing to stop her going to Haifa but that Palestine Government regulations came into effect on entering territorial waters, *Colon* got underway and steered in that direction.

At 1830 the immigrant ship approached the 3-mile limit and lowered a motorboat containing 20 men, which was dealt with by Palestine Police in ML 1145. Then at 1915 the *Colon* increased speed to 14 knots and failed to stop when called on to do so. *Venus* fired close-range weapons across her bows for seven minutes, at the end of which time the former corvette gathered sternway and went round in small circles, appearing to have lost control over her engines. At 2000, these gyrations ceased, allowing *Venus* to get alongside and transfer boarders; there was no trace of Master or crew and the *Colon* was taken into Haifa.

This episode demonstrated that the arrest of a really determined vessel inside territorial waters necessitated a warship going alongside her to transfer boarders and this might entail damage to both vessels. In such circumstances the police launches could no longer play a very active part, but might still be helpful in picking up swimmers or members of boarding parties so unfortunate as to end up in the water.

The next attempt to penetrate was by the *Akbel*, a small steamer. She sailed from Marseilles, was detected by RAF aircraft and intercepted by HMS *Virago* on 1 July. *Akbel* flew the Turkish flag. Her Master claimed that his 1,100 passengers had been transferred from SS *Norsyd*, encountered suffering severe engine trouble, and that he had been requested to take them to Cyprus. Later confirmation was obtained that 999 immigrants had indeed been transferred west of Crete from *Norsyd*. Mossad did not wish to risk the latter, the second of their two former Canadian corvettes, any closer to Palestine.

The Master of *Akbel* asked for a tow, a frequently-to-be-repeated attempt to enter Palestinian waters legally, but on this occasion possibly because the ship was indeed in danger of sinking through overloading. Food and water were also requested. Care had to be taken not to make an arrest in Cypriot waters and shadowing continued with HMS *Haydon* and HMS *Talybont* (Lieutenant-Commander N.J. Parker DSC RN) joining *Virago* early on 2 July. Eventually, the illegal vessel was ordered to stop and then boarded and handed over to the Police.

One Isadore F Stone, an American newspaper correspondent who specialised in news concerning the tribulations of Jews in post-war Europe, was found amongst *Akbel's* passengers. He held a US passport and a visa to enter Palestine but travelled as a refugee, intending to be transferred to Atlit Camp and then disclose his identity. This plan went awry due to the entry of a case of suspected bubonic plague on *Akbel's* Bill of Health. The passengers, including Stone, were placed in quarantine and transferred on the advice of the Senior Medical official at Haifa to isolation in the *Smyrna*.

7

Custody of Illegal Immigrants and the Diversion Proposal

NAVAL OPERATIONS: THE LONG-TERM TASK

The Commander-in-Chief, Mediterranean Fleet was by now increasingly concerned by the turn of events. His resources were being strained by four to six out of his Fleet's 14 destroyers having to be allocated continuously to the Palestine Patrol. He was also worried by the use of this type of ship to make arrests after the illegal vessel was inside the 3-mile limit and close inshore. Consideration was given to building up the Motor Launch section of the Palestine Police but by this stage larger vessels were being encountered and these could simply brush the MLs aside. Furthermore, MLs possessed neither sufficient speed and endurance nor indeed the radar and communications necessary for the tasks which had to be undertaken. For his part the High Commissioner did not wish to attempt the difficult task of forming a Palestine Government naval squadron to replace the Royal Navy. He held that in the long run the situation could only be resolved by a major change in policy and hinted to the Naval authorities that this might be forthcoming before too long. The Colonial Secretary shared the High Commissioner's hopes for a fairly early settlement and this misled the Admiralty into the belief that a solution was likely in the not far distant future and Navy would cease to be involved. So, recalling the earlier offer to provide additional MLs but not manpower, it suggested that additional Palestinian personnel should be trained in preparation for the day when the Palestine Police could resume responsibility.

CUSTODY OF ARRESTED IMMIGRANTS

By June 1946 the situation in Palestine was reaching a critical state, acts of terrorism being an almost daily occurrence, and a fresh attempt to rescue immigrants held in Atlit Camp was deemed likely. For some time the High Commissioner had been pressing the British Government for a decision on disposal of the ever-increasing numbers of arrested seaborne illegal immigrants, one alternative being to arrest immigrant ships on the high seas and then divert them elsewhere. Cyprus and Cyrenaica were possible destinations, both being under British administration at the time. But this course of action had, after much argument, been discarded.

Initially, General Cunningham had been opposed to diversion on the high seas, on the grounds that such an act would give rise to serious disturbances in Palestine and amongst the immigrants. On 29 June, however, he signalled:

MOST IMMEDIATE – TOP SECRET

2670 illegal immigrants were brought into Haifa today and are now lying offshore. At least one other ship with 500 suspected illegal immigrants on board may be expected .... We are quite unable at the moment to guard any more illegal immigrants in this country. I would urge that every other ship on the sea is diverted. Otherwise the situation here may become completely impossible.[30]

At this point the scale of Jewish terrorist activity ashore, which had been steadily increasing throughout the summer, reached a peak with the detonation of explosives placed by the *IZL* in the King David Hotel at Jerusalem, where, with other official sections, was housed the JHQ. This atrocity was the most destructive act of terrorism during the mandate, causing the death of 91 people. To add to the difficulties of the British Government, the US Government now made it clear they would not assist in implementing the programme suggested by the Anglo-American Commission.

The High Commissioner was entirely correct regarding an impending influx. By mid-1946 6,436 illegal immigrants had been arrested at sea, with some 450 escaping arrest, while only 500 had entered undetected by land and 54 had been arrested. At the start of the year caïques were mostly used but now faster ships were being employed and the majority were steam or motor vessels of 500 to 1,000 tons with a sea speed of about 7 knots and a carrying capacity of up to 1,000 passengers. Four of these were currently impounded at Haifa. Separately, Intelligence provided a fresh warning of the possible use of *Cutty Sark*.

The CinC added his thoughts, drawing the Admiralty's attention to parts of the world from which more illegal immigrant vessels could be expected. He was aware that illegal immigrants were receiving ample funds and considerable assistance on a worldwide basis and highlighted the activities of the Palestinian RASC troops who assisted the *Fede* and *Fenice* migrants in the Genoa–Savona region of Italy, where Army Field Security was now keeping a closer watch. He anticipated that the Adriatic could become a busy area, there were many rumours of large numbers massing in Greece and many more could be expected from the Black Sea area, with the Russians, the occupying Allied Power in Romania and Bulgaria, taking no steps to interfere. In his view the organisers of illegal immigration had abandoned concealment in favour of advertisement. They were gaining world sympathy, knowing perfectly well that illegal immigrants not only came to no harm but also were being housed in a comfortable camp until released. This was to the disadvantage of those with legally obtained papers, thus making a farce of the quota system and bringing the Palestine Government into disrepute. Although the Admiralty made these views known to both the Foreign Office and the Colonial Office, this was done without comment and with no pressure for, or suggestions on, action needed to deal with a deteriorating situation imposing increasing difficulties on the Mediterranean Fleet.

No Government decision on the High Commissioner's telegram message, quoted earlier, had been made before the Chiefs of Staff discussed the matter on 26 July. The First Sea Lord was by now Sir John Cunningham, previously the CinC Mediterranean, and he felt the High Commissioner's proposal to divert illegal immigrant vessels would put Commanding Officers in the position of giving orders which they were unable to enforce, with immigrant ships refusing to stop or alter course. Even if a master submitted to visit and search, the crew might refuse to work the ship to an alternative destination, in which case it would be necessary to put onboard a larger prize crew than could be found from the normal complement of the ships engaged in the patrol. The CoS therefore recommended to the Cabinet that diversion, either before or after arrival in Palestine's waters was not practicable. They would have preferred to see the flow of immigrants stopped at ports of embarkation and pointed out that the Law of the Sea authority Oppenheim held that states were under a duty to prevent activities of that kind. Neither were forces available to lie off ports and turn ships back. The Cabinet also received separate intelligence warnings that several attempts at landings were likely in the middle of August and by 30 July it was coming round to the view that some system of transhipment and deportation of immigrants was now necessary. The Governor of Cyprus was therefore warned to prepare camp facilities and the Royal Navy started to plan the provision of transports for arrested migrants and warships to escort them from Haifa to Famagusta. Subsequent events were to show that things might have gone better had the difficulties of diverting ships been faced up to and had immigrants not reached the Promised Land before being sent to Cyprus.

8

Introduction of Shipment
to Cyprus

Balboa, formerly HMCS *Norsyd*, has been mentioned earlier as having transferred immigrants embarked in France to the *Akbel* whilst at sea. The former corvette then returned to Greece for fuel and provisions before passage to the small Yugoslav port of Bakar at the north-east corner of the Adriatic. There, with the assistance of German prisoners of war, preparations were made to embark as many illegal immigrants as possible. The prospective passengers, refugees mainly from Transylvania, were brought to Yugoslavia by train. UNRRA provided free use of vehicles for their transfer to a camp, run by pioneer youth movements, supported by a field kitchen provided by the Yugoslav Army. On 22 July the migrants moved in two trains to Bakar for embarkation, a highly organised operation with a prearranged schedule, orderlies sent ahead to control movement and assist people with large bundles and a mobile hospital, formerly a mail van (in which a woman gave birth to a baby boy). In all 2,538 passengers, including 430 children, embarked in the 200-foot vessel. The Croatian authorities then passed on a message of thanks from the Jewish organiser to the central government in Belgrade, which readily granted permission for further sailings.

On 25 July Mossad signalled *Balboa* by radio to steer for Haifa and if intercepted allow herself to be taken to 'the State of Israel'. Mossad may have got wind of plans for diversions elsewhere since orders were given that if the Navy suggested any other destination then resistance was to be offered and the engines were to be sabotaged; in any case the crew and other workers must conceal themselves amongst the passengers. The number of passengers onboard necessitated strict discipline as the ship was inherently unstable. The engines also proved unreliable, for they stopped altogether 90 miles from the Palestine coast, at which stage the ship lost electrical power but was able to transmit an SOS. On 29 July *Balboa* was detected from the air and when intercepted by HMS *Venus* after dark she claimed to be broken down and in need of water and a tow. For legal reasons Venus did not become involved in towing at this stage. Assisted by HMS *Brissenden* (Lieutenant-Commander E.V.St.J. Morgan RN), she remained circling the *Balboa* as a guard against attempts by caïques in the vicinity to ferry passengers ashore.

Eventually, *Balboa* got under way again and at about 0200 on 30 July she crossed the 3-mile limit. When called upon to stop she failed to do so, despite bursts of 40mm Bofors gun fire across her bows. A burst of 40mm Bofors fired over her bridge caused an alteration of course favourable for *Brissenden* to attempt a boarding , which *Balboa* evaded by making a large alteration of course away from her towards shallow water. This enabled *Venus* to seize her moment, approach at 15 knots on the inner side of the turn, go alongside and put over her boarding party. Determination and good ship handling paid off, once onboard the boarding party were in control within ten minutes. They were assisted not only by police but also representatives of the Jewish Agency, the latter being instrumental in obtaining access to the engine room.

Events with *Balboa* demonstrated that the days of exchanging cigarettes and a cup of tea with the passengers once the naval party was onboard were at an end: arrangements had to be made for larger, better equipped and better organised boarding parties. The appearance of ships capable of at least 15 knots, greatly added to the difficulties of patrols, which would worsen when winter weather set in. With boarding restricted to use inside territorial waters, sooner or later there would be serious damage to an HM Ship, with the possibility of an overloaded immigrant ship capsizing. The event caused the CinC to consider again whether Commanding Officers should be allowed more discretion on where boarding might take place.

The next arrival was another former Canadian vessel; having started life in 1900 as an Austrian nobleman's yacht, she later became HMCS *Hochelaga*. Intelligence reported her as having sailed from Antwerp with 500 Jews embarked and that the Panamanian consul at Marseilles had issued a collective passport for those onboard; he was thought to have been bribed. The manner in which her voyage ended confirmed the CinC's view regarding Jewish tactics and 'gate crashing'. On 21 July *Hochelaga* was thought to be approaching but she choose the direction of her approach well and was not seen from the air. At 0409 on 31 July, HMS *Virago* detected two contacts by radar and the details were passed to the Officer of the Watch. One contact was found to be on the list of suspect vessels, and boarded, but everything was seen to be in order. The other contact was overlooked until at 0630 the Officer of the Watch in HMS *Saumarez* at Haifa observed a suspicious vessel closing the harbour entrance. This was the *Hochelaga* which then requested a pilot and was boarded in rapid succession by pilot, police and a party from *Saumarez*, who found approximately 550 immigrants onboard.

Hochelaga's Master later confirmed he had departed from Antwerp by night with 500 passengers bound for Panama who brought their own wireless equipment, there being no other equipment of that kind onboard. Off Cape Trafalgar he had been handed a wireless message diverting the vessel to Alexandretta and later a second message ordered a diversion to a rendezvous with three caïques, where he claimed that he and other members of the crew were overpowered and locked away.

TRANS-SHIPMENT TO CYPRUS

With the numbers of arrested immigrants held ashore increasing and the likelihood of fresh instructions for their disposal, the CinC arranged for the civilian manned HM Transports *Empire Heywood* and *Empire Rival*, each capable of carrying 800 passengers,[31] to be made ready at Port Said and then sail to Haifa. The High Commissioner reckoned that at the start of August totals of illegal immigrants in custody or transit were as follows:

Atlit Camp	2,252
Held onboard ships	2,232
Believed to be on their way to Palestine	2,500

This situation led the Cabinet to decide on 7 August that any further illegal immigrants were to be transhipped at Haifa and sent immediately to Cyprus. To enable British embassies to be warned beforehand, the decision was not announced until 13 August. By that time the embassies had been briefed . This was on the lines that no country had been a better friend to the Jews than the British, who had protested most vigorously when they were persecuted by Hitler and had accepted large numbers into the United Kingdom as refugees, both before and during the Second World War.[32] Under the British Mandate 400,000 Jews had settled legally in Palestine, which had been defended against the Germans, yet now Jews were killing and kidnapping British soldiers and civilians in Palestine in a manner more worthy of the Nazis than of the Jewish victims of Nazis. Although the quota of 75,000 legal immigrants permitted by the 1939 White Paper had been exhausted by December 1945, the British were permitting immigration to continue at a rate of 1,500 per month. Despite the knowledge that decisions on long-term policy were pending, the Jews had nevertheless refused to accept this provision even *pro tem* and there was an increasing flow of illegal immigrants. Sympathy for the suffering of Jews in Europe had hitherto led to illegal immigrants being allowed to land despite the difficulties this caused. But the point had now been reached where the traffic was not just by Jews seeing Palestine as their only hope for the future. Behind it were highly organised Zionists attempting to force the hand of the British

Government and maintaining a well-established network of agents for moving displaced Jews through Eastern Europe to the Mediterranean seaboard, there to embark in overcrowded ships in unseaworthy conditions. Finally, attention was drawn to illegal immigration holding up cases deserving of legal entry, the reunification of families for example. For all these reasons HM Government now stated that a decision had been made to convey all further illegal arrivals to Cyprus. HMG regretted that a small minority of Zionist extremists were exploiting unfortunate people in an attempt to create a situation prejudicial to a just settlement, which could only be achieved if Arabs and Jews were prepared to enter into constructive discussions and harmonise the claims of their two historic peoples.

Much later an announcement was made in Parliament that the expense of transferring illegal immigrants to Cyprus, entailing as it did the provision of camps, construction of hutted camps and extension of military medical facilities to non-entitled civilians, would be borne by the Palestine Government. This led to an immediate protest by the Arab Higher Committee, who represented that the Arabs in Palestine should not be taxed to meet a heavy financial liability caused by those who chose to violate the laws and were 'raiding the country like pirates'.

In order to make plans for transhipment, including provision of escort vessels, CS.1,[33] went to Haifa in the cruiser HMS *Ajax* (Captain S.B. De Courcy-Ireland RN) . and assumed the duty of SNO(A) in the cruiser HMS *Mauritius* (Captain C.A.E. Stanfield RN). A large number of illegal immigrants were reported by Intelligence to be on their way and he found the situation quiet but tense. A tanker had been sunk by an unexplained explosion, destroyer anchor berths had been moved further to seaward, recreational parties ashore had to be escorted by armed guards, libertymen had to keep in pairs and officers ashore carried small arms. Unlike the situation in 1938, the Army Commander was empowered to take control of everything on land and thus he anticipated that SNO(A) would be able to exercise similar powers over the other maritime authorities, rather than consulting and working with them. It had to be explained that such was not the case and even so there were still some misunderstandings.

AUGUST 1946

Although earlier in 1946 Mossad had difficulty in raising as many as 1,500 immigrants per month and the AJDC had announced the end of support, intelligence forecasts of an influx of landings in August now proved correct. On 5 August the British authority in Marseilles reported an old auxiliary schooner *Sagol* (250 tons) sailing from Le Ciotat on 29 July, being officially bound for Beirut with 754 passengers. The numerous attempts which soon followed are best summarised chronologically.

11 August

Aircraft reported the *San Pisero*, a coastal cargo vessel of about 400 tons, and after being watched for two and a half days she was intercepted by HMS *Talybont* on 11 August and shadowed. On the same day air reconnaissance reports led SNO(A) to despatch HMS *Brissenden* (Lieutenant-Commander E.V.St.J. Morgan RN) to intercept a second vessel. After investigating caïques reported by aircraft, *Brissenden* found *Sagol* flying Turkish and Zionist flags, with the name-board '*Yagur*' partially obscuring her original name '*Sagolem*'. With the very helpful assistance of her Palestine Policeman, *Brissenden* arrested the vessel. The Master asserted that he had been compelled by force to take immigrants onboard and sail for Haifa. This was substantiated by entries in the deck-log, but the fact that he still had a revolver and a box of ammunition in his possession indicated he had 'gone willingly'. Half of the 754 passengers (448 males, 302 females) had evidently been embarked at La Ciotat, later evidence suggests Toulon, and the remainder from another, unnamed vessel, two days before the arrest. The Master and crew were later deported.

With *Brissenden* and *Talybont* already shadowing suspects and strong evidence of an attempt at a landing during the night 11/12 August, SNO(A) stationed all four remaining destroyers (HM Ships *Saumarez*, *Venus*, *Virago* and *Volage*) on patrol. His foresight was rewarded when an aircraft reported another suspicious vessel and at 1715 the *Volage* was sent by SNO(A) from patrol to investigate. She was told to proceed at 23 knots, probably to economise in fuel, but her Type 293 surface warning radar was unserviceable and she increased speed to 28 knots so as to make contact before the aircraft ceased shadowing. When radio contact was established with the very helpful aircraft, *Volage* started taking Direction Finding (D/F) bearings of its transmissions. These were found to vary over a span of 50 degrees[34] but the aircraft also marked the target's position with Verey lights.

The suspect proved to a two-masted 200–300-ton schooner or brigantine proceeding at 7 knots under engine, with no flag or name visible. Hundreds of largely naked people were seen on deck and more formally attired and prosperous-looking men round her wheelhouse aft, an area they evidently kept to themselves. The identity of the vessel was unknown and *Volage* checked to ensure there was no confusion with the vessel being shadowed by *Talybont*.

12 August

At 0020 the last serviceable radar modulator valve held by *Venus* failed and this meant all her warning radar sets were out of action. A replacement valve was collected from *Volage* and enabled *Venus*'s 293 to be operating satisfactorily by 0420. Many years later an Israeli claimed to have played a part in the Haganah's preparations for baffling the British prior to massed landings by disguising himself in naval officer's uniform, obtaining access to destroyers at Haifa and sabotaged their radar equipment under the guise of 'maintenance'. This may have been the occasion.

At 0430 *Venus* detected a contact to seaward and 30 minutes later another to the north-east at a range of three miles, which turned out to be a caïque with engine and sails, packed with illegal immigrants, singing lustily despite the early hour. As an arrest and move to Haifa were likely to be a long slow job *Venus* requested the attendance of a Police launch and went to investigate the contact detected earlier, which proved to be the transport *Empire Heywood*. *Venus* returned to the illegal vessel and transferred a boarding party to the Police launch ML 1126 with orders to make the arrest inside territorial waters. This was done and as the caïque's engines had been rendered unusable, the ML towed her to Haifa. There were difficulties in identifying her and she was variously referred to as '*Ariete Salom*' or '*Henrietta Szold*', the latter being the name used by the Haganah. She had sailed from Greece and 535 immigrants were found onboard including a party of orphaned children.

In the meantime, and throughout the night, *Volage*'s companion headed roughly for Haifa, daylight revealing the name '*Katriel Goffe*' freshly displayed since the previous evening. When territorial waters were reached, she refused to stop until the third warning bursts of 40mm fired as low as possible over the wheelhouse. Lieutenant P.S. Hicks-Beach RN then led the boarding party across. He could find no trace of her real identity, nor any charts or wireless equipment, but some persons thought to be members of the crew were found in reasonable quarters aft and they were arrested by Palestine Police. The Boarding Officer had orders that Zionist flags were not to be allowed and those being displayed were removed, which caused many protests. There were two 'mess decks', fitted with tubular steel frames between which were slung hammocks in tiers of two, and throughout the vessel the customary state of indescribable filth prevailed. One man could speak a little English and he explained that 615 people were onboard with two seriously sick, both were sent on ahead in a police launch. Course was then set for Haifa.

Water had run out the previous day and the passengers were in a very poor state. A tank was found which had been reserved for the afterguard and this was now made available for use by others. A wild rush ensued, with women and children being struck and generally mistreated by the male passengers. One persistently attempted to kick a pregnant woman out of his way, causing her to scream. His activities were halted by a blow from Lieutenant Hicks-Beach, which caused some resentment until the Boarding Officer's bodyguard, an exceedingly tough sailor, called out 'Lie down when the officer hits you', and smacked him with a rifle. Thereupon he fell down into the hold and gave no more trouble. Lieutenant Hicks-Beach

62

then completed the restoration of order, arranged a fair distribution of water and improvised a sick bay aft for the fresh casualties.

Whilst approaching the anchorage the *Goffe* was passed by the transport making the first transhipment of illegal immigrants to Cyprus; fortunately the nature of her voyage did not become known onboard. There was a delay before the harbour authorities signalled an anchor berth and so the passengers were encouraged, as a means of keeping them content and occupied, to sing. In the meantime the *Goffe* flying the White Ensign and with the Boarding Officer ensconced in a chair on top of the wheelhouse, proceeded as though reviewing the Fleet at Spithead up and down both sides of the line of anchored warships, piping each one as she passed.[35] Once she had anchored, water was brought out by tug and four armed policemen arrived onboard. This also meant that news of the deportations to Cyprus reached the immigrants and 'all hell broke loose', a turn of events for which the boarding party was not altogether ready. No further police assistance was available, due to the numbers already taken up in Haifa with the task of the first deportations to Cyprus. Control was regained with assistance from *Virago*, who provided a relief boarding party which took over and enabled *Volage*'s boarding party to return to their ship so that she might resume her patrol.

13 August

Goffe's correct name was later found to be *Katriel Yaffe* and her arrival off Haifa proved not to be the end of the trouble she was to cause. During her first morning under arrest she quietly slipped both her anchor cables and drifted off across the bay. A boarding party from HMS *Mauritius* regained control and she was then placed close to *Mauritius* until the passengers could be despatched to Cyprus.

14 August

The suspect first shadowed by *Talybont* on 11 August had been turned over to HMS *Brissenden* and was found to be the *San Pisero* from Italy under jury sailing rig alone, making headway of about one knot as best she could. Some 600 immigrants were onboard and they claimed there was no crew and that they were making their own way from German concentration camps to Haifa. The boarding was not opposed and the vessel was towed to Haifa arriving on 14 August.

15–16 August

Air reconnaissance reported two caïques on 15 August and one, thought to be a French auxiliary schooner of about 150 tons built in 1913 named

Ideros was sighted and investigated during the forenoon by HMS *Saumarez* but allowed to proceed. She was not on the list of suspect vessels, probably being from Beirut, there was no evidence of illegal immigrants and the vessel appeared clean and ship-shape. During the night *Saumarez* continued to hold *Ideros* on her radar and although inside the patrol line and only six miles from Caesarea, she was thought to be coasting. It was not noticed that she had approached the coast until the suspicions of the Morning Watch Officer of the Watch (Lieutenant E.F. Gueritz RN) were aroused. He closed to investigate and at daylight a boarding party found unmistakable evidence that illegal immigrants had been present. By then the vessel was outside territorial waters and so she could not be arrested. The press later reported 180 illegal immigrants coming ashore that night, subsequent accounts give a figure of 183 and show her name as *Isle de la Rose*.

TRANSHIPMENT

Between 11 and 15 August, four ships, carrying a total some 2,700 passengers, had submitted to arrest without any great difficulty. But attitudes changed markedly when the immigrants learnt they were to be despatched to Cyprus. CS.1 reported that the level of force required to make the first to be transhipped embark in the transports necessitated the employment on two occasion of two brigades of troops. The fight against migrants armed with bottles, tins and staves, which was witnessed by press representatives sponsored by the Army, became a 'battle of some hours'. Nevertheless, with HMS *Ajax* as escort, the transports sailed for Cyprus only a few hours after the fresh British policy had been announced. The same day the police lost control onboard *Ariete Salom* and *Mauritius* again provided boarding parties to recapture the vessel.

Since the Cyprus camps were not yet completely ready, immigrants arriving in the *San Pisero* and *Katriel Yaffe* both very overcrowded, were kept onboard those vessels, secured astern of the warships, until on 17 August a boarding party from *Mauritius* assisted police and soldiers move the *Yaffe* into harbour. There was no opposition until after the first passengers had disembarked at 0110 on 18 August for transhipment to the transport *Empire Heywood*, when tear smoke and hoses had to be used to remove the remainder.

On 18 August the illegal immigrants from the *San Pisero* embarked in *Empire Rival* and departed. Those from the *Yaffe* could still not be accepted at Cyprus and had a longer wait at Haifa. On the night of *Empire Rival*'s return she was damaged by a limpet charge attached by underwater swimmers to her port quarter, about five feet underwater. Another charge is thought to have fallen off the starboard side some 30 minutes earlier when only the detonator fired. Temporary repairs were effected and the ship sent to Port Said for full repairs. On the same day two Landing Craft Infantry (Large) LCIs 258 and 278 arrived from Malta as a more substantial means than ships' boats for controlling illegal immigrant vessels in Haifa Bay, where police resources were proving to be inadequate.

A PAUSE IN OPERATIONS

Between 0930 local time on 9 August and 1200 on 16 August, when a lull began, six destroyers had been underway for a total of 525 hours and on at least two nights all those available were either on patrol or shadowing immigrant vessels. Intelligence reports now indicated a respite and so air reconnaissance ceased for the time being, whilst destroyer patrols were reduced to one on patrol with a second destroyer kept at short notice to assist her. From 17 August the task of SNO(A) devolved permanently on the resident Captain (D), currently D.3, and on 23 August CS.1 sailed in HMS *Mauritius* for Cyprus to help with the arrangements for deported illegal immigrants.

The 'Ch'-class destroyers of the former 14th Flotilla returned on 30 August as the 1st Destroyer Flotilla, which revived the pre-war designation of the resident Mediterranean destroyer flotilla. Breaks away from Palestine were essential to maintain morale and cruises amongst the Greek islands, visits to such ports as Venice and Palermo, together with sporting contests kept ships' companies reasonably contented. But after departing for Malta, *Saumarez* and *Volage* were shortly to be involved in a more hazardous naval operation in the Corfu Channel.

At much the same time the sloops and frigates of the Mediterranean Fleet were combined into the Fifth Escort Flotilla, Ninth and Tenth Divisions respectively. Events had by now shown that the Fleet Minesweepers were particularly suitable for boarding operations and three of these vessels relieved two destroyers. Whilst they lacked the speed advantage necessary for coping with illegal immigrant vessels, the majority were fitted with reciprocating engines which meant they had far more astern power. They were thus more manoeuvrable than the turbine-engined sloops, although the small size of their ships' companies meant they had to be on their guard against illegal immigrants swarming onboard and attempting to take control. Two RN Motor Fishing Vessels also arrived to reinforce Police launches and security patrols, joined later by a third. These rugged craft were found to be in poor mechanical condition and required ten-day refits before becoming sufficiently reliable to undertake their tasks.

PART III:

PALESTINE PATROL, 1946–47:
CONTESTED ARRESTS

9

More Difficult Tasks

After the successes achieved in early August, intelligence warnings of illegal arrivals dried up. But D.1 in HMS *Chequers* wasted no time after his arrival in warning his ships' companies that the policy of deportation to Cyprus would bring about a change of temper amongst immigrants. In anticipation of greater opposition he arranged for ships to be issued with glass tear-gas dispensers of the kind supplied to the Army for anti-riot purposes. The return of *Fede* and events during her arrest on 2 September soon demonstrated that D.1's forebodings were all too true and that a far more difficult phase of the operation had begun.

FEDE'S ARREST

Fede, now alternatively known variously as *Fede II*, *Arba Hiruyot* or *Cadio*, was sighted by an aircraft and then intercepted by HMS *Childers* on 2 September. The state of her boats, the wearing of lifebelts and swimsuits by passengers and the presence of small boats inshore made an attempt to land a proportion of illegals by swimming seem likely. The plan devised by the *Childers*'s Commanding Officer, Lieutenant Commander EAS Bailey RN, was that if, on reaching the 3-mile limit, the vessel did not stop in response to a signal to do so, his ship would:

- Fire underwater charges to discourage swimming.
- Fire across bows with 20mm Oerlikon guns.
- Fire overhead with 20mm and 40mm Bofors guns.
- Board by going alongside under way.
- Put the flare of her bow over *Fede*'s bulwarks and drop an anchor onboard as a grapple, thus securing the two ships together. Since *Fede* was a wooden vessel the risk of damage by doing so was not considered great.

- Grapple by means of kedge anchor, tailed with 3" berthing wire, fired from a depth-charge thrower.
- Employ physical obstruction.

Finally, the boarding party were not to shoot unless specifically authorised.

When called on to stop inside territorial waters the *Fede* paid no regard to shots across her bow and firing over her was ruled out by small fishing vessels fouling the range. *Childers* therefore approached from the port quarter, laid her port bow alongside the target's midships section and put an officer and twenty ratings across. The *Fede* turned sharply to Port and broke away, leaving a third of the boarding party still onboard *Childers*. About half of those who had reached the *Fede* were roughly handled and their Lanchester sub-machine guns were lost before they could recover themselves. Stiff opposition centred round the wheel-house and in the vicinity of the engine-room hatch, where 'toughs' wielded two-foot iron bars. One boarder, attacked with an iron bar, lost his Lanchester, and found the weapon, already cocked, being aimed at him. Fortunately the man holding the weapon did not know how to operate a Lanchester and threw it overboard. The migrants also prevented movement by the boarders by forming a human barrier, with the men hiding behind the women, then calling out 'You're no gentleman' if the females were touched!

Childers made a second approach but, owing to the *Fede*'s freeboard, failed in an attempt to grapple her by dropping an anchor onboard. However, another ten men got across and *Fede*'s crew stopped her engine and abandoned the engine-room. The boarders' numbers had increased to forty men and although uproar continued a towing wire was connected from the bow of *Childers* to *Fede*'s poop. *Fede* was then towed further out to sea with the aim of discouraging swimmers and obtaining more sea room in which to gain control.

HMS *Chivalrous* (Lieutenant Commander K.G.L. Southcombe RN) arrived at about 1840 and placed two officers and 20 ratings onboard *Fede* right aft, where the *Childers*'s boarding party were pinned down. There was too much swell for her to remain alongside. Although the immigrants had quietened down temporarily when the tow started, the situation then deteriorated until the Boarding Officer was forced to issue a warning that firearms might be used if necessary for self-protection. *Chivalrous* sent over another ten armed men at 1940 but the situation became worse still with a Police Sergeant being held hostage and his life threatened. By 2005 the situation had became very ugly with female migrants, whom the sailors were noticeably reluctant to take on, very much to the fore. Eventually at about 2025 a concerted effort, cheered on by the two destroyers, and a non-discriminatory approach towards men and women forced the bulk of the immigrants below. It then became possible for seamen to gain control of the forecastle and receive a tow from the *Childers*'s quarter deck which lasted from 2106 until arrival at Haifa at 0900 the following day. During the struggle several migrants jumped over the side, two were found drowned, and afterwards a Medical Officer and Sick Berth Attendants dealt with five injured ratings and 20 badly knocked-about migrants. A large number were in poor condition owing to the rigours of the voyage and the warships provided water for the 985 passengers. The *Fede*'s arrival at Haifa was arranged to coincide with the return of the *Empire Heywood* to which the immigrants transferred peaceably in Haifa Bay and they sailed for Cyprus the same evening.

The struggle put up by *Fede*'s immigrants took some 6 officers and 70 ratings to subdue and confirmed that the days of token resistance were over. Hitherto 20 men had sufficed for an initial boarding party and this figure was increased to 30. Lee-Enfield rifles had proved too cumbersome in crowded spaces and they were replaced by entrenching tool staves and pistols.

ORGANISATIONAL ARRANGEMENTS

CS.1 was back at Haifa by the time *Fede* was brought in but did not resume duties as SNO(A), his main purpose being a conference attended by Senior British Naval Officer Middle East (SBNOME) and the Principal Sea Transport Officer (Mediterranean) amongst others, regarding the handling and protection of shipping used for illegal immigrants. Measures now agreed included the formation of a Haifa Port Committee, whose purposes were to coordinate requirements for the movements and safety of vessels used for illegal immigrants within the port limits. Since NOIC Haifa was already very fully occupied, the task of chairing the new committee was allocated to the resident Captain (D) despite, it would seem, his seagoing commitments. CS.1 then departed, distracted by an underwater sabotage alert but rightly concerned that, divorced from direct contact with Jerusalem, SNO(A) would not be able to manage the patrols effectively. He recommended that either a subordinate should be put ashore to do this work or a senior officer with an appropriate staff should be established at the 1st Division's HQ at Mount Carmel. This suggestion bore fruit later.

CS.1's report commented on the wider implications of the transhipment policy as follows:

> The Jews' attitude to the British has a depressing effect on the sailors who have no wish to persecute them but are daily accused of doing so in the press. There is also a very genuine dislike of using force against the illegal immigrants especially as it entail fighting with women just as much as with men. The situation has become much more difficult

71

since the announcement of the policy of deportation and a battle must now be expected at some stage on every occasion that an illegal immigrant ship is intercepted. This most unpleasant and increasingly dangerous duty falls to the lot of a small pro-portion of the Fleet and I consider they deserve credit for the success with which it has been carried out so far.[36]

Although a cruiser ceased to be stationed at Haifa, the practice became to send one there to conduct transhipments (*Operation Seaside Wagtail*). HMS *Mauritius*, HMS *Phoebe* and HMS *Newcastle* all took a turn. Immediately the arrested vessel arrived she was placed alongside the cruiser together with one or more transports. The immigrants and their baggage were then moved to the cruiser, searched, sprayed with DDT insecticide and directed to a transport. A medical party was in attendance, as were the Police and female searchers. Drinking water and sanitary facilities were available. Some 350 of the ship's company had parts to play and in *Newcastle* the only seamen not involved were harbour watchkeepers. Precautions were taken against sabotage but it seems these did not include dropping charges into the water. The whole operation was conducted as an evolution and the *Newcastle* recorded some 550 immigrants, not all of whom cooperated, and their baggage being transhipped in slightly over 70 minutes. Also an average time for an immigrant to 'go round the course' – come onboard, being searched and sprayed with DDT and board the transport – as between two and four minutes. A record was set by a female immigrant who, after a lengthy argument, went round in ninety seconds.

If, as now seemed probable, transhipments were likely at such a rate that the camps at Cyprus became full it would have been necessary to send illegal immigrants to Kenya or some other distant destination. There were not sufficient warships to provide escorts and the Chiefs of Staff discussed whether the transports carrying illegal immigrants from Haifa to Cyprus should sail unescorted. Although the Commanders-in-Chief in the Middle East agreed this proposal, the War Department objected, on the grounds of the danger to military guards and the increased numbers of such guards which would be required. The Admiralty therefore withdrew the proposal and although the plan was to review the situation after six months, by that time the Mediterranean Fleet had been reinforced and so the question was not pursued again.

HMS *ROWENA* AND *ARIELLA*

Charts subsequently showed that the *Ariella* sailed from the Giannotri area of Italy and made a landfall off Tripoli and probably then crept down the coast of Syria and Lebanon. This tactic had been anticipated by SNO(A) and following an air sighting the minesweeper HMS *Rowena* (Lieutenant-Commander G.J. Cardew RN) intercepted the *Ariella* four miles north-north-west of Acre Light at 2345 on 21 September. She was lying stopped and on being illuminated set off for Palestine territorial waters at seven knots. Once there she refused to stop, the only response being the usual shouting and singing. *Rowena* placed her bow alongside *Ariella*'s starboard quarter in an attempt to put over a boarding party and was met with a hail of stones, iron bars, hatchets, nuts and bolts, knives and bottles. In spite of the use of hoses to drive the active opponents away no-one could get onboard but *Rowena*, taking care not to capsize the caïque, pushed her bows round to seaward and away from her original heading towards a point north of Acre. As the illegal vessel still did not stop, four 20mm rounds were fired across her bows and over her superstructure, but this action only excited the mob further and Lieutenant-Commander Cardew decided not to fire again. *Rowena* went alongside a second time and despite objects again being thrown at them four members of the boarding party got across. Her engines had then to be stopped to prevent rolling the illegal vessel over. This small party reached a position aft of the wheelhouse, where about 30 men and women rushed at them, causing an Able Seaman to issue a warning if they did not keep their distance he would open fire. Unfortunately, his warning was ignored, the mob continued to advance and when the boarders were on the point of being overpowered, he fired one round which hit a man, fatally wounding him.

The boarders remained in imminent danger of their lives and *Rowena* warned those aboard the caïque that all means of getting more boarders onboard would be employed, including the use of tear gas, which had not hitherto been used against illegal immigrant vessels. She then came alongside *Ariella*'s starboard quarter again and three tear gas canisters were dropped on to the deck house; this action cleared the after end of the caïque and enabled the remainder of the boarding party to clamber over. After a short fight, complete control was gained, an Engine Room Artificer went below and stopped the engine, enabling *Rowena* to lie alongside.

There was plenty of food onboard but the immigrants were suffering from the effects of the tear smoke and much needed water was passed across from *Rowena*. Medical aid was provided for casualties and the dead immigrant was placed in the wheelhouse out of sight, fortunately none of the others were aware either that he had been shot or was dead. One immigrant jumped over the side and set off for the shore but six rounds from a rifle fired in his vicinity persuaded him to return. No crew could be identified, all radio equipment had been removed from the W/T office and torn charts, files and notebooks were found in what appeared to be officers' quarters. The illegal immigrants, of whom there were 611, mainly members of youth organisations, transferred to a transport and sailed for Cyprus the following day, escorted by HMS *Charity*. Subsequent enquiries confirmed the vessel to have been recently purchased by Giacomo Viterbo, a Jewish resident of Milan. Her voyage was another example of the Italian Government's failure or inability to comply with the requests by His Majesty's Government.

PRECAUTIONS AGAINST SABOTAGE AND BOARDING PARTY EQUIPMENT AND TRAINING

D.1 observed that the attitude of Jews in Haifa towards the Royal Navy had hardened during this period and he curtailed leave to avoid incidents. The Navy had by now become viewed very adversely by terrorist organisations and the threat of sabotage whilst at Haifa had increased yet further. On 27 September police sources reported that a mine had been laid to sabotage an HM Ship. A local is said to have passed on this information to the police. But one account suggests that this coincided with the theft of 900 yards of cable, which led D.1 to surmise that a saboteur concealed onboard the wreck of the *Patria* could use it to touch off explosives placed at the fuelling berth when it was occupied by a destroyer. A 200-lb mine was found, probably by Lieutenant-Commander Crabb and his team, just where D.1 had anticipated. This led to a decision that until the port could be made more secure, ships would fuel at Port Said. An addition was also made to the training undertaken at Haifa by arranging for the Diving School at Manoel Island in Malta to train teams from each ship in shallow-water diving to counter the threat from underwater swimmers and divers.

Since arrested vessels would no longer stop when ordered and the use of firearms had to be avoided, boarding parties now needed to be increased in size and even better trained and equipped for overpowering opposition. These requirements were pressed by Lieutenant-Commander Bailey (HMS *Childers*) as a result of his recent experience with *Fede* and from 15 October courses were conducted at the Royal Marine Training Centre at Ghajn Tuffieha, Malta. The aims were to develop agility and physical fitness, give weapon training, accustom to working in and using tear smoke, ensure all equipment was properly fitted to individuals and, a vital consideration, be adept in quick release of equipment in the event of ending up in the water. One week courses were run for teams each consisting of one officer and fifteen men, including an Engine Room Artificer and a Leading Stoker or Stoker. It included accurate shooting with both 0.303in (7.7mm) Lee-Enfield rifles and 9mm Lanchester sub-machine guns and learning to jump down from heights safely, often boarders had to leap from decks 15 or more feet above the decks of the smaller immigrant vessels. Also runs with and without gas mask over an assault course, cliff and rope-climbing and a special night exercise. Ships sometimes found that the assault course was not an altogether suitable method for training boarders, since it caused more casualties than could be afforded from small ships' companies, so the enthusiasm of the RM Physical Training Instructors for subjecting sailors to this form of training had to be reined in.

Eventually each destroyer or frigate proceeding to Palestine waters had two complete and fully trained boarding parties. In addition new weapons, methods and devices were constantly tried out and supplied. Careful attention was paid to smart appearance by members of boarding parties, this being an important factor in giving an impression of efficiency and effectiveness, and those concerned developed much pride in their own appearance, also considerable *esprit de corps*. White No. 5 jumpers and white helmets were worn to make the members easily distinguishable among a crowd of immigrants and help them stay together, as well as enabling their progress to be observable at a distance from the boarding ships. As protective equipment boarders wore Royal Armoured Corps-type steel helmets, with special colours added to the white to distinguish officers, section leaders and engine-room personnel, together with leather arm shields. The threat from female migrants hat-pin-wielding became evident at an early stage and signals went seeking supplies of cricketers' 'boxes' for protecting private parts.

Entrenching-tool staves soon proved inadequate for overcoming opposition and were replaced by the 2-foot long baton or '*cosh*' developed at Ghajn Tuffieha through various 'Marks' by Major Price RM. The cosh could be used one handed and the point was employed for fending off opponents, whilst if necessary blows could be delivered with the body of the implement. Sailors were reluctant to hit out with this weapon, particularly if attacked by a woman. The rule that use of fire-arms could only be a last resort for self-defence remained paramount.

From the start of boarding operations, water hoses were found to be the most effective means of clearing the opposition from the decks of a vessel, but the boarding ship was seldom able to remain alongside long enough to provide sufficient support of this kind. Some ships embarked trailer pumps which provide two jets at 120lb/in^2 but these were wartime stock, feeling their age, and no longer reliable. Also trailing the inlet hose in the sea was not an effective method of providing them with water if the ship was under way.

Initially, few precautionary measures were taken onboard ships during boardings, apart from a general state of preparedness, including manning a proportion of the armament, in case of emergencies and also to impress the immigrant vessel. Later, ships were fitted with special wire netting and fendering and methods of grappling using kedge anchors fired from depth-charge throwers were devised. Things had moved on far from the days of sending a boarding party in the seaboat to a specialised form of the first degree of readiness with every man onboard taking an active part. In a destroyer, about 88 ratings were directly involved and allocated Boarding

Stations, 28 being in the Boarding Party and the remainder being given such tasks as a Counter-Boarding and Securing Party, countering snipers and manning short range weapons. The load on communications also necessitated destroyers, other than Flotilla Leaders, each employing five seaman on duties normally undertaken by communications ratings. Boy Seamen were not sent as Boarders and were carefully placed so that they were always under the supervision of an officer or a leading rate.

10

Further Arrests

Intelligence soon indicated another illegal vessel to be due and on 18 October the *Alma* (formerly *Fenice*) was sighted from the air and then intercepted by HMS *Chequers* 140 miles north of Haifa. She had 513 males, 261 females and 40 children onboard. *Chequers* shadowed her during the night and then turned the task of making an arrest over to HMS *Chaplet* and two minesweepers, HMS *Rowena* and HMS *Moon* (Lieutenant-Commander D.A. Dunbar-Nasmith DSC RN), after transferring some of her boarding party to the latter. Bad weather prevented boarding until *Alma* was 12 miles off Haifa when she stopped, claiming her engine had failed. No resistance was met when she was boarded by *Chaplet* and *Moon* and the vessel was towed to port by *Moon*. The immigrants left on 22 October in a transport escorted by HMS *Chivalrous*. The *Alma* had shown every sign of being a tough customer, well prepared to resist boarding, but D.1 made full use of a long period in company to persuade those onboard to yield to arrest.

COMMAND AND CONTROL

The CinC was back for a visit early in October. More comprehensive air reconnaissance was needed and after a discussion with AOCinC Middle East additional aircraft were made available. As CS.1 had forecast would be the case, Captain(D) was finding it difficult to manage the task of SNO(A), due to lack of communication links when his own ship took her turn on patrol. The Admiralty therefore agreed to provide a Commodore, 2nd Class and four watchkeeping Lieutenants to function ashore, other manpower requirements being met from 'on station'. On 27 October the post of Commodore Palestine was established and filled by Commodore A.F. de Salis DSO, himself a former Captain (D), sited in the 1st Infantry Division's HQ at Mount Carmel Lighthouse. D.1 relinquished chairmanship of the Haifa Port Committee and the duties of NOIC Haifa. Responsibility for administration of the few remaining establishments and personnel ashore at Haifa was transferred to NOIC Port Said. At much the same time instead of one complete destroyer flotilla being present, the force became six destroyers and two Fleet minesweepers, and periods of duty in the Patrol were reduced to six weeks.

THE *SAN DIMITRIO*

SS *San Dimitrio*, built 1879, was one of two small lake or coastal steamers bought in Sweden by a Swedish businessman. Haganah crews travelled to collect them but found neither suitable to bring passengers from the north. One ran aground and was lost but *San Dimitrio* made her way to the Mediterranean. Her agent was Ginesta and Co., a Marseilles company which later acted in a similar capacity for many other vessels intended for a similar purpose, besides providing a headquarters for purchase and management of illegal immigrant vessels. The *San Dimitrio* was reported by the press on 12 October to be anchored at La Ciotat with a Spanish crew. Despite British efforts through diplomatic channels, on 19 October she embarked 279 illegal immigrants, some apparently from Belgium, under the supervision of the local inspector of French Political Police. The Ministry of Foreign Affairs, more cooperative than the Ministry of the Interior, kept the British Embassy aware of what was afoot, being aware that visas held by passengers for Bolivia were forged, that a document purporting to be a collective visa issued for Ethiopia was also a forgery and that, although the vessel claimed Panamanian registration, the Panamanian authorities had cancelled registration for suspect vessels in France.

The *San Dimitrio*'s approach was reported by air reconnaissance on 30 October and two aircraft homed HMS *Chivalrous* to intercept her after dark. Large numbers of passengers were clearly present and the ship was noticeably unstable, lolling to one side or the other for lengthy periods. She claimed to have 140 passengers, all bound for Port Said via Beirut. At daylight her list became even more pronounced, due to many more passengers coming on deck, and a Zionist flag was now displayed, as were notices saying 'We are unarmed' and the name 'Latrun'. The *San Dimitrio* was still well outside territorial waters and so unstable that, to avoid attracting the passengers over to one side and capsizing her, *Chivalrous* withdrew to greater range. A terrible stench showed all to clearly how bad conditions were onboard.

When the *Chivalrous* next closed, two men were seen to jump overboard. Once retrieved by seaboat they were found to be Spanish crewmembers, who had signed on at Marseilles for a voyage to Beirut. Their tale was that Poles, Russians, Yugoslavs and Romanians had been embarked from the French coast. They were led by three American Jews, one being the wireless operator. Once the ship had been detected by aircraft, the immigrants locked up the Master and crew; they planned to run her up the beach near Haifa in accordance with beaching orders to be issued by Haganah.

A pair of minesweepers, HMS *Octavia* (Lieutenant-Commander T.C.U. Fanshawe RN) and HMS *Providence* (Lieutenant W.E. Messinger RN), joined during the second evening and when the convoy neared Haifa the following morning, *Chivalrous*, despite grave reservations concerning the target's stability, sent them alongside *San Dimitrio*. The boarders were met with cries of 'Gestapo' and 'Nazis', men threw broken bottles, tins and anything else portable whilst women and children were interposed to prevent access to the wheelhouse. At *Octavia*'s first attempt only one man, Abel Seaman C. Lewis got across, but he captured and held the foc'sle until reinforced from *Providence*. Opposition was not as fierce as seemed likely from the attitudes struck and the boarders were in control within ten minutes. The problem then became one of safety as the *San Dimitrio* seemed to be about to capsize. Efforts to prevent this by placing a minesweeper each side only made matters worse, whilst an attempt to tow was abandoned as it caused an even heavier lurch to one side. Despite a rising water level in the stokehold, the Spanish crew, who had now been released, and the boarders succeeded in raising steam. This enabled *San Dimitrio*, listing 45 degrees and rolling uncertainly in the slight swell, to make her way towards Haifa at five knots, *Chivalrous* watched anxiously, fearing that each roll might end in disaster. Eventually the vessel was handed over safely to the Palestine Police and the boarding party, who had done particularly well in alarming conditions in the engine room and stokehold, withdrew. Photographs taken when *San Dimitrio* was alongside in Haifa show her listed some 30 degrees to port despite the weight of passengers going to the jetty over her starboard side. The Attorney-General for Palestine later ruled there was insufficient evidence to prosecute Master or crew. Whitehall found such outcomes exasperating but when a vessel had been arrested using the latitude allowed by the Lord Chancellor, the Navy may have thought it best that officers should not be available as witnesses in court.

When transports reached Cyprus they did not unload at an alongside berth due to the risk of being sabotaged and then blocking the very limited port facilities. So migrants ashore were ferried ashore from an anchorage by means of Z-lighters.[37] Autumn was now advancing and disembarkation of passengers brought from the *San Dimitrio* was delayed by bad weather.

THE MARITIME SAFETY ISSUE

Illegal vessels which would not stop and manoeuvred evasively when warships tried to get alongside risked serious damage and greatly endangered their passengers. There was a risk that eventually one would be seriously damaged or might even capsize, with lives being lost. The generally bad state of the immigrant vessels added to the dangers. Placing a warship on each side of the suspect reduced space available for evasive steering, although ships needed to approach on relative bearings sufficiently far aft to leave no scope for the illegal vessel to turn towards and ram. At the same time care had also to be taken, bearing in mind the unstable nature of some illegal vessels, not to arrive alongside with such sideways force as to cause a capsize. Representations by the Commander-in-Chief, Mediterranean Fleet led to a statement in Parliament condemning the organisers of such hazardous voyages and rejecting any responsibility by HM Government for any catastrophe which might consequently occur. Strangely, the Colonial Office opposed this action and when it was finally decided upon, an unfortunate minister had only two hours warning that he had to read out a statement in the House of Commons. The redoubtable Leader of the Opposition, the Rt Hon W.S. Churchill MP, drawing on his long experience of the events concerning Palestine, treated the matter very seriously, posing questions which the unfortunate spokesman confessed inability to answer.

The Foreign Office also took a hand, sending a formal protest to the French authorities concerning the condition in which the *San Dimitrio* had been allowed to sail. The International Safety at Sea Convention, signed in London on 31 May 1929, included obligations requiring port authorities to obtain certificates confirming that vessels had proper arrangements for crew safety and were in a sanitary condition (Article 54). Also to be satisfied as to the destination of passengers and their travel documents (Article 21). If these requirements were not met, the country of the ship's registration was obliged to intervene. French law (the *Loi de 16 Juin 1933 sur la Sécurité de la Navigation Maritime*) made a vessel of any nationality subject to inspection to ensure she was in a fit state for navigation and also that the arrangements for safety of crew and passengers were in accordance with certain detailed regulations. Thus before embarking passengers in a French port a '*Permis de Navigation*' and a safety certificate had to be obtained.

Arrangements in British ports needed also to be reviewed. The Treasury Solicitor ventured no more than that a foreign ship could be detained in a British port under the Merchant Shipping Act 1894 if 'unsafe', within the rather limited definition of being 'unsafe by reason of defective condition of hull equipment, or machinery, or by reason of overloading or improper loading or by reason of undermanning'. His advice was to be chary of proceeding on those grounds. A meeting chaired by the Colonial Office considered this weak and unhelpful view and found that, whilst powers to detain merchant ships were indeed limited, the Act quoted enabled the forcible detention of an emigrant ship. Health standards, which

1. Rt Hon. A.J. Balfour MP on the steps of No. 10 Downing Street during the First
World War.

2. Arab demonstration in Jerusalem, 1936.

3. Coast guard station damaged by explosives, 25 November 1946.

4. The High Commissioner, General Cunningham, visits Senior Naval Officer Levant & Haifa, December 1947.

5. HMS *Superb* at Malta.

6. HMS *Phoebe* leaving the Mediterranean Station in September 1948 to pay off.

7. *Josiah Wedgwood* arriving at Haifa after arrest.

9. *Josiah Wedgwood* immigrants disembarking.

8. *Josiah Wedgwood* at Haifa. Palestine pol ceman on bridge.

10. HMS *Mauritius*.

11. *Sagolem*.

12. HMS *Chequers* (Captain (D), First Destroyer Flotilla).

13. *Merica* arriving at Haifa with RN boarding party.

14. *San Felipo* seen from HMS *Charity*.

15. *Galata*.

16. HMS *Cheviot* approaches *Galata*.

17. *Galata* alongside HMS *Pelican* after boarding and arrest.

18. Able Seaman J.B. Goodliffe after boarding *Galata*.

19. Boarding party in charge of *Galata*.

20. *President Warfield* prior to the boarding.

21. *President Warfield* after the boarding.

22. Arrested immigrants arriving at Cyprus camp.

23. *Pan Crescent* with HMS *Phoebe* beyond.

24. HMS *Phoebe* boarding party arriving at *Pan Crescent*.

25. HMS *Mauritius* boarding party approaching Pan York.

26. A typical caique in the eastern Mediterranean, 1946.

27. Wire netting protection against missiles thrown by illegal immigrants rigged in an RN ship.

28. Boarding platform in the raised position prior to boarding.

in the illegal vessels were almost non-existent, provided the firmest ground for doing so. Defence Regulations also permitted action to prevent the embarkation of aliens and if the ship concerned attempted to do so, she could be seized. Another useful wartime order was unearthed, the Control of Trade by Sea (No. 2) Order 1939 still required any ship of over one hundred tons to hold a licence granted by the proper authority before putting out to sea, whether or not passengers were embarked. There the matter rested.

LOCHITA'S ARREST

The next arrest followed an aircraft report on 24 November which led Commodore Palestine to despatch HMS *Haydon* from her patrol. She was homed by an aircraft towards the *Lochita*, sighted after nightfall completely darkened. She proved to be an 1,870grt vessel built in 1889 and grossly overloaded with the largest number of illegal immigrants hitherto encountered. The *Lochita* had sailed from Greece intending to pick up immigrants first from the Yugoslav coast and later at sea from the vessel *Athina*, which would probably have taken off some of her crew. But the *Athina*, a 273-ton Greek motor vessel built 1898, was not a lucky ship, she had sunk in 1941, had only been raised earlier in the year and another mishap, by no means the last, delayed her. When another illegal immigrant vessel was wrecked, *Lochita* rescued the passengers, revictualled at Split and then set off again.

Owing to the noise made by the passengers, the best means of communication with the *Lochita* was visual signalling, at which she proved very adept. She reported 4,042 passengers, including 1,587 women (about 240 pregnant), 453 children, ten of whom had been born onboard, some 300 old people, and gave her destination as Tel Aviv. *Haydon* suggested a diversion direct to Famagusta and appealed for good sense, to which the response came that the passengers would not exchange a German concentration camp for a British one and intended to put up a fight if necessary. Medical attention was politely declined. The following day HMS *Brissenden* arrived to assist and the CinC signalled a warning that it was of the greatest importance that the *Lochita* should not reach Tel Aviv – if necessary force could be used to prevent this. Further reinforcements, the minesweepers HMS *Octavia* and HMS *Espiegle* (Lieutenant-Commander R.W. Davis RN), joined during the second night and embarked boarding parties from the destroyers.

Lochita steered in the general direction of Tel Aviv until at 0545 she reported a man had fallen overboard about an hour previously. The convoy reversed course and *Brissenden* searched back, zig-zagging, despite a steering-gear breakdown which necessitated steering from her tiller-flat, along the trail of refuse marking the *Lochita*'s track. A little after an hour after the first report she found and rescued the man, Mr David Daid, no worse for his swim.

Daid, who came from Translylvania, had been a prisoner for two years at Dachau and had made his way to Split with a forged passport. *Lochita*'s passengers were, he said, funded by an American organisation in Europe and had called at Crete, where 12 Greek sailors deserted. On the night prior to interception radio contact had been established with the Haganah, who directed the vessel to Tel Aviv, where strikes and demonstrations were planned. Orders were also given that firearms brought onboard by most of the young males were to be destroyed. Stocks of food, water and fuel were said to be very low onboard and sanitation non-existent.

On hearing Daid was safe, the *Lochita* altered course for Haifa and at 1109 agreed to be boarded so she could be taken in. At the 3-mile limit three police launches were waiting and the two minesweepers went alongside 2.2 miles off Carmel Light to transfer boarding parties, totalling three officers and seventy men. The boarding was unopposed; the tact, efficiency and enthusiasm of the boarders meant that the *Lochita* was under control by 1215 and she was then towed into port and berthed alongside the same quay as transports on which the immigrants were to be embarked. A British press representative later found ample stocks of food supplied by UNRRA.

This peaceable arrest was facilitated by the interception being made in plenty of time to try prolonged and skilful persuasion, fine weather, goodwill caused by the recovery of the man overboard and, as it turned out, an immigrant leader in firm control. His final, very helpful, suggestion was that if disturbances were to be avoided, no mention should be made of transhipment to Cyprus. Indeed the Boarding Party noticed that the passengers evidently believed they were home and dry with the Promised Land in their grasp. It was no surprise that when transfer to transports was attempted the mood changed completely. The Army authorities were warned accordingly but were unable to prevent violent opposition developing into a pitched battle, the Jews producing a large number of missiles and lead-weighted wire 'stonachies'. For a time the Army personnel lost control, there was shooting and two immigrants died.

The three transports available for the *Lochita*'s migrants each had capacity for only 800 passengers, but retention of any of her 4,000 in the illegal ship herself was impracticable on sanitary, security and humanitarian grounds. The distance from Haifa to Famagusta being only 170 miles. all the immigrants were therefore embarked in the transports. At this point the Jewish Agency started a legal action aimed at preventing their removal and the transports had to be retained in territorial waters until the case was decided. They left Haifa and steamed slowly up and down the Palestine coast, escorted by HMS *Cardigan Bay* (Captain G.K. Collett RN – Captain (F) 5th Frigate Squadron). Once the law case was cleared all the transports departed for Famagusta with *Cardigan Bay* and HMS *Octavia* in company. The outcome of the case caused a three-minute silence to be observed by Jews in Palestine, also concern by Jewish authorities that the restraint which had been exercised following the Palestine Government's concession allowing arrested immigrants detained in Cyprus to enter Palestine, might suffer. Indeed there was renewed activity by the Stern Gang, and, the other side of the coin, fresh accusations by the Arabs that the Palestine Government was facilitating Jewish illegal immigration.

DISEMBARKATION ARRANGEMENTS AT CYPRUS

Recalling the difficulties with putting *San Dimitrio*'s migrants ashore at Cyprus and with a likelihood of winter weather, Commodore Palestine enlisted the aid of the GOC 1st Infantry Division to urge the Cyprus military authorities to expedite the forthcoming disembarkation. F.5 signalled ahead to the same effect, but when the convoy arrived at 0600, the time notified, nothing was planned until 0800 and then only one ship would be unloaded at a time. The Army Camp Commandant proved unhelpful and his superiors at General Headquarters, Nicosia declined to intervene. By the end of the first day, therefore, only one transport had been cleared and very careful precautions had to be taken to guard against any of the ships being attacked by underwater swimmers during the night.

The following day, a Sunday, F.5's requests for urgency appeared at first to be more successful, unloading started two hours earlier and by 1430 a second transport had been cleared. In the meantime news came that unloading of the third transport would be left until Monday morning. This caused further representations to GHQ Nicosia, more successful than earlier, since the Camp Commandant was then overruled, disembarkation continued and by the end of the day all the passengers were ashore. Only the baggage was left until the third morning, when at the last moment the Camp Commandant produced 300 legal immigrants to be embarked and taken to Haifa. By good luck the weather caused no difficulties with an operation which, with better preparations and a greater sense of urgency, could have been completed in one day. Subsequently, the naval CinC took the matter up with CinC Middle East Land Forces. The need to maintain precautions against underwater sabotage when off or in Cyprus ports was demonstrated in the early hours of 3 April 1947 when a swimmer was sighted near the transport *Ocean Vigour*, anchored two miles from the shore off Famagusta. He was fired on by a sentry and at dawn an underwater explosion blew a hole three feet by six feet in her starboard quarter. A man seen coming ashore was arrested. This was a Palyam operation mounted from the Cyprus internment camps where training in military matters proceeded briskly with messages being smuggled in.

The Captain of HMS *Stevenstone* later visited a section of the internment camp and found that, due to the refusal of the inmates to clear up or clean up or to respect the needs and comfort of their successors, conditions were deplorable with torn-up tents, used tins, broken crockery and debris of every kind present in profusion. The Army in Cyprus had a very trying task, since living conditions were deliberately made most unpleasant by the immigrants as a 'dirty protest'. Soldiers were not stationed inside the camps but still had to live under canvas in a sea of mud and had a very unenviable task, dealing, as they were, with uncooperative, treacherous and destructive people. The Chiefs of Staff had long considered there should be more permanent accommodation for at least 20,000 illegal immigrants in Cyprus. Construction of winter hutted accommodation for up to 10,000 men, women and children was due to be completed by mid-January, whilst a start was about to be made on construction of accommodation for a further 10,000. By late autumn 1946 all those held in camps in Palestine at the time when deportation to Cyprus started had been released against the quota. A decision was now made that the quota of 1,500 per month would in future be split in equal proportions between 'gatecrashers' held at Cyprus and legal immigrants, with a high priority for Second World War ex-Servicemen.

The first sign that President Truman's personal support for Zionist aspirations was less strident came in November when the President, increasingly harassed by individual Zionists and with elections out of the way, shed the greater share of the responsibility for handling the problem of Palestine to his Secretary of State. At the start of the New Year this post was taken by the greatly respected General George Marshall, the Second World War Chief of the US Army Staff. At much the same time the French Government suggested tripartite talks with the British and Americans to discuss the problem of travel by displaced persons in the three nations' zones of occupied former enemy territory. The underlying issue was the attitude of the Americans and the French which enabled Jews to make their way through the American zone of Germany to the French border. There they were admitted as travellers on their way to other lands, went on to the Mediterranean coast and embarked under false pretences for Palestine.

11

The *Athina* Rescue

At the end of November the 8th MSF left the Mediterranean, reducing the number of 'Algerine'-class minesweepers available for the Patrol to eight. However, the onset of winter appeared to reduce Zionist zeal for difficult sea voyages and from 26 November until 9 February 1947 there were no arrivals or arrests. During this period it was possible to reduce the force level to three destroyers, two minesweepers and one sloop or frigate. However a major rescue became necessary after a final unsuccessful voyage by the *Athina*, which started from Bakar in Yugoslavia, where she received two railway wagon loads of UNRRA foodstuffs and two wagon loads of fuel sent from Zagreb. These were embarked with the open assistance of the Yugoslav authorities. Illegal immigrants followed, mainly from Poland, travelling by night in horse drawn vehicles for anything from two to five months. The ship then sailed flying the Zionist flag and a Reuter's source indicated that she had been intended to tranship her passengers to another vessel. The Naval authorities had wind of her intentions and the Admiralty authorised an attempt at voluntary diversion to Cyprus.

In the event the *Athina* did not need to be intercepted. Immigrants were sometimes transferred between ships in the lee of the island of Sirina to the North-East of Crete. As early as 1940 the *Panchem*, a paddle steamer carrying immigrants, came to grief there. *Athina* suffered a similar fate when after twelve days at sea bad weather caused her to seek shelter. On 7 December she inadvertently grounded on Sirina, slipped off the rocks after 40 minutes and sank. There were 784 illegal immigrants onboard and about eight, including three children, were lost when the survivors struggled ashore onto the island. Its only inhabitants were a Greek farmer (the proud possessor of a letter of commendation for services rendered during the late conflict signed by Field Marshal Alexander) and his family. The *Athina* had a radio put together by amateurs in Athens and the operator succeeded in getting it and one of the two batteries ashore. The rescued battery was slightly damaged but produced just enough power for a transmission reporting the predicament to Mossad in Palestine and

Athens, this led the Jewish Agency to seek assistance from the High Commissioner. The latter passed the request on to the Air Force and naval authorities, at the same time recalling the precedent of the Agency paying the costs when Jews reached Turkey in 1942 and were transferred by the British to Cyprus. The RAF immediately delivered medical and supplies by parachute to what the High Commissioner described very accurately as 'this desolate isle'.

HMS *Chevron* restricted by bad weather to 20–23 knots, arrived after dark on 9th December and found that the Greek destroyer HHMS *Themistocles* had put some men ashore and was evacuating eight casualties assisted by a very able English doctor who had come from Rhodes. Supplies of tea and food were landed at daybreak; later the CinC signalled authorization for embarkation to start and during the forenoon HMS *Providence* arrived to help. In driving rain and very difficult conditions, which twice caused operations to be suspended for long periods (during one of which the unexpected culinary skills of CPO Mortar, the Gunner's Mate of *Chevron*, were much appreciated), shore parties, led by the First Lieutenant of HMS *Chevron*, Lieutenant G.C. Leslie RN, brought off all the survivors. A very reluctant (due to the weather) British Military Authority caïque, commandeered by Lieutenant Leslie, 'In the name of the King', assisted. *Themistocles* and HHMS *Agean*, another ex-British 'Hunt' now present, did not attempt boat work in such adverse conditions.

With *Providence* pitching and rolling heavily, each survivor had to be secured by a line and hauled onboard, and the women, clinging to their bundles, showed considerable pluck and fortitude. However, when her whaler first brought survivors alongside they panicked, became out of control, rushed to get aboard the 'sweeper' and capsized the boat, leaving two crew, six men and seven women in the water. All were safely rescued and the whaler was later recovered too. *Providence*'s First Lieutenant and Landing Party Officer, Lieutenant A.F. Wilcocks RN, found the survivors' morale good during his period ashore and heard constant expressions of appreciation and not one word of complaint. Another onboard *Providence* recalled 'the pot-mess (already) prepared to feed them, the razors given to them to remove lice-infested hair and the pervading smell of death on the mess-decks and the utter desolation of them all...'.[38] Soon bathrooms onboard both vessels were being put to good use by passengers all keen to clean themselves up.

Embarkation was completed[39] by 0300 and the two British ships then went to Suda Bay in Crete, arriving the same day. There the survivors, after formally thanking their rescuers, transferred to Landing Ship Tank (LST) 3016 (Lieutenant-Commander A.M. Sullivan RN). HMS *Stevenstone* escorted the LST and provided her with a guard. The immigrants included a large proportion of modest, middle-aged men and women of the genuine refugee type, more than half being mothers or grandmothers, with many children and elderly men, all still dazed from their ordeal and grateful for being rescued. But before long a deputation appeared requesting a voyage (without delay) direct to Palestine.

Accommodation in the LST was on the tank deck where hot soup, food and bedding awaited the passengers. There were insufficient camp beds and the men regarded themselves as having first priority in that respect. This unchivalrous tendency was corrected as far as possible before the LST set off eastward into bad weather, which kept the immigrants in a subdued state. The sailors spared no effort in caring for them, a complaint of lack of food proved unfounded and although the passengers lacked the ability to organise themselves domestically, they helped with washing up dishes. Quarters were comparatively spacious but when a complaint was made of congestion by night the Captain offered space on deck under an awning. This was accepted by the males present, who added that it would allow them more space and comfort below and thus was very suitable for the women, which selfish view led to the offer being withdrawn.

During the voyage from Sirina *Athina*'s former radio operator read messages exchanged by signal lanterns between ships and thus learnt their destination. On the second day out ringleaders began to renew 'claims', principally the demand to go to Haifa, but eventually the chief trouble-maker was warned that if he made any more difficulties he would be locked up. Before arrival at Cyprus on 14 December all possible weapons, down to razors and fountain pens, were removed from the passengers. *Stevenstone* and the LST berthed alongside in Famagusta where representatives of the Civil Administration of internment camps, the Jewish Agency, migrants already at the camps and the press met the immigrants. By this time the LST's tank space was ringing to cries and shouts of 'Haifa' and 'Palestine' and Jewish anthems, whilst the passengers smashed 600 or so cups and soaked and damaged bedding to the best of their ability. These activities increased the costs due to be met by the Jewish Agency, whose representatives did their best to persuade those involved to disembark. Although the bulk of the refugees, including the women, children and older men were prepared to comply, they were prevented from doing so by ring-leaders and 30 or more thugs who blocked the exit and threatened violence. Eventually the only solution was to lower a tear smoke generator through a skylight into the tank deck and this produced tearful assurances that a very early stay in Cyprus was the passengers' most earnest wish. True to previous form, the male passengers tried to be first and there was a short delay whilst sailors introduced the practice of women and children first. At one stage two sailors standing quietly to one side were suddenly attacked by some 30 men with such fury that the Petty Officer in charge fired one round at the legs of the assailants, causing them to disperse, one male being wounded in the wrist by a ricochet. When at last the whole party were clear, a start was made to the 24-hour task of cleaning up the

LST. Women and children ex-*Athina* were later reported to be at one of the internment camps in Palestine about to be released against the quota for May 1947.

The Captain of *Stevenstone*, Lieutenant-Commander Owen, subsequently reported that illegal immigrants should never be trusted, being unreasonable people who, when roused, became 'utterly ruthless'. Vigilance could not be relaxed, firm measures were necessary at all times, particularly as the mood could change very suddenly and when reason failed tear gas, backed up with determined but economical use of force, was the best way forward. Ringleaders and thugs were always conspicuous and if they could be isolated from the start then much of the trouble could be avoided, in some case immigrants being glad to be rid of them.

The need for additional transports resulted in four more ships being transferred to this task. Laid down as 'Castle' Class corvettes but completed as merchant-manned, Red Ensign 'Convoy Rescue Ships', the *Empire Comfort*, *Empire Lifeguard*, *Empire Rest* and *Empire Shelter* had been modified while fitting out to carry up to 400 survivors with enhanced medical facilities. They were thus particularly suitable for shuttling the illegal immigrants to Cyprus.

12

The Legal Issues

The turn that events were now taking meant that the Patrol needed instructions on what was to be done if an illegal immigrant vessel used firearms to resist arrest. Whilst the CinC Mediterranean Fleet held that the more the show of force and determination, the less the risk there would be of such a very undesirable development, he authorised opening fire if necessary to suppress opposition of that kind. But he added that response was to be proportionate and no more than absolutely necessary to overcome opposition.

Even larger and faster vessels were becoming liable to be encountered and to prevent any reaching the shore boarding operations needed to start before the 3-mile limit, in practice one mile offshore for every knot of which an illegal vessel was capable. The ships and craft being intercepted were frequently ex-enemy vessels or wore no recognised flag and generally the presence of illegal immigrants was obvious. After the *Ariella* the CinC suggested to the Admiralty, at the same instant as the High Commissioner made a similar proposal to CS.15, that arrests be made outside territorial waters and illegal vessels then escorted direct to Cyprus. Air searches would need to be extended to a greater range and the Air Officer Commanding-in-Chief was agreeable to providing additional aircraft for that purpose.

This question was to prove crucial to whether or not the naval blockade remained effective and continued to serve a useful purpose. However, Admiral Willis's predecessor, now First Sea Lord, remained adamant that diversion was impracticable. He held that a vessel intercepted or arrested would decline to go anywhere but Palestine and foresaw lengthy tows to Cyprus. The Admiralty's Military Branch advised that carriage of illegal immigrants was not sufficient justification for arrest, but otherwise they supported the proposal. Two precedents were cited, the first being when the Royal Navy put a stop to the slave trade early in the nineteenth century, and the second the American 'anti-hovering' practice, which was discussed earlier. Both the Secretary of State for the Colonies and the Foreign Secretary agreed proposals put first put to them by the Admiralty at the end of October, which suggested that illegal immigrant ships might be arrested on the high seas if they:

    a. had no identifiable master or crew. Hence failed to fulfil the requirements of international law, which requires the carrying of proper ships' papers, including a muster roll identifying master and crew;

    b. wore no recognised flag;

    c. wore an ex-enemy flag (i.e. Italian, Bulgarian or Romanian flag (until peace treaties were signed). These ex-enemy countries were scarcely in a position to object.

The Admiralty also proposed that:

    a. authority be given for intercepting vessels to divert illegal vessels direct to Cyprus in cases where this was feasible;

    b. legislation be introduced to permit the ships to be confiscated at Cyprus and their Masters detained.

Finally, the Admiralty was of the view that Palestine's right of self-defence justified arrest on the high seas. Although illegal immigration did not go so far as to constitute a body of armed men landing for the purpose of an attack or raid, it was considered that such activity constituted a direct incitement to civil war and even more serious disturbances.

These suggestions were considered at a Cabinet meeting on 10 December 1946 with the First Lord and the First Sea Lord present. Both intended that whenever a suspect vessel was known to be approaching Palestine, the Admiralty should have a period of 48 hours to consider whether the extreme measure of arresting her on the high seas was to be adopted or that an interception of this kind was likely to be more trouble than it was worth. If an arrival did not become known 48 hours or more beforehand there might not be sufficient time for a decision to be made at the Admiralty. In those exceptional circumstances, the CinC would be permitted to order the arrest or stopping of a ship flying a foreign flag outside territorial waters.

British support for the creation of the United Nations Organisation had already led to the Prime Minister instructing ministers to tread warily where international law was concerned and at the Cabinet meeting the Lord Chancellor raised questions concerning the propriety of what was proposed. The argument concerning no recognizable flag dated from the days of countering piracy and the 'Jolly Roger' so was in his view no longer relevant. The US 'anti-hovering' legislation had not turned out satisfactorily. An even more compelling argument was that at just that moment a case was being brought by the British Government in the International Court of

Justice following Albania's mining of the Corfu Channel, an international straits, which seriously damaged HM Ships *Saumarez* and *Volage*. Anything which smacked of taking the law of the sea into Britain's own hands would thus be singularly inopportune.

Nine days later the Lord Chancellor told a subsequent Cabinet meeting that he concluded strongly against stopping vessels on the high seas, holding that visit and search was solely a belligerent right, which could not be exercised in peacetime. As to the right of self-defence, this could only be justified by a need for self-preservation. Even in such an extreme example as a vessel attempting to bring in arms and ammunition, a case would have to be put in an International Court that her activities would lead to civil war. But, as has been shown earlier, it was just that threat which necessitated limits on Jewish immigration and when, 16 months later, these ceased, a civil war followed. Nevertheless, the Admiralty considered the Lord Chancellor had 'cut the ground from under our feet' and thus it did not pursue the point that subsequent events in the courts showed, as we will see, to carry greatest weight.

Informally, however, the Lord Chancellor could see no objections to attempts to 'persuade' illegal immigrant ships to go voluntarily to Cyprus. In view of the Prime Minister's directive concerning strict observance of international law, this caused the First Sea Lord some surprise but the Lord Chancellor later confirmed that there was no objection to 'peaceful persuasion being by means of a strongly armed vessel'. Subsequently, as will be seen, the question had to be confronted of being able to produce written evidence from a vessel that she had *gone willingly*. The Lord Chancellor also volunteered, quoting Nelson's use of a blind eye, that there should be no practical difficulties in taking certain liberties with the 3-mile limit, since a Master would be unlikely to know whether he had been arrested just inside or outside the limit. Bearing in mind the shortcomings of navigational methods available at the time, this was entirely realistic. That settled the matter to the Admiralty's satisfaction. Some three months after the CinC started to press the question he was able to issue instructions to Commodore Palestine and Commanding Officers that seizure if necessary up to six miles from the shore was permissible, although in such cases HM Government and the Admiralty would be embarrassed to know precise positions. The involvement of Commanding Officer in court proceedings, i.e. appearing in the witness box, was inconvenient and undesirable. Indeed, the presence of an onboard Palestine Policeman should make this unnecessary. That did not suffice when use was made of the latitude now allowed by the CinC and eventually arrests were being made up to 16 miles from the coast. In such cases the Attorney General for Palestine held that Palestine Municipal Law allowed a ship to be brought in outside the three mile limit but, although their vessel was forfeited, the crew were free to go. In particular, he preferred to admit that an arrest had been made outside territorial waters rather than have a Commanding Officer called into the witness box.

Later, in 1947, the Government of Honduras agreed that ships flying the Honduran flag and reasonably suspected of engaging in the illegal immigrant trade could be arrested on the high seas. The Lord Chancellor had no objection to this arrangement, but a separate proposal that an arrest could be made if the vessel's registration certificate had been withdrawn at British request did not meet with his approval. However, the Board of Admiralty opposed both options for two reasons. First, because it was contrary to Britain's interests to encourage interference with merchant ships on the high seas in peacetime. Second, because reliance could not be placed on an arrangement with a state such as Honduras made by an exchange of telegrams or letters and without a written treaty. Pressure from the Foreign Officer legal adviser on the latter point, and indeed Military Branch, its own secretariat, failed to change the Board's view and so the matter was dropped. Later, in May 1947, political and diplomatic pressure led to certain foreign states, notably Panama, agreeing to cancel the registration of ships shown to be engaged in the illegal immigrant traffic. Once again Their Lordships would not agree to arrests using this procedure, since in the longer term the precedent might encroach on the freedom of the seas for British vessels.

LEGAL STEPS AGAINST IMMIGRANT VESSEL CREWS

The desirability of using the full rigour of the law to discourage Masters and crews from assisting illegal immigration was made clear to the Palestine Government in the late winter of 1947, when the Foreign Office pressed for a Master and crew to be brought rapidly to trial. Stiff prison sentences would, it thought, have a deterrent effect on potential crew members. However, the Colonial Office raised legal difficulties, noting the difficulty of identifying crew members, and advancing the suggestion that martyrdom might aid Zionist propaganda in America. The first of those arguments was a matter which could be handled locally. The second is one prone to use by policy makers not directly involved at the scene of conflict. Having committed its forces to upholding the law, laxity of that kind by government increases their difficulties, morale can suffer and, as was the case with boarding parties, it is they who endure martyrdom. Judging by desertions known to have taken place from illegal immigrant vessels once the purpose of their voyage became clear, a surer prospect of a spell in Acre jail might well have increased the difficulties of the organisers significantly.

13

The Second Winter: Arrests

The discussions between the High Commissioner and Jewish Agency representatives at the time of the *Athina* incident revealed that no further ships were expected to arrive for two or three months. This period coincided with an unsuccessful final attempt to bring Jews and Arab representatives together in London and secure agreement on Palestine's future. The success of the Patrol in 1946 had been due very largely to good and timely information but the illegal immigrant organisations' security was tightened, and during the winter the Joint Headquarters in Jerusalem found detailed intelligence more hard to come by: some of the sources were not to recover their full reliability until mid-May 1947. In November 1946, the 800-ton Italian motor barquentine *Merica* had been reported at Marseilles for conversion as an illegal immigrant vessel. On 17 January she moved to Sête and embarked migrants, the majority coming from two UNRRA camps in Bavaria. Every effort was made to persuade the French authorities to prevent the passengers, who held forged Cuban visas, departing on a voyage to a country where they would not be admitted. The *Merica* sailed giving her destination as Cuba, this was apparently believed and as air searches were not flown. There was no further warning of her approach until she encountered HMS *Chieftain* (Commander G.E. Fardell RN) unexpectedly after dark on 8 February.

HMS *Welfare* (Commander Q.P. Whitford RN) (Senior Officer MSF.2) joined later and the *Merica* was boarded at 0244 the same night whilst underway; according to the Palestine Police officer present, this was done nine miles west of Caesarea. To enable a boarding party to gain control of a vessel's wheelhouse and engine room the best position to arrive onboard was at the after end but evasive steering could result in a blow on the quarter which might result in a capsize. *Merica* took violent avoiding action and the risks to passengers were increased by the bunks below decks being so constructed that many would have been trapped had she rolled over. Portable gangways rigged on the minesweeper's bow provided shelter but otherwise were not of much value. Resistance onboard necessitated the use of tear gas and after some small arms fire, *Merica* was under control in six minutes. On this occasion the automatic weapons carried by some members of the boarding party were found to have a sobering effect. The training provided at Ghain Tuffieha stood the boarding party in good stead and the newly supplied cosh was a great success, but in consequence of the use of firearms one passenger died from head injuries. Leather arm shields proved invaluable and men working on the *Welfare*'s upper deck were provided with large wooden shields. Another innovation was standard warning addresses in both English and German.

Water onboard the *Merica* was found to be bright green and the smell onboard was, as ever, terrible. One of *Welfare*'s ship's company recalls a female migrant onboard going into labour and that the others would not help, in his view because they were always looking for an atrocity. The *Welfare*'s Gunner's Mate and a Leading Stoker set to and, with advice culled hastily from medical manuals by her Leading Sick Berth Attendant and then passed across by Aldis Lamp, successfully delivered a baby girl. No crew members could be found and *Merica*'s engine eventually broke down, so she was towed into territorial waters and on to Haifa, where her 657 passengers were transferred to *Empire Heywood* for passage to Famagusta. The Palestine Police officer witnessing the arrest reported of the transfer:

> A number of women showed signs of hysteria and a few men had to be dragged down the gangways of 'MERICA' but the troops conducting the operation employed no harsher methods than were necessary to coerce these delinquents off the vessel.[40]

The 3rd DF now returned. The ships companies of HMS *Saumarez* and HMS *Volage* had collected as replacements from England HMS *Troubridge* and HMS *Verulam* (Commander L.H. Stileman RN), the latter having been scheduled to come out to Malta as a reserve in any case. HMS *Volage* was repaired at Malta, and became available to rejoin the Patrol at an opportune moment later.

ARRESTS

The 500-ton packet steamer *San Miguel*, alias '*Hama'apil Ha'almoni*' ('Unknown Immigrant'), built in 1876, was the first arrival of four Swedish ships purchased by a suspect Panamanian company in the autumn of 1946. Two of the four, dating from 1876 and 1868 respectively, had their Panamanian certificates of registration withdrawn and never left the Baltic.

The *San Miguel* reached Marseilles from Copenhagen on 19 January and sailed on 1 February, purportedly for Oran but in fact to Sête, where she embarked migrants ostensibly bound for Cuba. *San Miguel* was detected by the RAF and intercepted on 16 February by HMS *Welfare* and the frigate HMS *St Austell Bay* (Lieutenant-Commander E.M. Harvey RN). MSF.2 attempted to dissuade the vessel from attempting to land her passengers but the only responses were missiles and cries of 'Nazi swine'. Once inside the 3-mile limit south-west of Jaffa both ships closed and whilst *Welfare* played hoses on those on the *San Miguel's* deck, *St Austell Bay's* boarding party clambered onto the poop-deck and, with the assistance of tear gas and men from *Welfare,* gained control. One passenger, a Polish migrant, attempted to swim ashore but the distance was too great and he was recovered from the sea, as was one member of the boarding party. No crew could be found, and six passengers needed hospital treatment but the remaining 798 transferred, the large majority cheerfully, at Haifa to the *Empire Rival* and she sailed for Famagusta at 0630.

The *Ulua*, the former 880-ton US Coastguard Cutter *Unalga* built in 1912, was tougher meat. She was purchased in the USA and known in December to be at Marseilles converting for illegal immigrant traffic. *Ulua* then went North and in January the *New York Times* reported her at Trelleborg embarking illegal immigrants; these totalled 600, again carried forged Cuban visas and were originally intended to travel in one of the four Swedish ships. On 3 February, whilst crossing the Bay of Biscay, flying the Jewish flag, the *Ulua* encountered HMS *Vanguard* conveying HM the King and Queen together with the Princesses Elizabeth and Margaret to South Africa.[41] After fuelling at Algiers, to the chagrin of the British consul who failed to be aware of her presence until after departure, the *Ulua* went to Italy and embarked 700 more migrants south of Taranto by night using rubber rafts.

The RAF located the *Ulua* at 1345 on 27 February and she was closed by HMS *Chieftain* at 1800 in 31°45'N, 32°45'E, further to the south and west than any other interception hitherto. She flew the Honduran flag and signalled, using Naval procedure and twin yardarm signal lamps, that she had an American crew, was registered in Honduras, and carried 600 passengers embarked in Sweden and bound for Alexandria. She pretended that the passengers fom Italy were survivors from a Jewish refugee ship picked up off Malta and announced that these would be landed at Tel Aviv. *Ulua* was overheard transmitting on a powerful radio transmitter in an unknown language and was thought to be talking to a shore station.

HMS *Chevron* joined *Chieftain* at 2207 and shortly after midnight the Senior Officer 2nd Minesweeping Flotilla (MSF.2) arrived in HMS *Welfare* with HMS *Rowena*. As the *Ulua* was probably capable of 12 knots, there were some doubts whether the minesweepers were fast enough to do the boarding, but it was decided to try. HMS *St Austell Bay* arrived during the night, throughout which *Ulua* signalled changes of course and speed as though she was the senior officer, adding at midnight a signal that by general consent she had been renamed Chaim Arlosoroff. To this *Chieftain* replied 'Happy Birthday'.

The *Ulua* would not stop when ordered and took violent avoiding action when approached by *Rowena* at 1040. She had wooden booms rigged on both sides and a boat full of passengers on her starboard quarter provided a further obstruction, so she had to be boarded over her stern. *Rowena* used ramps with heavy grapnels on their outboard ends attached to a wire spring and a head rope. These worked successfully but only one officer and six ratings from the *Welfare* and one officer and four ratings from *Rowena* succeeded in getting onboard, before the two minesweepers found themselves forced away by the *Ulua*'s wash. This small party were met by fierce resistance and a hail of bully-beef tins, nuts and bolts and iron bars. After two minutes their supply of tear gas was exhausted and although permitted the use of firearms for self-defence they did not shoot, a restraint which was thought to have probably reduced the opposition later. The boarders were soon overwhelmed, disarmed and beaten up, with one rating forced to the ground and seriously injured by having his stomach jumped on. The remainder took the first opportunity to jump overboard and were recovered by *Chieftain* and by the police in ML 1145.

The *Ulua* was now making 12 knots and, as had been feared, the minesweepers proved not fast enough to catch up sufficiently quickly. Twenty minutes passed before *Rowena* managed to get to her again and, by means of boarding ramps with grapnels at their ends secured to wires leading back inboard, she remained alongside for long enough to transfer 27 boarders before the *Ulua* broke free. This time the boarders fired bursts over the immigrants' heads and gradually achieved the upper hand, although they were unable to reach the wheelhouse and take control. *Rowena* made another attempt at a boarding but had to draw clear, first to avoid rolling the ship over when she altered violently to port, and later to avoid running up the beach. *Welfare* also made a second boarding attempt but was forced to stop engines and sheer off to avoid ramming *Ulua*. The immigrant ship then stopped her engines and drifted ashore, fortuitously grounding close under the Army Barracks at Mount Carmel. Nine immigrants swam ashore but the others, seeing them being very easily rounded up by soldiers, choose to remain where they were. Later 1,398 immigrants were taken off by Army manned Z-Lighters and moved to transports awaiting them at Haifa. Attempts to tow off the *Ulua* were not pursued, since she had been holed in her engine room by the grounding.

A total of 84 personnel were employed as boarding parties against the *Ulua*, one rating being seriously injured and two others badly hurt; there were also 30 immigrant casualties. The Master handled his ship in a resolute manner but the strong resistance by the immigrants was, not surprisingly, disorganised and hysterical and could be progressively overcome as soon as there were enough sailors onboard. The immigrants were at their boldest when they had got their man down, and it was the *Ulua*'s crew which prevented them from using firearms taken from the first boarding party. The Master and crew were, once again, not prosecuted, since the Palestine Government could not prove that they abetted illegal immigration inside territorial waters.

The latest arrests demonstrated afresh the risk of an overloaded, unseaworthy illegal immigrant vessel capsizing during an arrest. The CinC signalled the Admiralty to request that the Government issue another warning placing responsibility for any disasters or mishaps on the organisers of the traffic. Some dissatisfaction was again felt at a senior level in the Foreign Office at the Palestine Government's inability to prosecute Masters and crews who claimed they had been over-powered by passengers before entering territorial waters.

In Haifa a Government fishery protection launch and two Royal Army Service Corps craft were damaged by explosions on 13 February and during the transfer of immigrants from *Ulua* on 28 February a bomb was planted in Barclay's Bank by men disguised as soldiers. This damaged the nearby offices of the Admiralty Cashier and injured two Admiralty civilians, one of whom died later. By now naval personnel and Admiralty civilians remained inside 'cantoned areas'. A purely maritime problem in Haifa was the wreck of the *Patria* which *Talybont* touched whilst berthing, necessitating eight weeks of repairs at Malta. A little later *Chieftain* chipped her port propeller on the same obstruction whilst going to the same berth and had to make a three-day passage back for repairs at Malta.

There was good reason to believe that the next arrival SS *Abril*, the former 753grt yacht *Argosy* built in Germany in 1930, would offer violent resistance. The *Abril* was unique in being the only ship prepared by the IZL with financial help from Revisionists in New York and the 'American League for Free Palestine', an organisation headed by Mr GM Gillette, former Iowa senator, with prominent non-Jewish members who supported militant steps against the British. Funds were also raised by a theatrical production written by the Jewish American Ben Hecht, known to be a supporter of the IZL. The *Abril* was operated by the 'American Sea and Air Volunteers for Hebrew Repatriation', an offshoot of the American League for Free Palestine and the Hebrew Committee for National Liberation. There was little secrecy concerning the purchase and repair of *Abril* (alias '*Ben Hecht*'), the American Master, Clay, was known to be a tough customer and the passengers, who embarked at Port de Bouc in France, were expected to be armed.

On 8 March at 1040 an RAF aircraft sighted the *Abril* approaching and since she was likely to make a determined effort to beach near Tel Aviv at 16 knots the interception was undertaken by destroyers and not minesweepers. HMS *Chieftain* was in company at 1215 being joined by HMS *Chevron* (Lieutenant-Commander R.W. Mayo RN) two hours later. The

Abril claimed to be bound for Arica in Chile and hoisted the Honduran flag. The usual warnings were passed by loud hailer, on this occasion in German as well as English, the former being a language understood by most Eastern Europeans. The Master appeared cooperative, stopping his ship at 1615, when the passengers were seen to be sent below and a discussion took place. HMS *Chivalrous* and the frigate HMS *St Bride's Bay* (Captain R.A.St.C. Sproule-Bolton RN) joined at 1730 but despite the *Abril* being in the presence of overwhelming force, the situation then became difficult and by 1915 she was getting close to Tel Aviv and still making 10 knots. When ordered to stop and head to seaward, the *Abril* feigned a misunderstanding and increased to 13–14 knots, so *Chieftain* went alongside her. She succeeded in getting the whole of her boarding party of 32 officers and men across, as well as pushing the illegal vessel round to a westerly heading: slight structural damage was caused but there was no opposition. *Chevron* added thirty boarders and *Chivalrous* another 20. Control was rapidly established.

Contrary to expectations the boarding parties were well looked after onboard by the American crew, being offered tomato soup and fudge from modern galleys. The Master turned out to be not Clay but a Jewish ex-US Navy officer who had assumed command at Marseilles, where the passengers embarked; Clay had found a French girl on whom to spend the crew's pay roll, with which he absconded. His absence may have been the reason for a lack of resistance, but the immigrants were of a better class and cleaner than the usual types, beside being completely under the control of their leader, an American. The only casualty was a *Life* magazine representative seeking, he said, a non-political human-interest story, who was accidentally kicked while taking a photograph of the boarding party jumping down. This boarding showed that voice radio circuits were insecure when dealing with such ships and also that red lights should be fitted to the life-jackets worn by boarding parties. From enquiries by an Army field security officer it seemed that discipline onboard an illegal immigration vessel was good but 24 hours prior to arrival orders were given to convert the vessel into a pig-sty and the passengers made themselves out as poverty-stricken. It had already been observed that the great majority of illegal immigrants arriving at Haifa were fit, healthy and well fed, and the impression gained was they were colonists not refugees. The *Abril*'s passengers were transferred to transports peacefully and left for Cyprus before dawn. A *Chevron* officer removed her Honduran flag and many years later he presented it to the Immigration and Naval Museum at Haifa.

The civil authorities did not prosecute the Master and crew of the *Abril* due to lack of evidence that she had been arrested in territorial waters. After being held in Acre prison they were, nevertheless, deported and thus several members were encountered again later. The Colonial Office was displeased at this lack of effective action and pressed the question of legal action a little further by requesting details of confiscation of vessels after arrest. The Palestine Government responded with a list of vessels held and this showed the situation with each case being pursued through the courts, including those subject to appeals to the Judicial Committee of the Privy Council; details are shown at Annex A. The *Abril*'s voyage was not a success for the IZL and was not repeated.

SUSANNAH

The motor schooner *Susannah* behaved suspiciously off the coast of Sicily on Christmas Day 1946 and when brought into Reggio di Calabria was found to be on passage to Venice to engage in the illegal immigrant trade. The Italian authorities took firm action to remove the Master's certificate, equipment for passengers and wireless equipment and she was then sent to her port of registry for a formal inquiry. Her next appearance was when, having evaded air searches and patrols, she was sighted from the air at daybreak on 12 March attempting to land her immigrants, said to number 823, five miles north of Askalon. Four ships had been on patrol but patrol lines were not normally maintained south of Jaffa. When located, weather and sea conditions made it very difficult to rescue the *Susannah*'s passengers and those not already ashore could not be removed from her for another 24 hours. HMS *St Bride's Bay* was sent to stand by and very unfortunately lost Sub-Lieutenant Hodgson RN, a well liked officer, and two men when one of her boats capsized in the surf, just at the moment when Commodore Palestine was signalling instructions that attempts of that kind were not to be made.

The aftermath to the *Susannah*'s arrival demonstrated to the Palestine Government and to the military the value of the service provided by the RAF, whose resources still limited their capability for air searches to half the days in each month, and by the Royal Navy, who were dependent on the Royal Air Force for early detections. Sorting out immigrants who had reached the shore from 1,030 people who were arrested there, and then transporting them in two batches half the length of Palestine to be deported, set the authorities a very difficult task and occupied two full days. Many Palestine citizens from Jewish settlements had helped provide a reception party and, being unable to produce identity cards, some 390 of their number were also despatched to Cyprus, where it took a fortnight to identify them. The Jewish Agency subsequently claimed, very unwisely, that 350 immigrants had evaded the authorities and this figure was therefore taken off admissions against the next month's quota.

The last of the old Swedish steamers, *San Phillipo*, fitted out at Marseilles. She held provisional certificate for a Panamanian flag and when the Panamanian Consul was instructed by his own authorities to remove it, he failed to do so, claiming no support whatever from the French port authorities. The *San Phillipo* was still in very bad order on departure and her voyage could well have ended in tragedy. She was sighted from the air approaching Palestine on 29 March and Commodore Palestine despatched HMS *Charity*, which reached the quarry 86 miles north-west of Carmel Point during that afternoon and was joined just after dark by HMS *Haydon* (Commander J. Mowlem DSO RN). The illegal vessel was seen to be dangerously unstable but declined assistance although she claimed to have defects and no Master. The passengers sang lustily. *Haydon* remained in her vicinity overnight. When daylight came *Haydon* and *Charity* shadowed from over the horizon, being suspicious of a ruse until the Marine Police Wireless station ashore heard SOS signals. The warships closed again and water was reported entering the ship. *Haydon*'s Engineer Officer (Lieutenant (E) H.W. Nichols RN) led across a salvage party, which had been refused earlier, with a 70-ton/hour-capacity diesel salvage pump, hoses and other gear and instructions to reduce free-surface water, close the scuttles and keep passengers low down in the ship. A boarding party also went across. HMS *St Bride's Bay* and HMS *Octavia* joined during the late afternoon.

When the salvage party arrived *San Phillipo* was listed 18 degrees to port. She then rolled over to starboard and listed 23 degrees. She was in grave danger of sinking due to flooding through insecure lower-deck scuttles, with little prospect of the passengers being able to extract themselves. Within 90 minutes, the salvage party succeeded in clearing the boiler and engine-rooms of water, this caused the ship to roll back to starboard and remain listed at 25 degrees. No more could be done until passengers were cleared from the holds, and so *Charity* and later *Octavia* went alongside and, greatly aided by *Haydon*'s cheerful and cool salvage party, took off some of the passengers. During this delicate operation, which halved the list to 12 degrees, those onboard appeared to have no inkling of the dangerous condition of the vessel in which they were embarked and harboured doubts as to whether they should leave. There was some fighting between those who thought discretion was the better part of valour and others who wished to resist. A somewhat scared deputation went over to *Haydon* and agreed to persuade passengers to disembark, and later sign a request for aid and guarantee of good behaviour. There were many pregnant women, some of whom had to be transferred on stretchers. *Charity* embarked 556 migrants (including forty-nine pregnant women, 18 children, one doctor and two nurses) and the *Octavia* 265 (including 65 women and four children), leaving practically no women onboard.

Octavia transferred her load of immigrants to *St Bride's Bay*, singing the Hatikvah as they went, with some of the *Octavia*'s joining in. Despite short notice, both the aptly named *Charity* and *St Bride's Bay* settled their passengers down quickly and fed them. Even after so many passengers had left, the *San Phillipo*'s condition necessitated the remainder be kept as low down as possible in order to reduce risk of capsize, but the *Octavia* was now able to go alongside, secure a tow in six minutes and take the vessel to Haifa Bay. She was arrested on reaching territorial waters at 0533. The party arrived just as Zionist saboteurs set the refinery alight, with the loss of 16,000 tons of oil.

San Phillipo's passengers proved to be mostly northern Europeans who had embarked in Stockholm; they were aware of the likelihood of diversion to Cyprus, but expected eventually to reach Palestine. On arrival at Haifa a delegation of passengers thanked *Haydon*'s Captain for saving their lives and for their treatment onboard. Commander Mowlem later reported that '... there is no doubt in my mind that the ship was in grave danger of sinking and that those responsible for her loading were nearly accessories to mass murder.'[42] He added that those onboard had not the slightest knowledge of seamanship. He praised the men in all the warships involved as 'magnificent, good humoured, tireless and humane'.

When the time came for the remaining passengers to leave the *San Phillipo* they barricaded themselves onboard until a tear smoke capsule was dropped into the lounge set disembarkation in train. Troops involved suffered some slight cuts and bruises. This would have been avoided if they had been willing to use more force to suppress resistance when migrants indulged in a certain amount of playing to the gallery of reporters and press photographers on the jetty. They wished to make the point that they were Palestine subjects returning home, that they had owned Palestine for thousands of years and should be able to enter the country as and when they liked, since it was theirs by right of birth, and especially in view of the recent persecutions.

Haydon suggested that texts in German, French, Polish and Italian be provided for use by the warships, but the manner in which ships should be recommended to submit to arrest was considered of great importance, a mixture of confident commands with cajolery and compassion being recommended. The *San Pisero*'s immigrants had called over that they had fought alongside the Allies and so *Haydon* suggested mention of Britain having been the Jews' best friend might help. Also that provision of a small cinematograph camera would enable valuable propaganda to be obtained.

PUBLIC ORDER IN PALESTINE

Events in Palestine led the authorities to impose martial law for a fortnight in March 1947 but at a Cabinet meeting the results were thought to be unsatisfactory and the Chiefs of Staff were instructed to report on the measures necessary for maintaining law and order. The Navy had already arranged for four frigates to be brought from the British Pacific Fleet to reinforce the Mediterranean Fleet. This enabled preventive measures against

101

seaborne illegal immigration to be strengthened without calling even further on the minesweepers and thus prejudicing clearance of the many wartime minefields. The First Sea Lord was more concerned that vessels eluding the Navy were being beached since, bearing in mind the extent to which they were overcrowded, this practice risked heavy loss of life. He warned the Cabinet accordingly. In the meantime the danger to boarding parties if they failed to gain control in the short period available before reaching the shore, the ugly situation for the Army and Police which would follow and the possibility of bloodshed if the ship reached, for example, Tel Aviv, led the CinC to issue instructions permitting boarding to start 'the necessary number of miles offshore'.

14

The *Guardian*: A Very Hazardous Arrest

A very difficult situation was experienced with the next arrival. The *Guardian*, alias '*Theodor Herzl*', sailed from Sête on 2 April after Gendarmes at the brows had shepherded over 2,600 immigrants onboard. During her voyage a Mossad escort group leader trained resistance groups to oppose boarders and provided them with rubber clubs and gas masks. She was reported by aircraft and intercepted after nightfall on 13 April by HMS *St Bride's Bay* whilst making for Tel Aviv at four and a half knots with only ten miles to go. With a gale blowing, weather conditions were adverse for boarding and the Promised Land being so close at hand, those onboard were not in a mood to give up easily. Nor was there time to call in reinforcements, demonstrate the Navy's capability or try persuasion. Preparations to repel boarders were very evident and although HMS *Haydon* was detailed to assist, she was still ten miles from the scene when Commodore Palestine ordered immediate boarding.

Difficulties with communications and weather bedevilled the *Guardian* operation. First, Commodore Palestine's signals made early on 14 April were undecipherable, due to being enciphered in the previous day's codes and then *Haydon*'s signals could not be decoded by Commodore Palestine, this being put down to an unreliable Typex machine. For much of the arrest *Haydon* was stopped and rolling heavily beam on to a heavy swell with seasickness greatly affecting the manning of her small wireless office.

The gale, a heavy swell and evasive manoeuvres by the *Guardian* made the transfer of boarders difficult, but at the second and third attempts, the entire boarding party from *St Bride's Bay* was put across, aided later by boarders from *Haydon*. Fierce opposition was met but within an hour the immigrants, some 50 of whom were wearing anti-gas respirators, were subdued, and the wind and high seas were 'thought to have been of considerable assistance in damping any remaining ardour in the immigrants'.[43]

The most unusual feature of the arrest was the level of employment of firearms by the boarding party: of over a score of casualties among the immigrants ten suffered gunshot wounds, of whom two died at the time and one died later. One other was said by the immigrants to have been shot and fallen overboard. The first occasion on which the boarding party opened fire was on the advice of the accompanying Palestine policeman, to bring down wireless aerials liable to be used for communicating with a reception party or Jewish propaganda stations. This was neither effective nor a matter of sufficient priority to merit diversion from the aim of securing control of the vessel's movements. As was the case during the *Ulua's* arrest, it was also thought necessary to order the firing of bursts of sub-machine gun fire over the heads of 'rioters'; but on this occasion the shooting became a little wild. With so much gunfire, the immigrants and elements of the boarding party may have gained the impression a fire-fight had broken out, making the latter more inclined to greater use of their weapons for self-defence. There is also a belief in some quarters that resentment at the loss of life when *St Bride's Bay's* whaler capsized during the earlier incident caused shooting. However, Commodore Palestine commented 'the use of firearms in the circumstances experienced was fully justified.[44] Fourteen immigrants in need of hospital treatment were transferred to *Charity*, which was then detached to land the casualties, together with one of the boarders, an officer who also required hospital treatment. The boarding parties sustained five other casualties, none of which were found to be serious.

When brought under control, the *Guardian* lay stopped, her rudder jammed 20 degrees over, only five miles north-west of Jaffa Light and since her engines were unusable, *St Bride's Bay* passed a tow. Towing of the relatively small ships hitherto encountered had not normally presented any particular problems, generally being undertaken by the minesweepers using their sweep wires. Other ships held in readiness tows made up from extra-length 3inch berthing wires and hurricane hawsers; as the need was for haste the usual length of anchor cable, intended to provide some 'spring', was not included. On this occasion conditions were very difficult due to the bad weather and the tow parted at the first attempt to get the *Guardian* underway. Fortunately, the light cruiser HMS *Phoebe* (Captain A.R. Pedder RN) happened to be in the vicinity and she provided a 5½-inch wire hawser with which to reconnect the tow. Strong winds then made keeping the right heading increasingly difficult and, with a leak also reported, the force had, in sheer desperation, to stop. But members of the boarding party, including a very determined Palestine police officer, succeeded in freeing *Guardian's* rudder, enabling progress to be resumed.

Whilst the gale had possibly helped during the boarding, it also meant that arrival off Haifa was by no means the end of the affair. A tug took over the tow but thirty minutes later, with half a gale blowing onto a lee shore, the tow wire parted. HMS *Cheviot* (Commander R.A. Ewing DSC RN) attempted to pass a fresh tow from her forecastle and, when this was unsuccessful, another tug passed a tow, which again parted. The *Guardian* with 2,622 immigrants and the Naval boarding parties still onboard was now within a few hundred feet of being driven into the heavy surf and wrecked in Acre Bay. At this point *Octavia* was called in, whilst *Espiegle*, another minesweeper, stood by preparing a further tow. True to her previous form and despite room for manoeuvre being limited by mooring buoys and small craft, *Octavia* succeeded in passing across an 8 inch manila cable within three minutes. This held whilst she first hauled the *Guardian* off the lee shore and then, keeping her own heading with difficulty due to the high crosswind and the slow speed to which towing had to be limited, brought her into sheltered water well inside the harbour. This episode was the nearest point to disaster during the whole period of the Palestine Patrol and reflected great credit on HMS *Octavia*.

Reduced complements, both ashore and afloat, were shown during the *Guardian*'s interception to be taking their toll on the reliability of communications, as was inexperience and a lack of personnel available for machine cipher maintenance. In consequence the CinC's staff took steps to rectify a major shortcoming in Commodore Palestine's staff by adding to it a specialist Signal Communications Officer.

After arrival at Haifa the leaders of the *Guardian* immigrants made difficulties which held up disembarkation. Then the rank-and-file passengers decided for themselves to go ashore, walking down the brow with cheerful expressions and helped by Airborne troops amused and pleased to find themselves entrusted with carrying well wrapped-up babies. Arrival in Haifa had caused little interest and a local newspaper stated '...and some of the soldiers were very helpful'. A magazine photographer and correspondent was found onboard the *Guardian* and he recounted a disagreement onboard as to whether resistance should be offered if boarded or not and that, in the event, those not in favour of resistance stayed below decks. His photographs showed the passengers to be generally well-fed and well-clothed, again contrary to the impression of being reduced to rags with which illegal immigrants often used to impress outsiders, during and after arrests. When Cyprus was reached two passengers came forward claiming to represent the French Press and were found to hold visas issued by the British Embassy in Paris.

The last arrest in April was that of the *Galata*. This small ex-Turkish steamer sailed from Italy and disembarked a part of her crew into a small diesel motor craft named *Albertina* shortly before interception by *Cheviot* and *Pelican* (Commander M.G. Goodenough RN) on 23 April, the method of operation practised on several occasions. A new means of quelling opposition by stunning opponents was tried out when Chinese firecrackers were employed for *Galata*'s arrest. As a surprise venture these were successful in causing temporary alarm amongst the 761 immigrants, even so tear gas had to be employed, there was some fighting and both sides received minor injuries.

DEVELOPMENTS IN MAINTAINING THE PATROL

By February 1947, 42 officers and 626 ratings and Royal Marines had completed boarding and unarmed courses at Ghajn Tuffieha and recent experience in boarding Jewish illegal immigrant vessels had shown them to be of great value. RAD considered equipment was capable of considerable improvement. Type 91 smoke grenades had been found successful in producing a powerful emission without harming people in the vicinity, but there were not enough of them, and a representative of the Admiralty's Gunnery Department had visited Malta to assist in finding a more effective means of applying tear smoke. A 'Zulu'-type shield made of plywood was being tried out in response to a request from sea for a light arm-shield capable of protecting both boarders and men working hoses or wires.

Trials to find a reasonable means of stopping illegal immigrant ships without firing a projectile had proved unsuccessful. Whatever method or scheme was used it had to be easy to manufacture or implement, must not endanger either illegal passengers or our own ships and had to be effective quickly (i.e. inside the 3-mile limit). Two possibilities had been considered, either using gunfire to shoot off the rudder or propeller or entangling the vessel's propeller in wires or chains. Although trials showed that the 4.5-inch and 4-inch guns mounted in the warships of the Patrol could be fired at ranges of about 40 yards with sufficient accuracy, their use was ruled out because of the propaganda and panic effect such methods would cause. It also proved not possible to find a means of fouling a propeller sufficiently effectively to ensure a vessel came to a halt before reaching a beach. Boarding to take control thus remained the only certain means of stopping an illegal vessel determined to break the blockade.

By March Haganah had announced full scale illegal immigration and there were reports of a small fleet of vessels sailing from the USA to pick up migrants in European ports. To meet this 'surge', warship numbers were brought up to eight ships – four destroyers and four minesweepers, sloops or frigates – by the middle of April. Earlier the CinC had reminded Commanding Officers to continue in peacetime the methods brought into use during the war for keeping their ships' companies better informed. Jewish illegal immigration and the part played by the Navy in countering it were currently the subject of a great deal of comment in the Press and in Parliament, with questions being put chiefly by the Government's Jewish supporters, and the task of the patrols needed to be explained and justified throughout the Navy. An unclassified supplement to the naval Monthly Intelligence Report was issued for this purpose. Onboard *Childers* Arthur Koestler's book *Thieves in the Night,* written from the point of view of a British Jew who had joined those attempting to establish a Jewish state in Palestine during the 1930s, was passed round officers and Senior Rates. One of the latter commented recently: 'It gave us an insight into the motivation of those trying to establish the state of Israel. It did not, and was not intended to, cause us resentment towards the Jews.' The same person added that only on one occasion did he hear resentment expressed against the Jews as a whole and this was a comment by a Ghajn Tuffieha instructor. He also summarised the attitude within the warships of the patrol as follows:

> As far as I can recall those of us involved did not relish the task, and felt antagonism only to the people such as Haganah, Irgun and the Stern Gang who were responsible for shipping Jews, who had suffered horrendously already in their lives, in dangerous and appalling conditions. Added to this were the acts of terrorism by the above organisations committed against our troops in Palestine at the time.[45]

RECOURSE TO THE UNITED NATIONS ORGANISATION

By February 1947 the final attempt to reach agreement between the Arab and Jewish leaders had failed, the Arabs still refusing to accept partition. To impose partition would do great harm to Britain's wider responsibilities, relationships and interests in the Middle East. The only alternative, an independent Palestine with an Arab majority, would have further compromised Britain's relationship with the USA on many vital post-war matters, in particular the very serious economic crisis which increasingly beset the British Isles in 1947. However, the United Nations had by now come to undertake functions which ceased when the League of Nations became inactive and thus the problem could be referred to that body. The Chiefs of Staff favoured this course, balancing the British relationship with Arab states and the military situation in Palestine against Palestine's suitability to station and train the Middle East strategic reserve. On 2 April 1947 a request was made for the matter to be placed on the agenda for the next meeting of the General Assembly, which later the same month appointed a commission to study the question and deliver a report by 1 September.

Reference to the UN led to a belief, agreed by the CoS, not that attempts at illegal immigration would abate but rather that a large scale increase was likely. The Joint Intelligence Committee estimated that at this stage over 35,000 Jews were strategically located for embarkation to Palestine and that there were nineteen vessels (eleven reliably reported, eight suspected) immediately available to bring in over 20,000 illegal immigrants. Another eighteen ships were thought to be in various stages of preparation and these could transport 21,600 illegal immigrants during the summer. In addition some 110,000 to 140,000 Jews were present in the American zone of Germany and the final figure for immigrants might be considerably in excess of 22,000. The JIC included in its list ex-HM Ships *Lowestoft* and *Shoreham*, mentioned earlier and currently at Cardiff, considered to be under the control of Haganah. They were not amongst the immediately available vessels but there was still a lack of confidence in being able to detain a suspect vessel even in a British port.

REFOULEMENT AND REINFORCEMENTS

With the illegal immigrant trade likely to continue in full flood, the possibility of the accommodation at Cyprus becoming fully occupied had once again to be considered. The Chiefs of Staff, amongst others, were therefore invited to make plans for transporting arrested immigrants to other destinations. The First Sea Lord forecast to the Cabinet that this would entail a heavy drain on transports and their naval escorts. One possible way ahead now started to be considered, the sending back of arrested immigrants to the country where their voyage had started; a practice known in the League of Nations era as *'refoulement'*. The case of Italy was in mind, since the Italian Government professed the inability to prevent vessels embarking illegal immigrants and departing, and since it was from Italy that the majority of voyages currently began. The Italian Government represented a defeated nation, although latterly a 'co-belligerent', and with peace terms still being negotiated, it was not in a strong position for resisting British pressure. The Cabinet also considered the possibility of applying refoulement to immigrants embarked in France. Another rather different suggestion was that the Italian islands of Pantelleria and Lampedusa, at one time under consideration for settling the surplus population of Malta, should be borrowed from Italy and used for arrested immigrants. But peace treaty negotiations had already been very long drawn out and it was not thought wise to prolong that situation, incur additional Italian hostility or import into the western Mediterranean the problems of the eastern Mediterranean.

At the end of April the frigates HMS *Bigbury Bay* (Lieutenant-Commander H. Hutchinson RN) and HMS *Whitsand Bay* (Lieutenant-Commander R.P.C. O'Sullivan RN) followed by HMS *Veryan Bay* (Captain R.S. Welby RN) arrived as the temporary attachments to reinforce the Mediterranean Fleet. The Fifth Escort Flotilla (5th EF) was then re-numbered as the 2nd EF with the sloops forming the Third Division and the 'Bays' the Fourth Division.[46] The fleet of transports provided by the Ministry of Transport (formerly War Transport) for moving arrested immigrants included HMTs *Empire Rival, Empire Heywood, Ocean Vigour* and *Runnymead Park*, each with a normal capacity of 800 but capable of carrying 1,400 people for the short voyage to Cyprus. There were also the four Convoy Rescue Ships with capacity for 400 each. Although conditions for immigrants onboard transports were adequate, if very basic, the immigrants were, as has already been shown, frequently unhygienic in their habits and there had also to be physical measures to guard against attempts to overcome the crew and seize the vessel. The Haifa–Cyprus transport task was not only an unusual one, it was often also most unpleasant. At a fairly early stage some of the United Kingdom crew members in the transports raised objections to the employment in which they found themselves and were therefore replaced by other nationals.

MAY ARRESTS

The *Trade Winds*, another ex-US Coastguard Cutter, was the first of three vessels arrested in May. She had been purchased in the USA and was taken to Portugal, but had to be moved on hastily when police removed the local Mossad agent. *Trade Winds* eventually sailed from Italy with 1,413 immigrants and was found approaching Palestine by an aircraft. When intercepted by HMS *Venus* on the afternoon of 16 May there was no response to signals by light or loud hailer, but eventually humanity poured on deck from forward and aft. The *Trade Winds* was well prepared with handrails and ladders covered in Vaseline; tops of ladders, wheelhouse and deckhouse wired off; hoses rigged all round the upper deck and three-legged stanchions protruding five feet out from the side. Her davits were turned out; the usual tins and ironmongery had been prepared as ammunition and parties of toughs on the forecastle and afterdeck house were armed with wooden and iron coshes. HMS *Brissenden* (Lieutenant-Commander C.T.D. Williams RN) joined shortly after midnight and dummy runs undertaken.

At 1100 on the following day the *Trade Winds* increased speed to 12 knots and it was deemed desirable to arrest her as she crossed from Syrian to Palestinian waters. Only five minutes elapsed between HMS *Venus* and HMS *Brissenden* starting their approach and boarding parties being onboard, with hoses, tear gas and firecrackers all in operation. Within a few minutes everything was under control, except in the Engine Room, where the situation with machinery necessitated a tow by the minesweeper HMS *Espiegle* to Haifa. The success of this boarding operation was felt to be due to the despatch with which it was carried out. Slight damage was caused by one of the destroyer's anchors which the immigrants tried to persuade the Press was caused by a shell or deliberate ramming. Amongst the passengers was found a correspondent from a New York newspaper.

A few days later (23 May) aircraft reports led HMS *Brissenden* to intercept the three-masted 200-foot schooner *Agha Oriente* at 1030 when ninety-two miles from the Palestine coast. HMS *Haydon* arrived in the early afternoon and the force was joined later by the sloop HMS *Magpie*. At this juncture a Polish passenger decided to try and swim ashore but he was picked up by *Brissenden*. Approaches from an unstable vessel's quarter risked rolling her over and ships had found it preferable to come up abreast an illegal vessel before boarding and then close in. The usual preparations to resist boarding were observed but when *Brissenden* and *Haydon* went alongside at 1446 opposition onboard the schooner soon collapsed, and she was towed to Haifa. The minesweeper HMS *Skipjack* joined to take over the tow but this was found unnecessary. The total number of immigrants arrested proved to be 1,459.

The third ship to be arrested in May, *Anal*, must have been the most elderly to make an attempt. She had been built in 1877 and plied among the Shetland Isles before being put up for sale at Aberdeen in 1946. Bought, despite the precautions by British authorities and mentioned earlier, by the notorious Greek shipping agent Pandelis, she steamed to Marseilles to be fitted out for illegal immigrants. The crew were mainly sailors who had served the defeated Spanish Republican Government and so were very anxious not to return to Spain. As usual Mossad provided an overall commander, an escort and a radio operator.

Mossad had been recruiting with missionary zeal in North Africa, where the Jewish inhabitants were at first not inclined to see much point in going to Palestine. Mossad persevered and as time went by the animosity felt by Arabs towards Jewish activities in Palestine spread westwards along the southern shores of the Mediterranean, leading to many more volunteers. The French authorities in Algeria were not inclined to be openly helpful but Mossad found sympathizers. The *Anal* anchored off the Algerian coast and 400 illegal immigrants began to embark by means of two ship's boats and two of her life rafts until some 300 were onboard. Soldiers nearby observed unusual activity and then intervened, but whilst they were obtaining reinforcements, the remainder of the passengers made their way onboard. When the *Anal* called at Palermo for coal, water and food the Italian authorities inspected the vessel and she was shadowed by both the RAF and the Navy when she finally departed for Palestine on 19 May.

HMS *Talybont* intercepted the *Anal* on 30 May and she was joined by HMS *Peacock,* whose commanding officer (Commander E.N.V. Currey DSO DSC RN) became Senior Officer. He was reinforced by HMS *Whitsand Bay* and later HMS *Skipjack*. *Anal* agreed to alter course for Haifa but she refused to stop on entering territorial waters and hazarded herself by altering course across *Peacock*'s bows just as the latter approached to board. This did not prevent *Peacock* and *Talybont* putting parties across and slight resistance, not of an organised or spirited nature, was overcome with the assistance of tear gas, hoses and Chinese crackers. The *Anal* was then towed by *Skipjack* to Haifa, where 339 unusually clean and healthy immigrants were later transferred to transports, during which process some of the passengers were found to be wearing bandages stained with red ink for propaganda purposes.

Commander Currey reported that sloops were unhandy for boarding purposes since despite being twin-screw ships, they were slow to accelerate or decelerate, a comment which Commodore Palestine supported. *Peacock* also noted that the *Anal* had been rolled first 20 degrees and then about 40 degrees the other way, due to being taken further aft than intended. Fortunately, unlike several other illegal immigrant vessels, she was strongly built and fairly stable.

15

'Exodus 1947': The Arrest of SS President Warfield

The Mediterranean Fleet was now to be involved in the most difficult operation to take place and one which passed in its true form into Israeli history and with embellishment into Zionist folklore. This concerned the illegal immigrant vessel *President Warfield*, also known to posterity as *Exodus 1947*, which attempted to land 4554 immigrants, the largest number yet encountered. Her arrest entailed prolonged fighting but it was the subsequent fate of her passengers, which came to attract increasing worldwide interest.

Launched in 1928 in America as the flagship of the Old Bay Line, the 330-foot *President Warfield* was built to run as a passenger steamer on Chesapeake Bay. War came and in late 1942 craft of this type were sent to England for ferrying troops in case an opportunity suddenly arose for cross-channel operations. The US authorities requisitioned the *Warfield* and other vessels for the British Ministry of War Transport; she embarked a British crew and set off across the Atlantic in convoy with other vessels of the same type. A U-Boat erroneously identified the ships as fast troop transports and, seven days into the voyage, they came under heavy attack. Once safely arrived, the *Warfield* proved unsuitable for her intended purpose and she was transferred to the US War Shipping Administration. Thereafter she served in 1944 as harbour control vessel off Omaha beach, supporting the campaign in Normandy, and later she transported US troops up the Seine. Returning in 1945 to Norfolk, Virginia, *President Warfield* received something of a local hero's welcome. Seaborne passenger traffic up and down the Chesapeake having by then ceased, the *Warfield* was put up for sale. She attracted the eye of Haganah agents in possession of money provided by sympathetic Americans and was bought by what the Security Service described as the 'bogus firm The Chinese American Import-Export Company' and passed on to the Weston Trading Company. She was a faster ship than any used hitherto, being capable of 16 knots.

Although lacking assistance from the US State Department, the British soon became aware of what was afoot. The British Consulate in Baltimore was in touch with the Chief Engineer, a full and accurate crew list was obtained in March and steps were taken to prevent the *Warfield* being registered in Panama. At this stage the President of the Weston Trading Company of New York (Mr W.C. Ash) personally testified on oath before an attorney that the company would not use the vessel for illegal immigration into Palestine. The owners then achieved registration under the flag of Honduras to the extent of a temporary permit for navigation issued by the Honduran Consul General in New York. This document was cancelled, but not removed from the vessel before she sailed and was later to prove useful when shown to port authorities.

After one false start, the *Warfield* arrived in the Azores. The British ambassador in Lisbon had made efforts for her to be denied the fuel necessary for the voyage to be completed but the firm concerned was obliged by its contract to provide a supply, although it agreed to limit this to 'the minimum'. Some accounts indicate she was denied any oil but succeeded in obtaining some by such efforts as tapping into oil pipes under the jetty at which she was berthed. The Ambassador later reported that she had sailed on the morning of 9 April, after being delayed and supplied only with 1,000 barrels of oil, against a request for probably 2,000 barrels. Her radio transmissions indicated she had been unable to obtain all she required, even so the Master telegraphed the owners that he now had sufficient oil to go to Marseilles and this information also reached the British. A Royal Navy vessel was stationed to identify the *Warfield* in the Gibraltar Straits and when she arrived at Marseilles the Haganah took over command. A 22-year-old Israeli (named Itzhak Aronwitz) who had been sent to the United States and embarked there in the guise of the Chief Mate became the vessel's master.

Between November 1946 and March 1947 four ships carrying illegal immigrants had sailed from southern French ports and, as the British Ambassador, Mr Duff Cooper, pointed out, Marseilles was virtually a Mossad naval base. The French Foreign Minister (Monsieur Bidault) was favourably disposed to requests to end the assistance Mossad was receiving. In his absence, the Prime Minister (Monsieur Ramadier) chaired a meeting of ministers which agreed to apply laws regarding safety at sea and also that collective visas held by Jewish refugees en route through France should be examined to discourage unlawful sailings to Palestine. There was a strong body of support for the Zionist cause in France and two issues were skirted round – whether travel documents produced for inspection were genuine and whether travel would indeed be to the country stated and not to Palestine. In the meantime the watch kept by the British on Marseilles made further preparations very difficult for the *Warfield* and she departed, being thought to be heading for Italy, and arrived there, at Porto Venere, on 24 April.

Whitehall's efforts to prevent illegal immigrant vessels sailing from foreign ports and harbours were by now proving much more successful. The General Assembly of the United Nations Organisation had agreed unanimously a resolution calling on all nations to refrain from any actions prejudicial to the Assembly's work on Palestine. For their part the Italian Government had denounced the activities of UNRRA, which was about to give way to the International Refugee Organisation, and the AJDC in assisting illegal immigrants. It had also instructed Captains of all Italian ports to report details of any vessels suspected of illegal traffic to Palestine. Thus there was little prospect of the intended passengers being allowed to embark at Porto Venere.

The *Warfield* problem was broached at a British Cabinet meeting on 1 May when the Colonial Secretary represented the need for every possible step to prevent the arrival of an unnamed ship carrying some 5,000 would be immigrants. For Mr Attlee and his ministers this must have seemed a minor matter, the spring of 1947 marked the trough of the British population's fortunes and conditions after 1945. No more was agreed than that ministers directly involved should consider further the arrest of any ship on the high seas whose flag state had agreed to interception of this kind. This was of course the procedure agreed by the Lord Chancellor. The Secret Intelligence Service (MI6) had reported that the *Warfield* still held the cancelled temporary permit for navigation issued by the Honduran Consul General, evidently she was making good use of it. Two weeks after the Cabinet meeting, the Honduran authorities agreed to the interception on the high seas of any vessel flying their flag and suspected of carrying Jewish illegal immigrants. In addition, if she proved to be so engaged then Honduran registry was automatically cancelled. For reasons given earlier (see Chapters 5 and 12) the First Lord of the Admiralty remained firmly opposed to taking advantage of this kind of arrangement.

A convenient means for discussing such problems as arrest on the high seas was provided when the Prime Minister approved the setting up of a Cabinet Illegal Immigration Committee (ie Minister level) supported by a Cabinet (Official) Illegal Immigration Committee (ie Officials as members) to coordinate departmental action. Refoulement was still being considered. All possible methods by which the traffic in illegal immigrants could be stopped at source, in other words in European countries came under scrutiny. Under the aegis of the committee, the Security Service (MI5) provided a fortnightly list of suspect vessels, with amendments being provided more frequently, and coordinated production of a periodical Illegal Immigration Review to which the Secret Intelligence Service, Naval Intelligence Division (NID) and other Government departments contributed. These reports show that the movements and intentions of vessels later encountered by the Navy were invariably made available from an early stage of their preparations. In the case of the *Warfield* there were additional very accurate and up-to-date signals and telegrams originated by British representatives abroad.

The Italian authorities decided to delay *Warfield* by means of a thorough inspection to establish whether she could pass safety tests, and sent a minesweeper to assist the process, but they stated she could not be detained after 17 May. The British ambassador was therefore instructed to insist on the ship returning to Marseilles and the Italians undertook to despatch and shadow her, although she could not be detained forcibly if she sailed unannounced. In the meantime two UNRRA lorries delivered stores. Eight tons of fuel were taken onboard on 23 May and further Haganah personnel embarked including Mr Yossi Harel, who was to take overall charge of the attempt. Those onboard the *Warfield* have subsequently claimed that owing to British intervention, food and fuel could not be obtained.

The British naval authorities were kept fully informed via HM Ambassador and planned for an HM ship to take over from the Italian shadower. *Warfield* eventually departed from Porto Venere on 12 June at 1100 with a crew of 58 but no passengers and was shadowed by an Italian warship until seen to enter French territorial waters. Berthing at Port de Bouc on 14 June, she obtained ample fuel together with a certificate of seaworthiness for a voyage to the Black Sea without freight or passengers and in fine weather. The French authorities interpreted the fine weather proviso as applying to the conditions prevailing at the time she sailed from a French port. Although ostensibly bound for the Black Sea she arrived at Sête during the night 9/10 July, berthed stern to in the Outer Harbour and embarked 4,229 men, women and children, mainly Czechoslovaks, Hungarians, Germans and Poles equipped with visas for entry to Colombia. The Mayor of Sête was subsequently reported by passengers to have been most cooperative, although one said he had been bribed.

The local Lloyd's Agent passed news of events to the British Consul-General at Marseilles and the Director-General of the Inscription Maritime, whose jurisdiction covered Sête, gave orders that on no account was *Warfield* to be permitted to sail. Five minutes before her intended time of departure, the ship was detained and there may have been an attempt to disable her by removing machinery. The services of tug and pilot were then withdrawn and a picket was placed on the jetty to prevent mooring wires being cast off, but the passengers were not brought ashore. In the meantime HM Ambassador reminded the French Foreign Minister of the limitations set by the clearance certificate and received a response that the ship was being held and the passengers forced to disembark. She was reported by an RAF aircraft at 1000 and the same afternoon the British Consul-General estimated the passengers to number about five thousand.

Earlier in the year a meeting at the Colonial Office had agreed that the

Master of an illegal vessel would be unlikely to attempt to leave a port if the services of pilot or tugs were not provided. The *Warfield* lay in the Outer, not Inner, Port and even so those onboard at first believed her departure to have been ruled out. Nevertheless, at some time between 0200 and 0400 on 11 July she severed or cast off her lines and moved off. After clearing one of her wires which fouled the propeller, she made a turn of some 135 degrees, during which process her stern grounded in shallow water, escaped from Sête and at 0600 was out of the harbour steering for Palestine

The Foreign Secretary (Mr Ernest Bevin) was in Paris and protested strongly to his French opposite number, Monsieur Bidault, at the failure of the French authorities to prevent the immigrant vessel sailing. Although Italy had been the country to which Refoulement was likely to be applied, the unprecedented number of passengers in *Warfield* led Mr Bevin to request she be obliged to return to France and he called for cooperation in receiving her back. To this request Monsieur Bidault gave verbal agreement, but he was not thought to be in a sufficiently strong position to win over his Prime Minister and colleagues.[47] Mr Bevin therefore visited Monsieur Ramadier, who professed never to have heard of the ship, and reminded him of the duties laid on the Mandate Government by international agreement, the support which was due from other governments and the obligations of the French Government for safety at sea. However, Mr Duff Cooper warned the Foreign Secretary on at least two occasions that forcible removal of Jewish illegal immigrants from British ships in a French port would be viewed by the French public as a further persecution of Nazi victims who now sought no more than refuge in a national home.

HMS *Mermaid* (Lieutenant-Commander A.P. Davey RN) was already lying in wait and, assisted by RAF aircraft, shadowed *Warfield* until relieved by HMS *Cheviot* (Commander J.V. Wilkinson DSC GM). HMS *Ajax* was sailed by the CinC from Malta on 13 July and leaving the Grand Harbour on a serene summer Sunday morning past other ships of the Fleet at Sunday Divisions, she was in company at 1400. In Palestine arrangements were being made already for all the large transport vessels to be provisioned for maximum capacity of passengers for a seven-day voyage. The *Warfield* convoy continued Eastward at 10–12 knots, with the choice for a naval flag hoisting exercise on Monday being, very suitably, a biblical quiz. *Ajax* made a determined effort to ascertain whither the *Warfield* was bound but, despite much confabulation being observed on her bridge, there was no response. During the afternoon of 15 July, *Cheviot* was relieved by HMS *Childers* (Lieutenant-Commander E.A.S. Bailey RN), veteran of the very difficult *Fede* boarding.

The CinC instructed *Ajax* to start a verbal softening up process, on the lines that the passengers would not be allowed to land in Palestine and that the Royal Navy had the duty of carrying out the law, if necessary using overwhelming force, so resistance would be useless and could only lead to injury. During the dogwatches on 16 July this message was passed on in as many European languages as possible, and nothing was said about the destination planned for the passengers. The purport of the messages was evidently taken in and only when addressed by the versatile *Ajax* in German was annoyance demonstrated.

South of Crete, a stiff head wind came up from the north-east, this lasted for the rest of the voyage and slowed *Warfield* down. D.1 held drawings of *Warfield* provided by the Admiralty, these proved invaluable, and on 15 July *Childers* signalled more details obtained by observation. Her appearance had been aptly described by an Italian observer as 'like a giant packing case'; being designed for use in sheltered waters and a hot summer climate, her steel hull had little freeboard and above it stood a high wooden superstructure containing her original passenger accommodation. The top level of the steel hull was open only at the Forward Well and Poop decks, where awnings and canvas side curtains obstructed access from outboard. Above that Upper Deck there were three decks vulnerable to boarding and D.1 estimated their heights above her waterline as follows: Lower Promenade deck – 24 feet; Upper Promenade or Boat deck – 32 feet (with a deck edge 2 feet inboard of the Lower Promenade deck edge); and Top Deck – 40 feet. Access to most of the Lower Promenade deck was obstructed by Carley Rafts, oval buoyant rafts designed for lifesaving purposes, suspended vertically. A prominent Wheelhouse or Pilot House, described by one observer in HMS *Ajax* as 'like a summer house', stood at the forward end of the Upper Promenade deck and it was from there that navigation was conducted and the vessel's movements controlled. From the Wheelhouse accommodation ran aft for about two-thirds of the length of the Upper Promenade deck, leaving a large open space where there were two pairs of lifeboats on davits. The deck head of the accommodation formed the under side of the Top Deck at a level slightly above the Wheelhouse deck head. Abreast the superstructure vertical rails were fitted, each set bearing a heavy raft which could be dropped down the side. During *Warfield*'s transatlantic adventures the join where the wooden superstructure met the steel hull had proved weak and it was this area which was soon to prove vulnerable. But the hull itself was protected by a very prominent rubbing strake fitted six feet above the waterline and of the kind intended to protect ferries constantly berthing and unberthing on piers and wharves.

After matching her own dimensions to those of her target, Lieutenant-Commander Bailey constructed a boarding platform onboard *Childers* at the level of his own bridge, 33 feet above the waterline. He intended to board using this platform and from the Flag Deck below it, 26 feet above the waterline.

Commodore Palestine sailed D.1 (Captain R.D. Watson RN) in HMS *Chequers* with HMS *Chieftain* and HMS *Charity* to rendezvous early in the morning on 17 July. HMS *Cardigan Bay* joined a little over an hour later and D.1 assumed command of the force. *Warfield*'s heading was far to the South of the direct course for Palestine and at 0700 the Rosetta Light House at the North end of Aboukir Bay on the Egyptian coast rose above the horizon. She continued on a course leading into the shallow water at the northern end of the Nile delta. The accompanying warships gained the impression she was uncertain of her geographical position and might have been establishing it with sufficient accuracy to ensure a better landfall when Palestine was reached. However, *Warfield* drew less water than the warships and her Master intended to exploit this feature to help him reach a beach. When at the seven fathom line off the Egyptian coast *Ajax* drew off into deeper water he would have gained a better knowledge of the limits which his most formidable adversary set for herself. After steaming another three miles Warfield altered course to the north-eastward and *Ajax* was able to close her again.

In the British force, the rest of the day was spent making preparations for an arrest, each of the warships taking the opportunity to close their quarry and familiarise themselves with her layout. She flew the Honduran flag, large numbers of still polite, quiet and peaceful folk, including many children, were on deck and further messages were passed verbally, to which the responses were 'in American'. The weather was not favourable for boardings, the wind being a steady north-west Force Four, and weather forecasts for the area ahead were requested, including report from HMS *Rowena*, which had been positioned off Jaffa and Tel Aviv. The destroyers were stationed so they could construct boarding platforms, similar to those devised onboard the Childers, on the side out of sight from their quarry. D.1 decided his objective should be to put onboard the largest possible number of boarders in the shortest possible time and thereby achieve a quick capture. To provide maximum numbers onboard the first pair of destroyers, three boarding parties from *Ajax* were transferred by boat to *Childers* and *Chieftain* and each then had 50 boarders. D.1 felt confident that *if* the augmented boarding parties onboard the two ships got across successfully *Warfield* could be seized without too much difficulty.

Written orders were transferred by heaving line to all ships during the First Dog Watch. The destroyers were to attempt to get their people across as close to the wheelhouse as practicable, with each ship sending over three boarding parties, as many as possible onto the Boat Deck. Having made the first boardings, *Childers* on *Warfield*'s port side and *Chieftain* on her starboard side, were to remain alongside giving all possible support if the situation warranted this. Meanwhile, *Charity* and D.1's own vessel, *Chequers*, were to follow astern, prepared to put two parties each onboard when ordered. This put D.1 in the best position for seeing how the situation developed so he could control the force and signal reports to Commodore Palestine, the link with GOC 1 Division and other authorities ashore. At the same time his ship would be available to attempt boardings if the first pair of destroyers had to be replaced. *Cardigan Bay* was also to have two boarding parties ready but the primary duty of this less speedy vessel was to act as '*long stop*' and recover men from the water, deal with any boats lowered by the immigrant ship and, if no minesweepers arrived in time, tow her if necessary. *Ajax*'s part was as a last resort to prevent *Warfield* beaching herself by riding her off.

D.1 nominated his Flotilla Gunnery Officer Lieutenant R.J.G. MacPherson DSC RN to be in overall command of the boarding parties. His instructions were to gain control of the Wheelhouse, then clear the Top and Upper Promenade decks from for'ard to aft and establish a 'citadel' at that level. Once those tasks were completed, control was to be gained, using a strong party, first of the steering engine, to ensure it was not tampered with, and then the engine room. Finally, if a tow was required then a party was to be established in the eyes of the ship to receive and secure the towline.

At 2045 the warships darkened themselves and fifteen minutes later an RAF aircraft arrived overhead, evidently unexpectedly as it was some time before radio communication be established. The destroyers now started making hourly visitations to *Warfield* in order to wear down the opposition's alertness. D.1 observed that it was the Lower Promenade deck which was by far the best prepared for repelling boarders, whilst the women and children had been massed on the Upper Promenade and Top decks, an arrangement which indicated a good chance of achieving surprise. From 2200 *Warfield* was overheard transmitting radio broadcasts in Hebrew, English and French.

THE ARREST

After sunset the wind decreased to Force Three and the swell also decreased, but even so conditions were such that Commanding Officers doubted if boardings could be made successfully. However the CinC's instructions to D.1 stressed the importance of preventing the immigrant ship from reaching the Palestine Coast, including the likelihood of very serious and widespread disorders if a landing in the Tel Aviv area was achieved. He was left in no doubt that neither the risk of casualties amongst his own people nor serious damage to his ships were to deflect him from his aim.

At 0152 ships were ordered to take up stations on *Warfield* in preparation for boardings:

a. Two cables on her port quarter: HMS *Childers*, followed by HMS *Charity*.

b. Two cables on her starboard quarter: HMS *Chieftain*, followed by HMS *Chequers*.

  c. Long stop five cables astern: HMS *Cardigan Bay*.

  d. Between *Warfield* and the land: HMS *Ajax*.

Situation reports were being made regularly to Commodore Palestine and at 0200 D.1 signalled that verbal exchanges had given some hope that resistance would be light. The ships were now approaching the low lying Palestine coast; no marks were available for navigation but D.1 estimated by the best means available that *Warfield* was approaching territorial waters West of Gaza and at 0244 he put his plan into execution. *Chieftain* and *Childers* closed simultaneously, but their target made a well timed reduction in speed. *Chieftain* was not successful in getting anyone across, whilst *Childers* overshot. The alarm having been raised, the *Warfield* increased speed to 13 knots and started violent alterations of course; she proved to be more manoeuvrable than her antagonists and, as D.1 noted, she was handled with skill. The swell, her heavy construction, the opposition mounted by those onboard her and the fact that the boarding platforms were sited at the destroyer's pivoting point made getting alongside and remaining there for a sufficient length of time to transfer boarders very difficult indeed.

Despite the hour and also the earlier attempts to exhaust the opposition, the *Warfield*'s Top and Upper Promenade decks remained crowded with singing people, and the continued presence of women and children confirmed that the assault on this area was unexpected. *Childers* mounted two 'storming parties', as her Captain termed them, each of one officer and fifteen ratings. At her second attempt, at 0305, the First Storming Party, under Lieutenant A Stein were unable to get across from her Flag Deck due to wire netting onboard *Warfield*. However, Acting Lieutenant K.P. Shallow RN with one Leading Seaman and four Able Seamen of the Second Storming Party went across from the boarding platform and reached the Top Deck at a point about 30 feet aft of the port side door into the Wheelhouse. Chinese crackers were used to bring the opposition to their knees, attacks from aft were repelled and, since *Childers* had swung away and there was nothing to be gained by maintaining a bridgehead for reinforcements, Lieutenant Shallow led a direct assault on the Wheelhouse. Despite being a target for missiles, which landed mainly on their tin hats, his party drove away opponents in front of them with coshes. They reached their destination at about 0307, drove out the occupants and steered the ship round to steady on a course to the westward. But the engine room telegraph had already been rendered unserviceable and within a few minutes the Master resumed control of his vessel's movements by steering from aft, a measure planned earlier. Nevertheless, the citadel sought by D.1 had now been established, albeit not in much strength.

During the seizure of the Wheelhouse, one rating was injured in the shoulder and the extent of the fighting is shown by Lieutenant Shallow's estimate that between 15 and 20 crewmembers and immigrants became casualties. One of the mates, an American named William Bernstein, returned after being forcibly expelled, attacked the boarders with a fire extinguisher and received head injuries later to prove fatal. Attempts to recapture the wheelhouse continued, including efforts to insert burning distress flares. By 0330 a hole some 30 inches by 18 inches had been cut through the deck head and a man thought to be Murray Aronoff then called on the boarders to surrender or be shot. He fired two shots at them through the hole and fire was returned, limited to two shots, without causing casualties but reducing enthusiasm for breaking in through that route.

At about 0320 *Chieftain* made a second approach and reached the *Warfield*'s starboard side, enabling Lieutenant MacPherson, Sub-Lieutenant Ure RNVR and two ratings to clamber onboard via one of her lifeboats, which had conveniently been left turned out. The air was thick with smoke and missiles so they took cover in a cabin, expecting reinforcements, which were not forthcoming since their destroyer had been unable to remain alongside. An angry mob threw missiles through doors and windows, shouted abuse and attacked them with oars and sticks, whilst the boarders defended themselves with coshes and two rounds were fired by the ratings into the crowd outside the windows. In an attempt to abate the fury of the mob, Lieutenant MacPherson made insistent demands to see the Captain in order to deliver an urgent message. An American named Grauel, taken by MacPherson to be a chaplain, but in fact prominent in the American-Christian Committee for Palestine and a correspondent for the American publication 'Churchman', now intervened and took the boarders to his cabin. He appeared throughout to wield considerable influence and be genuinely seeking to avoid bloodshed. On the way forward one of the ratings unobtrusively dropped two tear gas grenades and these held off attackers until just outside Grauel's cabin.

Childers came alongside for the second time at about 0332. This time Lieutenant Stein with three seaman and one Royal Marine went across via the boarding platform, but, like *Chieftain*'s boarders, were forced to take refuge in cabins. The scale of resistance met by the destroyers now and later, was heavier and more effective than anything encountered in previous arrests. The large rafts and the lifeboats were dropped onto the destroyers and the immigrants attacked boarders with twelve foot iron scaffolding poles, crow bars, oars, horsewhips, axes, coshes, sticks and buckets, as well as throwing a rain of missiles – nuts, bolts and tins of all descriptions, including whole cases of food. The food could be put to some use, and the messman from *Childers*'s Chief Petty Officers mess was seen gathering in this manna. Less welcome were distress flares of American origin in large canisters, these burnt with a fierce flame and generated large quantities of smoke. Tear gas grenades, whether part of the *Warfield*'s equipment or taken from boarders is not known, were thrown on board the ships. The principal belligerents were youths, based on upper deck cabins, many between the ages of 16 and 18.

In a third run, *Childers* put across Lieutenant D.G. Gill RN and her reserve storming party from her Flag Deck to the Upper Promenade Deck, where they joined up with two other ratings from their ship. Augmented by a fresh boarding party, some managed to get inside the Wheelhouse, but the door was only opened for a split second due to attempts to hurl missiles inside. The remainder, Lieutenant Gill with Engine Room Artificer (ERA) E. Ravenscroft, one badly injured Petty Officer and six boarders from different parties, took refuge in cabins, at one stage being attacked by migrants who attempted to break in through the deckhead. A shot was fired to deter this activity, not at any individual. Ravenscroft encouraged Lieutenant Gill to take the initiative and with some others they made their way to the top of the main stairway, hemmed in by hostile passengers.

In the meantime Grauel had left the cabin containing Lieutenant MacPherson and his party, saying he would find the Captain, and leaving two Poles as guards. Each bore a concentration camp brand and both made it quite clear they had no intention of being put by the British into another institution of that kind. When the next destroyer came alongside, MacPherson succeeded in getting away, the only one of his party to do so, and reached what he expected to be the Wheelhouse, but which turned out to be a cross-passage. After his departure, Sub-Lieutenant Ure and the two ratings were attacked by a gang led by Murray Aronoff which removed their lifebelts and threatened both to throw them overboard and shoot them with their own weapons. One rating's pistol was removed, causing Ure and the other rating to hide their weapons under a bunk mattress. These weapons were recovered later.

After the third run by *Childers*, her boarding platform was not in fit state for further use and this combined with other damage, caused mainly by the *Warfield's* rubbing strake, meant she had to be relieved shortly after 0330 by *Charity*. She put across one officer, Lieutenant J.R.S. Gerard-Pearse RN, one Petty Officer and three men who clambered onboard via the *Warfield's* foremost lifeboat. Another lifeboat was dropped on her foc'sle, fortunately without causing severe damage or casualties. But in any case the destroyer became so badly damaged that she was unfit to continue. Gerard-Pearse and his party encountered a bombardment with tins which forced them to take refuge in a cabin which already contained some of the boarders from *Childers*. An attack having been beaten off the party broke out and reached the Wheelhouse, but they were unable to enter and had to split up and take refuge in cabins again, with attackers attempting to break in through the deckheads. Gerard-Pearse became separated from the others and eventually succeeded in making his way via the Charthouse into the Wheelhouse. Others from *Charity*, including Petty Officer Harris, fetched up in a cabin further aft full of women and children. The presence of these immigrants hampered attacks on them through the door and Harris attempted to dress the severe head wounds of a girl. The party were prevented from leaving the cabin and attempts were made from outside to open the deckhead with axes before those outside started to evacuate the other occupants through a serving hatch. An American constantly made threats that the boarders would be killed.

About 0345 things quietened down on the *Warfield*'s port side decks and MacPherson and about six men were able to rush forward to the Wheelhouse. There they found the *Childers* boarders whose numbers had grown to a total of two officers and nine men. Eventually Petty Officer Harris and his men escaped from the cabin and met no resistance whilst making their way to the Wheelhouse. *Chieftain* made a fourth run but only one Able Seaman reached the target, he was immediately overpowered, and damage meant *Chieftain* had to be relieved at about 0415. She had used small arms fire on two occasions. A revolver shot was fired at a migrant with an axe apparently about to cut off the head of a boarder[48] and a short burst of fire from a Vickers machine gun was directed at an immigrant with a rifle on the Top Deck. The sound of automatic fire was not welcomed by some of the boarders who felt it would 'stir things up'.

Despite signalling frequent situation reports to Commodore Palestine, D.1 was being pestered by GOC First Division with requests for information. His ship now took *Chieftain*'s place and approached the Warfield's starboard side with Lieutenant R.B.W. Bundle RN and five ratings on her boarding platform. Tear gas, probably obtained from boarders, was used against her and was effective against the bridge personnel. At the critical moment the *Warfield*'s for'ard starboard lifeboat rolled up under the platform and forced it upwards, but three ratings (Stoker Petty Officer Fynn, Petty Officer Green and Stoker Moreton) managed to jump into the lifeboat and then reach the deck. They were immediately overpowered and their revolvers removed, but Green and Moreton succeeded in recovering their weapons and then throwing them overboard. Fynn was hit by an axe and jumped over the side, followed by Green when he was free. Moreton was by then badly injured and only semi-conscious. American crewmembers prevented the immigrants from attacking him further and removed him to the sick bay.

At about 0400 the team in the Wheelhouse were able to start the next phase of the operation and an expedition led by Lieutenant Stein and including Lieutenants Gerard-Pearse and Shallow set off to investigate the situation elsewhere. After a brief encounter with a large body of migrants armed with coshes, a search was made to find the Engine Room, Boiler Room and Steering Compartment. The party had to make their way through crowded passenger decks but there was no further opposition and everybody below decks appeared to 'have had enough'. It slowly became clear that the mass of people below decks were taking no part in the fight and had little idea of what was going on. Doors to Engine Room and Boiler Room were found to be of steel construction and firmly locked whilst the Steering Compartment was isolated by extensive barbed wire and could not be reached. The team therefore made their way back, walking through the crowds without a struggle but having to enter the Wheelhouse via the Top Deck and the hole in the deckhead.

RESISTANCE COLLAPSES

The *Warfield* had, like the destroyers, suffered damage; some of the hull plating to which the rubbing strake was attached had been torn, a large portion of superstructure woodwork had been damaged on the port side and a smaller section on the starboard side, both areas being low down and close to the waterline. The persistence of the destroyers in coming at her was inflicting increasingly serious damage and more and more water was washing onboard due to sea conditions and their wash. Conditions onboard were becoming very bad with many people badly frightened. All the navigation equipment had been lost with the Wheelhouse, although those in the Steering Compartment had a not very reliable compass. At first light Murray Aronoff again appeared, heavily bandaged; he told Lieutenant Gill of his concern that the ship might sink and asked to be taken to the Commanding Officer of the boarders. Aronoff stopped all opposition in the area and was taken to the Wheelhouse.

Shortly after 0430, the Haganah Commander, Yossi Harel, Grauel and other members of the crew also became concerned that the lives of the passengers were being endangered. Casualties were crying out for medical attention, about 30 needed hospital treatments, in particular blood transfusions, and babies were exposed to tear gas. Grauel brought a person described by MacPherson as 'the senior Jew' to parley at the Wheelhouse window. Despite pleas that the ship was sinking, backed up by frenzied ravings from Aronoff alleging 'babies shot' and 'women and children drowning in the bilges'. Lieutenant MacPherson refused to evacuate the Wheelhouse or allow the ship to be headed for the nearest land and demanded the Captain be found and come forward to restore control.

D.1's appreciation at 0445 was based on the fact that in two hours only some forty boarders had been put onboard and they were split up into small parties, from whom nothing had been heard. He believed they had probably been overpowered. All four of his destroyers had buckled plates and frames and slight flooding, leaving only his own ship in a fit state to attempt further boardings. Thus at 0500 he requested *Ajax* place herself on the Warfield's port beam to act as buffer whilst his ship attempted another boarding. *Ajax* went to boarding stations and with hatches and scuttles closed, gratings, stanchions and davits stowed away, boats turned in, hoses rigged and trailer pumps ready, closed her quarry at sixteen knots. Being so well prepared and after such a long wait, those onboard were keen to take a decisive part and outdo the destroyers. They were about to be disappointed, by now a senior member of the *Warfield*'s crew, the youthful Chief Mate, had gone to her Wheelhouse and passed instructions to the Engine Room and Steering Compartment by telephone as requested by Lieutenant MacPherson. Trouble onboard then ceased and at 0515, to D.1's great relief, a figure appeared on top of the wheelhouse and signalled by semaphore that resistance had died down and order could be maintained. A little later MacPherson added that the Master, as he believed the Chief Mate to be, was willing to steam his vessel to Haifa and that medical assistance was urgently needed.

At 0540 the *Warfield* stopped and *Chequers* went alongside her to transfer Surgeon-Lieutenant D.C.S. Bett RN and her Sick Berth Attendant (SBA). Bett treated three British casualties: two fractured scapula, one each from *Childers* and *Chieftain* boarders, and one case of head injury and lacerated ear, a *Chequers* boarder. There were three fatal casualties amongst crew and immigrants: the American crew member Bernstein who had attempted to recapture the Wheelhouse and two male immigrants died of gun shot wounds, one being a 15-year-old youth who had not been the target. In all there appeared to be less than ten serious cases amongst the crew members and their passengers plus assorted mild concussions, odd cuts and one or two fractures, but there were many onboard sick from other complaints.[49] Bett found a sound and well-arranged medical organisation with first aid stations on deck and a hospital section manned by male and female nurses designed to deal with casualties. Three Jewish doctors presided, but even before the boarding began the situation with the sick had gone beyond their control. One English-speaking doctor alone had 35 severe cases in his care, believed many others should have come to him and had also seen seventy-five women in the last stages of pregnancy, some with complications. A dead baby was found but death had been due to earlier natural causes. Having established the situation as best he could, Bett signalled that proper nursing assistance was needed for about two hundred cases. Surgeon Lieutenant-Commander Gaskell and two more SBAs, all from *Ajax*, were brought over by *Childers* at 0830 with further medical supplies. The naval doctors set about applying what treatment they could, but refrained from surgery on severe head wounds as in the conditions onboard and without very specialised equipment, this would have done more harm than good.

Bett found that those who had fought against the boarders, including the 16 to 18 year olds, had come off very much the worse, in his view to a degree which had been instrumental in resistance collapsing. He added that once control had been gained and fighting stopped, the sailors were extremely helpful in tending wounded and sometimes took the initiative by rendering first aid themselves. Considering the violence which had been used against them, he found the limited extent to which the boarding parties had opened fire very commendable.[50] During the arrest three boarding party members were picked up out of the water and an efficient check of numbers could not be made under current conditions. HM Ships *Charity*, *Cardigan Bay* and also *Rowena*, which was now in the vicinity, were therefore directed to search the area and an air search was requested. Fortunately, there was no one still in the water.

The *Warfield* now took station astern of *Childers*, continuing to communicate by semaphore, and the force steamed towards Haifa following a route which kept the ships out of sight of Tel Aviv. Her decks were patrolled as a measure to deter groups forming and organising further resistance. ERA Ravenscroft, the only naval engineer onboard, was steering in the Wheelhouse when the Engine Room crew indicated they would not assist further and Lieutenant MacPherson, a little surprised to find an engineer at the helm, despatched him to take over. Collecting a National Service Ordinary Seaman, whom he knew to have a public school education and therefore likely to possess good intelligence, Ravenscroft set off escorted by a Petty Officer and six men. There was still some turbulence amongst the passengers but having made their way through decks packed with passengers looking rather sorry for themselves, and after some difficulty at the Engine Room door due to it being padlocked on the outside, Ravenscroft and the Ordinary seaman obtained access. The Petty Officer and six had by now disappeared and the *Warfield* engineer inside turned over the main engine throttle and left too. Four boilers were found, each with only one oil sprayer to fuel them, a rather rudimentary system and, the engine room telegraph being out of action communication, engine orders were passed from the wheelhouse by telephone. Hearing the Ordinary Seaman being instructed in his new duties, an affable American thought to be a fireman, but in fact the Second Engineer, introduced himself as 'Sol' and volunteered to remain and help. There were five thousand of his people onboard and he knew the consequences of a boiler blowing up would be disastrous.

At 1330 Lieutenant MacPherson reported the spirits of the passengers and crew reviving and requested forty additional hands to keep order and help enter harbour. Twenty were sent over but the swell made boat work difficult and D.1 decided not to send more. Things onboard remained under control and *Charity* led the *Warfield* into Haifa at 1545, followed by HMS *Providence*, probably in case a tow became necessary. As at the start of her voyage no assistance was provided by pilot or tugs, although these were sent out to meet her. With ERA Ravenscroft operating the engine and the Ordinary Seaman assisting with the boilers, the President Warfield, flying the Zionist flag prominently above her wheelhouse, entered the port of Haifa in full view of the population and the press looking down from Mount Carmel.

CONCLUSIONS

In his report on the arrest D.1 noted the inability, contrary to his earlier hopes, to get substantial numbers of boarders onto the *Warfield*. This meant that they were in insufficient strength to fight their way through to the steering compartment, force the door and steady the ship so overwhelming reinforcements could be put onboard. But the operation had ended successfully and he attributed this outcome to: the use of boarding platforms at bridge level; fine ship handling by the destroyer Commanding Officers; and the resolute behaviour, courage and initiative of each member of the boarding parties.

D.1 also considered that his decision to place his own ship where he could best exercise control had been proved correct, as indeed it was. He identified as the chief factors in causing the collapse of opposition: the loss of the Wheelhouse, thereafter he believed the crew lacked navigational information necessary for reaching their destination, not knowing even the course being steered;[51] casualties crying out for medical treatment, he considered the injuries suffered by Bernstein frightened the American crew; and severe damage to the superstructure, which caused some onboard to think the ship was sinking. Finally, the naval party patrolling the decks between 0400 and 0500 gave the impression that the Navy were in control. He added that although the destroyers had only been able to get small numbers onboard, their repeated attempts and support distracted the opposition, whom he described as 'hooligans', from liquidating boarders already amongst them. D.1 saw a requirement for some sort of grappling equipment so a target could not break away from warships as the *Warfield* had done. Wire netting was also necessary to protect the open bridges of boarding ships from missiles, expanded metal screens had been tried but provided only limited protection, and better equipment was needed to cut barbed wire, force doors and blow locks. Fortunately, the boats and rafts dropped on to the destroyers had not fallen on their bridges or further aft where they would have done a great deal of damage. He also called for provision of special boarding platforms, on the lines of those devised by *Childers*, which could be quickly assembled from tubular scaffolding poles. Finally, with so much hard fighting and men going overboard in the dark, he considered that the fact that British casualties amounted to only three hospital cases was providential.

Commodore Palestine singled out the Commanding Officer of *Childers* for particular praise, it was he who had devised the boarding platforms, which had been the decisive material factor. Through superb ship handling his destroyer had put across over half the total number of boarders to reach their target. They included Lieutenant Shallow, whose dash and determination captured the Wheelhouse in the first few minutes and then held it against prolonged opposition before leading a party down to the steering compartment. Lieutenant MacPherson was also praised for the skill and courage with which he carried out a difficult task.

The CinC considered that in the circumstances casualty totals were in his view extremely light, largely due to very restrained use of firearms. He attributed success to three factors: the presence of two very experienced destroyer officers; sufficient opportunity to study the *President Warfield* and make detailed arrangements to board at her highest level using the platforms; and the element of surprise achieved by the boarders arriving where they were not expected amongst the women and children. Although only a few men were put onboard, and there were some 20 attempts to do so, they were able to concentrate on the Wheelhouse until in sufficient force to attack elsewhere. He added that only the destroyers had the speed to compete with a vessel capable of 13 knots or more and that if the immigrant vessel had not been so strongly constructed she would have been so badly holed as to sink. Indeed, the damage inflicted on *Charity* during her one run necessitated such lengthy and extensive repairs that the ship's company left her and recommissioned HMS *Volage*, whose repairs were now complete.

The CinC also praised the ingenuity put into the preparations whilst D.1's operation order was held up as a model of clearness and brevity. He believed the operation would have failed but for the determination and good ship handling by Commanding Officers and, although D.1's report expressed regret for the severity of damage to destroyers, this might have been much greater.

For the parts they played Lieutenant MacPherson was subsequently awarded a bar to the Distinguished Service Cross he already held and Lieutenant Shallow the Distinguished Service Cross.[52] The Commanding Officer of HM Ships *Charity, Chieftain* and *Childers* were mentioned in dispatches and a number of others received awards including Distinguished Service Medals for ratings.

16

The 'Refoulement'

As soon as the *Warfield* docked Royal Army Medical Corps doctors took over the medical arrangements and evacuated the casualties and sick with efficiency and dispatch. Although the Foreign Secretary intended the ship be returned to France, and the French Government sought her return, even if she was no longer capable of carrying the passengers, the condition of her hull did not permit this. The remainder of the passengers were tran-shipped to HM Transports *Ocean Vigour*, *Runnymead Park* and *Empire Rival* by 0600 the following day. This was a quick and efficient means of finally denying them access and removing them from Palestine, but it meant that they could only be disembarked at a place which either suited them or where the authorities ashore would countenance the use of force.

The transfer went peacefully and allegations that it entailed use by British troops of rifle butts, hosepipes and tear gas are not true; in any case the immigrants believed their destination was Cyprus and that like all other 'gatecrashers' they would be eventually admitted through the quota. During the transfer to the transport the immigrants were separated from their baggage, so that the latter could be searched more quickly, and the fact that some items were subsequently loaded into a different ship to their owners had unfortunate consequences. A few members of the crew were detained but about forty Haganah people (including the Master) remained hidden, as instructed, until they could escape disguised as workmen. This phase of the operation was watched by some members of the United Nations Special Committee of Inquiry into Palestine which, in response to the British reference to the United Nations, was studying the situation, including the problem of Jewish Displaced Persons. Their Chairman, Justice Sandstroem, was accosted by a passenger alleging the arrest took place 200 kilometres off Jaffa, which he refused to accept. But the fact that the boardings started in International Waters was kept very quiet by the Admiralty.

The three transports departed on 19 July at about 0600, ostensibly for Cyprus but in fact, on instructions from Whitehall, for Port de Bouc. An escort was led by HMS *Ajax* accompanied by HMS *Providence* and HMS

Cardigan Bay carrying 40–50 additional Army guards. The speed of the convoy was lamentably slow, between 5 and 8 knots, with occasional halts to enable the warships to send medical staffs to the transports, including attendance at the birth of baby in the *Runnymede Park*. HMS *Providence* was relieved by HMS *Brissenden* on 22 July and the next day HMS *Troubridge* (Captain C.L. Keighley-Peach DSO RN – Captain D.3) with additional medical supplies relieved the *Ajax* and took charge. The mine-sweepers HMS *Welfare* and HMS *Skipjack* joined from Malta later and *Brissenden* then detached. When a passenger fell into the sea, he was recovered by one of the escorts, given a glass of Gin and some other 'goodies' and then returned to his original ship. At the time he was thought to have fallen overboard accidentally; in fact, this was an attempt to communicate with passengers in another transport.

The attitude likely to be taken by the French government became clearer on 23 July when the Minister for Ex-Servicemen (Monsieur Mitterand)[53] specifically stated that whilst France had no objections to the immigrants landing there, the French would not use force to make them do so. Little or no notice seems to have been taken of this utterance, possibly because Mitterand's responsibilities did not directly cover such matters and con-sciousness that, more generally, the French Government was embarrassed by their failure to halt the *Warfield*'s voyage. Indeed the Minister accen-tuated such sensitivities by observing that immigrants left France with visas for Colombia and so could not have been prevented from departing for that destination. He omitted to mention that French authorities had denied certification for any such voyage whilst his utterances caused the Colomban embassy in Paris to declare that if visas were held they must be forgeries and in any case the immigrants would not have been permitted to land in Colombia.[54]

Shortly before reaching France, *Cardigan Bay* transferred her extra guards to a transport and went on ahead to Marseilles for discussions between the Senior Military Officer (O.C. Troops – a Lieutenant-Colonel who had supervised disembarkations at Haifa many times in the past), a member of the British Ambassador's staff (Mr J. Coulson), the British Consul-General and French officials. A suggestion had been made that the message giving news of their future should be passed to the passengers by means of loudspeakers but at the request of the authorities in Whitehall, the message was to be conveyed by a French representative through translators. This decision and the moment chosen for the delivery of the message were both to prove disastrous. Mr Coulson's instructions, issued by the Ambassador and approved by the Foreign Office, included doing all he could to make the offer of French hospitality effective and avoid a serious Anglo-French incident. Although the resident French Admiral (Commandant Marine Marseilles – Rear Admiral Tanguy) proved very helpful, it soon became clear that the French authorities were determined to keep numbers disembarking as low as possible. After this inauspicious start, *Cardigan Bay* rejoined the convoy, which was planned to arrive on 29 July and anchor off Port de Bouc at 0400.

On the appointed day the local French Sous-Préfet (Monsieur Colaveri), Mr Coulson, the Consul-General and other British representatives all gathered on the shore ready to meet the convoy. D.3 kept the escorts outside territorial waters and instructed the transports to anchor at 0400. Owing to delays caused by *Runnymede Park* they eventually arrived three and a half hours late. (O.C. Troops later vouchsafed to Mr Coulson that the Master of the *Runnymede Park* had been under the influence of alcohol, muddled his instructions and caused the delay.) Thus by the time of the first visit to a transport, the sun was well up and the heat started to take effect on the Sous-Préfet, clad as he was in an official uniform most unsuitable for activities onboard overcrowded ships at the height of the Riviera summer. Seeing the party arrive onboard the immigrants clustered together in the hold under their leaders ready for whatever came next. M. Colaveri then read out the French Government statement, a text worked out with British approval offering hospitality to all who disembarked in France. The Ambassador had suggested to the Foreign Office that the immigrants be told that if they did not land they would simply be taken back to sea but no mention was made of this or any other alternative.

Once the message had been delivered the immigrants were asked if there was anything they wished to say. This enabled a spokesman to orchestrate and lead a hysterical response after which few, if any, were prepared to disembark. The Sous-Préfet and his companions therefore retired ashore for lunch. There they encountered large numbers of Jews streaming into the port area, already congested by lorries ready to transport disembarked passengers, stocks of bread, medical supplies and large numbers of security police. During the pause Mr Coulson established from M. Colaveri that the French had instructions only to accept those who specifically volunteered to come ashore and not to provide any facilities if the British used force. Things went from bad to worse when, in the second ship to be visited, there were people who were clearly willing to land but the Sous-Préfet insisted on interrogating each of them to confirm they were genuine volunteers. D.3 reported that '... by clever insinuations, and discussions with the Jews, which it proved impossible to prevent, he succeeded in working up the illegals up into an hysterical frenzy in which state they volubly announced they would not disembark in any circumstances'.[55]

By the time of his final return to shore, the Sous-Préfet was almost prostrate from lack of sleep, the suffocating heat in the holds and, above all, the very wearing negotiations with individual immigrants. The day was made complete when he announced that there were no volunteers who wished to land and so no craft would be provided for disembarkation. The British representatives immediately challenged this announcement. From their standpoint, the mission had ended in complete failure: the French emissary had proved ineffective and his British companions were unable to achieve anything better. Essentially, the lukewarm offer worked out between the French and British lacked substance and was not accompanied by a clear and convincing, or indeed any, alternative, backed up by a deadline. Since the leaders of the immigrants had been allowed to retain control, any attempt to bring the passengers ashore not backed up by force was probably doomed from the start. Even the planning had been unsound: the naturally suspicious immigrants would have had less time to gain their bearings if the transports had arrived in the dark and then been visited simultaneously before or at first light. By midday, the immigrants in the two ships still to be visited could see for themselves that no one was disembarking from the first ship. For a great many the separation from their few belongings, stowed in different ships, was an important factor.

By the afternoon of the first day a small fishing vessel, thought to be hired by Haganah, in fact by Mossad, was circling the Transports and calling through loudspeakers for the immigrants to remain where they were. Although steps to prevent this had been agreed before the convoy arrived, the French authorities became reluctant to prevent such activities, which continued intermittently throughout the stay. Haganah also infiltrated the passengers and Palyam, which had a more aggressive approach, smuggled explosives onboard one transport. A few immigrants did wish to land but were subjected to angry shouts or beaten up by a hooligan element. The Navy was surprised to find that the Army guards, who had been given orders not to use force to eject the immigrants, interpreted these to mean that force should not be used to prevent such incidents. There were also some 1,500 Jews gathered ashore who further deterred landing, to the extent that D.3 described the situation facing those who wished to land as 'a double gauntlet, the fanatics onboard and the thugs ashore'.[56] Those in close touch with the immigrants nevertheless still felt that there was a majority of volunteers to land, providing their baggage accompanied them. The British Government's decision that in no circumstances would the immigrants be returned to either Cyprus or Palestine was announced to the 'illegals' on 1 August. But this was not believed and any effect was cancelled by a man in a motorboat calling out to each vessel that he had recently returned from an important conference in London which had decided they should go to Palestine. Thus by 5 August, only 96 volunteers had disembarked, described by D.3 as a small but steady stream; he added that the immigrants simply did not believe that return to Cyprus had been ruled out.

The stay off the French coast became prolonged and to the naval posts in the Mediterranean was added Senior British Naval Officer (SBNO) Port de Bouc, a task which fell to D.3 with *Welfare* and *Skipjack* remaining in company. One ship anchored off Marseilles, the remaining warships patrolling outside territorial waters, and each transport went to Marseilles in turn to coal. A tanker, RFA *War Bharata*, brought fuel from Malta and emergency provisions arrived from Gibraltar but proved to be of poor quality, those in boxes marked 'Not to be used after 1945' being completely rotten. Entr'aide Français, an American-financed Jewish organisation, provided food for the transports and International Red Cross doctors went onboard and remained for the rest of the voyage. On 16 August HMS *Phoebe* relieved the much tried D.3. He had found the Consul-General lacking in drive and his experience of French officialdom caused him to describe them, from Minister of Interior to jetty gendarme, as 'bought'. The use of this method of persuasion later claimed on behalf of Mossad would indicate that he was not far off the mark. A hunger strike was staged on 18 August, but the passengers consumed their own food stocks and returned to normal meals the following day, *Phoebe* describing the event as 'a routine publicity stunt and means a few miss their lunch'.[57]

Any hope of disembarkation having proved impracticable, the Illegal Immigration (Official) Committee considered alternative destinations for the passengers and, after rejecting a number of alternatives inside the British Empire, recommended the British zone of occupation in Germany. Accommodation in Displaced Persons Camps was available there and providing the French maintained their offer of hospitality, the immigrants need only remain in Germany until they travelled on to France by land. The view that world opinion was likely to take on Jews being sent to the country which had caused them their worst sufferings was evidently not a factor which weighed much with the Committee. Their recommendation was agreed on 18 August and those onboard the transports were informed at 1100 BST on 21 August of the consequences of continued refusal to disembark. *Phoebe* had already commented that hysteria meant immigrants did not believe one word of what was said to them, and indeed the news was received with amusement and disbelief. The French Government allowed a further and final approach by their representative emphasising the advantages of landing in a free country but the response to this was signalled by O.C. Troops 'Reaction absolutely nil'.[58]

The convoy sailed again with 4,294 immigrants still embarked[59] at 1800 BST on 22 August, a time chosen to allow a period for consideration of the final offer but, to avoid an outcry, before the Sabbath started at sundown. During the 25-day stay only 130 immigrants had landed. Escorted by HM Ships *Phoebe*, *Chevron* and *St Bride's Bay*, the ships reached Gibraltar on 26 August. There the transports replenished with coal and lay at the detached mole when not at the coaling jetty. The local Jewish community sent presents of food and clothing but showed no other interest. Even so, very thorough precautions were taken against underwater sabotage; these were entirely justified since they deterred an attempt to swim from a transport and mine the cruiser with explosives embarked off France.

THE ROYAL NAVY AND THE PALESTINE PATROL

The voyage on which the convoy now embarked had been brought about by persistent Zionist threats and propaganda and its influence on the French Government. Also the Jewish Agency could, if it really had the well-being of those concerned at heart, have used its influence to bring them ashore and thus make the journey to Germany unnecessary. These points were made in a forthright statement by the British government, issued abroad through diplomatic representatives. It drew attention to the Mandatory Government's responsibility for preserving the balance of the population in Palestine and not causing further bloodshed between Jews and Arabs. The British had found that transfers to Cyprus had only encouraged organisers of illegal immigration, many legal immigrants had been pushed aside by 'gate-crashers' and the *Warfield* passengers need not go to Germany unless they continued to refuse to land in France. Unfortunately the French Government had not yet agreed to receive back ex-*Warfield* immigrants landed in Germany, thus the intention that they should be free to do so could not be included either in the announcement or when dealing with the Agency. This shortcoming caused terrible misunderstanding, besides allowing free rein to Zionist propaganda.

The CinC Mediterranean Fleet wished to avoid sending escorts from his Fleet any further: maintenance and refit programmes would be disrupted. Besides he was short handed and once in Home Waters the ships' companies, who were on Foreign Service commissions for periods of up to two and a half years, would expect to be granted leave to see their families and friends. The Admiralty concurred, reliefs were provided from local squadrons at the three Home Ports and the task was taken over initially by Commander (D) Plymouth in the frigate HMS *Burghead Bay* (Lieutenant-Commander M. Harris RN) with HMS *Tremadoc Bay* (Lieutenant-Commander D.J. Godden RN) and the destroyer HMS *Finisterre* (Commander D.F. Chilton RN). The transports carried Army guards totalling 319 officers and men plus 75 officers and men described as 'permanent staff'; in each ship about six of the guards carried firearms and the remainder were armed with 'entrenching tools and their natural charm[60]'. One warship was provided as escort for each transport and each transport carried one officer and twenty seamen to assist the Army guards. These arrived untrained and without their anti-gas respirators; equally, the relief warships had of course not undergone the same training as the Mediterranean Fleet. Onboard the transports, a Medical Officer and a Sick Berth Attendant assisted in caring for the immigrants. The O.C. Troops remained unchanged. He expected to be able to land the passengers without bloodshed but anticipated a certain amount of trouble, particularly if the business was handled as the BBC was predicting, with the world Press and public allowed to watch proceedings.

The voyage to the English Channel at 8½ knots was uneventful except for a thirty-minute halt for the funeral at sea of a baby born 24 hours earlier, colours being half-masted and the escorts closing the transport concerned as a mark of respect. Aircraft taking photographs made an appearance as land was neared. Lack of Signalmen and Telegraphists in all the ships hampered communication and manoeuvres, orders for emergency turns taking up to ten minutes to get through and one of the escorts was therefore stationed five miles ahead to warn approaching vessels and keep then clear. In the Channel, Commander (D), the Nore, in HMS *Zest* (Lieutenant-Commander P. Bekenn RN) with two other destroyers, HMS *Bicester* (Commander A.G. Forman DSC RN) and HMS *Bleasdale* (Lieutenant-Commander C.E. Blackmore RN) took over the escort.

On 27 August the French Government agreed to receive the refugees back, on two conditions, first that they went voluntarily, and second that no precedent was set for the reception of a higher number of refugees in France. The transports arrived in the Elbe on 6 September and anchored, except for the *Ocean Vigour*, which was delayed by fog until 7 September and went alongside into the berth to be used for disembarkation late the same day. Flag Officer Commanding British Navy Germany's plan was for one transport to be unloaded each day and for each transport to be escorted up river by two escorts. Arrangements were made for both representatives of the International Red Cross and the press to attend the disembarkation, whilst the International Refugee Organisation, successors to UNRRA, was invited to consider whether any of the immigrants were eligible to be treated as Displaced Persons under the IRO charter.

The O.C. Troops set odds of 6–4 on for peaceful disembarkation, except in the *Runnymede Park*, where the odds were 3–1 against due to the presence of several fanatical Polish leaders and strong centralised leadership. On the first day, 8 September, onboard the *Ocean Vigour*, where the leader was an American who did his best to secure a peaceful disembarkation, 20 immigrants offered slight resistance and 10 offered major resistance, 1 suffering slight head injuries. On 9 September no force was necessary during the disembarkation from the *Empire Rival* and this allowed disembarkation from the *Runnymede Park* to start at 1250, but there the passengers would not at first come out. They had destroyed some of the ladders and as the use of tear gas might have precipitated a dangerous rush up those which remained, soldiers had to go down, resist attacks by immigrants and drag some out: 22 slight casualties resulted. Disembarkation was complete by 1400 and the fact that the soldiers who had accompanied them from Palestine had established a working relationship with the immigrants was seen to be a restraining factor. Although an army report mentioned that some of the more inexperienced soldiers over-reacted on this occasion, a newspaper reporter present at the scene commented that the troops had taken 'no reprisals'.

Press and a representative of the International Committee of the Red Cross were allowed to witness the operation, on the grounds that if they were excluded atrocity stories would undoubtedly be spread by the immigrants and their supporters. Precautions were taken to avoid the returned immigrants gaining the impression that it would be worth demonstrating as a means of influencing the press and these were successful. Mr Buckhardt (ICRC representative) subsequently reported he had no adverse comments concerning the disembarkation and that he was favourably impressed by the behaviour of the troops when difficulties were encountered, and saw no case of excessive force.

The expedition with which the passengers left the *Empire Rival* roused the suspicions of the officer in charge of the army escort. He was entirely correct, a bomb made up from the explosives embarked off France was in the bilge timed to detonate after the passengers disembarked. It was found and removed by a Royal Navy Explosive Ordnance Disposal Team to a safe place where it exploded. Fortunately no casualties or damage were sustained. Much later a former passenger claiming to have been the Haganah commander in *Empire Rival* attributed the explosion to the bomb being fitted with two fuses, of which only one had been found before the bomb was moved.

The Foreign Secretary's first priority remained that the ex-*Warfield* passengers should return to France, which remained acceptable to the French providing those concerned volunteered to do so. A statement to that effect was read out to the immigrants in the camps and the two nations formed a commission to make the arrangements for travel there by train and also to take steps to prevent further clandestine departures. For their part, the French authorities levied a charge of ten million francs on the Weston Trading Company for the *Warfield*'s illegal departure. This sum was secured by the seizure of SS *Northland*, a vessel also owned by the Weston Trading Company and currently preparing to embark illegal immigrants; it was widespread knowledge that the money would be readily forthcoming from Zionist funds. The French authorities also informed all Préfectures in the south of France that embarkation of illegal immigrants to Palestine was to be prevented, not that there was much prospect of such instructions being effective. Mossad's position in France did suffer some deterioration, despite bribery, and although one source claims that the DST continued to assist by actively working against Britain, the newly arrived Head for the French Mediterranean littoral actively assisted the British. Certainly, Mossad found greater secrecy necessary and, as will be seen, the French coast ceased to be favoured for embarkation of large numbers of Jews.

17

Policy and Incidents after the *President Warfield* Episode

Through news reports made at the time and subsequent accounts, including the introduction of a high degree of fiction, the so-called '*Exodus*' episode has passed into legend. The fact that the immigrants, seen as concentration camp survivors, were not only denied access to the Promised Land but were returned to the country which had caused their suffering continues to attract much hostile comment, particularly in Israel and the United States. No other post-war event lent itself more to attempts to attract sympathy for the Zionist cause but this standpoint overlooks the illegality of attempting to enter Palestine other than through the quota and the connivance of the French authorities. Ignored above all else is the fact that the would-be immigrants refused to disembark in France. Thus the route by which they had to be returned was via Germany but the destination remained France and there was no intention that they should be forced to remain in Germany.

The Foreign Office subsequently informed the Colonial Office that before refoulement was ever tried again, the receiving country must agree beforehand to the use of force if the passengers refused to disembark. There must also be an agreed alternative destination in case things went wrong. Not long before the despatch of the *Warfield* passengers to his area, CinC Germany had been informed that the British zone would not be required to accept any more refugees and the Foreign Office noted that since he was faced with many other difficulties, never again could he be saddled with a commitment of this kind.

Until the transports carrying the *Warfield* passengers returned to Palestine no shipping was available for further refoulement. Despite the current odium attaching to this practice, the Cabinet (Official) Illegal Committee recommended that although there would be considerable difficulties with the Italian Government, once there was proof of a large-scale embarkation from Italy the illegal immigrants concerned should be returned to Italy. Considerable difficulties were foreseen and this proposal was not acted on.

The Committee accepted that refoulement to France was ruled out, as was further use of the British zone in Germany. Apart from the difficulties of clearance for an escort to go through the Turkish straits, recent events in Romania and Bulgaria, now both in the increasing grip of communist regimes, showed all too clearly that the necessary co-operation would not be forthcoming from those nations either.

BOARDING MEASURES

Two large ships, the *Paducah* (940 tons), an ex-cross-Channel steamer, and the *Northland* (1,280grt), a former US Coastguard vessel, were known to be making arrangements for an illegal immigrant voyage. In the light of the immediate consequence of the sizeable problem posed by the *Warfield* and the difficulties of her arrest, the CinC broached the question of the likely effect on world opinion if an interception led to heavy casualties amongst immigrants. He doubted whether extreme measures were worthwhile at a time when the Palestine question was before the United Nations Organisation and reluctantly proposed that Senior Officers be permitted to hold off from boarding if the anticipated scale of casualties and damage appeared excessive. The best alternative would be agreed diversion direct to Haifa and if successful then the Army would not have the problem of rounding up immigrants who reached the shore. The latest Intelligence indicated organisers of immigrant voyages were unlikely to risk their passengers unduly. They felt Cyprus presented them with a satisfactory compromise, whilst refoulement, which the Zionists clearly thought the worst alternative, did not.

The Cabinet's 'Illegal Committee' discussed the CinC's proposals, members agreeing that refoulement to France could not be attempted again. The Admiralty viewpoint was that when there might also be heavy loss of life on both sides and serious damage, discretion should be granted the senior officer present not to attempt boarding. The General Staff doubted if the Navy could predict the position of an eventual beaching point and the High Commissioner was concerned by the possibility of a large ship beached on the coast, with a likely water gap of 400 yards, making landing or rescue very hazardous. On these points the CinC felt that whilst the Navy could not ensure a ship beaching at a spot selected by the Patrol, warships could, particularly if a cruiser were present, prevent her from doing so where she herself chose. Even so a ship might be beached and wrecked in bad weather due to the Master's better judgement being overruled by impatient but ignorant immigrant leaders; in this case the Navy would do all that it could to save lives, whilst the Army cordoned off the beach.

The Committee debated these matters but postponed a firm conclusion, possibly because some success was being achieved in efforts to obstruct preparation of the *Paducah* and *Northland*. However, the CinC Mediterranean Fleet gleaned enough to issue instructions which can be summarised as follows: considerable risks had to be expected and accepted when boarding and getting control of illegal immigrant ships; if damage or casualties, however great, were sustained by HM Ships they could count on his support. If, nevertheless the vessel encountered was so large and well prepared that an unacceptable level of damage and casualties seemed likely, then this appreciation was to be signalled to Commodore Palestine and CinC Mediterranean Fleet. Commodore Palestine was given authority to signal instructions in response, if possible after receiving the CinC's views. Finally, if time did not permit consultation, the Senior Officer present had, subject to existing orders, authority to hold off if he considered the risks too great. Every endeavour should then be made by means of 'persuasion' to get the ship to go to Haifa or to delay her beaching to give the Army as much time as possible to make arrangements for meeting the immigrants ashore. If beaching could not be prevented, it was better done in shoal water as far as possible from the shore as this meant less risk of a Jewish reception party being at the spot. After a grounding, every effort was to be made to hamper disembarkation by gaining control of the ship, not forgetting the possibility of laying a small shallow draft warship alongside a deep draught ship after she had beached. But Commanding Officers were not to be lightly diverted from making an arrest since this could have serious consequences for the Army, could damage the Navy's prestige and would encourage all those engaged in the illegal immigrant traffic. The CinC's instructions were welcomed by the Admiralty and approved by the Cabinet Illegal Immigrant Committee, and it would seem, by Ministers, which concluded the matter.

ARRESTS

Since the start of the Palestine Patrol in November 1945 only one ship had reached Palestine without being identified beforehand as a suspect, and only one interception had not been assisted by Intelligence identification of the ship concerned. Haganah's security was proving inadequate and a Jewish news agency reported in June that measures taken by the British authorities to prevent sailings had become so effective that there would be no more for the time being. Although that statement must be seen in the light of events in July, diplomatic representations and the hindering of preparations by suspect vessels had, in the view of the Joint Intelligence Sub-committee, taken their toll. Although estimates for intended immigrants had risen to 600,000, the assessment was that shipping immediately available had capacity for less than 20,000.

On 19 July, the day that transports left with the *Warfield*'s people, HMT

Empire Lifeguard, one of the corvette-type rescue ships, was alongside in Haifa disembarking quota immigrants when she was seriously damaged by an explosive charge. It was probably placed by one of the immigrants being brought from Famagusta to Palestine and so, at Commodore Palestine's request, immigrants still onboard ships at Cyprus due to sail for Palestine were taken ashore, the ships thoroughly searched and then returned empty to Haifa. That this delayed the arrival of 'quota' immigrants was a price organisers of the sabotage had chosen to pay. Two cases of sabotage by 'quota' immigrants from Cyprus having been experienced, the Jewish Agency was now invited to provide the shipping necessary for them to reach the place where they would be.

By 21 July the Jewish Agency was aware that the *Warfield* immigrants would be returned to France. A few days later two other immigrant ships, the three-masted Italian schooner *Bruna* (alias 'Yod Dalet Halalei Gesher Haziv') and the *Luciano M* (alias 'Shivat Zion') were known to be approaching Palestine. On 27 July the Palestine Government requested the Jewish Agency call off resistance onboard, giving an assurance that the passengers would not be sent back to Europe. Two destroyers and one minesweeper were available to deal with each of the new arrivals. The *Bruna* sailed from France and carried refugees from Poland, Hungary and Romania. She was shadowed by HMS *Espiegle*, which kept her target supplied with fresh water, bread and medical supplies. The convoy was joined by HMS *Verulam* and HMS *Childers* (Lieutenant-Commander M.C. Morris RN) on 27 July, with HMS *Rowena* (Lieutenant-Commander D.A. Dunbar-Nasmith DSC RN) arriving later the same day. Faced with such overwhelming strength, the *Bruna* agreed to steer for Haifa and, on the grounds she had no chart of Haifa onboard, to accept a pilot, but not a guard. The risk of deception could not be run and this refusal resulted in the *Verulam* and *Childers* going alongside her at 0612 on 28 July and, in one minute, putting across four officers and 59 ratings. There was no opposition but the engines were sabotaged and she was towed by *Rowena* to Haifa.

The *Luciano M* sailed on 16 July with immigrants from Algeria who had earlier been unable to embark in the *Anal*; they were supposed to have been transferred at sea to the *Bruna*, but the latter did not make the rendezvous. The *Luciano M* had been in wireless touch with another station and this may have led to a voluntary statement eventually being made that arrest would not be resisted because children and also old women were onboard. She was intercepted by HMS *Chivalrous*, HMS *Widemouth Bay* (Lieutenant-Commander J.S. Kerans RN) and HMS *Providence* on 28 July. The *Luciano M* did not stop when ordered to do so on approaching territorial waters and was boarded by the *Providence*. No opposition was offered but the engine-room was sabotaged as soon as the boarders arrived and *Providence* towed her to Haifa. The passengers were filthy, with 100 young children and babies, many covered in sores and skin diseases and they appeared not to have seen daylight for a long period. Difficulties with identifying crewmembers continued but this was primarily a matter for the police.

A number of youths, male and female staged a demonstration of resistance when the *Luciano M*'s passengers disembarked but this was brought to an end without the use of much force. When two hours later the *Bruna*'s immigrants came ashore, the Officer Commanding Airborne Division Security Section described relations as excellent with the soldiers having 'an almost professional air of travel agents, carrying, directing and helping...'.[61] He added:

> Disembarkation began quietly and smoothly – almost gaily, as soon as the word was given by the Commander of operations. The gangway was rather steep, and Airborne soldiers were to be seen running up and down, hugging dirty little Jewish children in their arms, whilst plump Jewish mothers struggled along behind: the father was usually in the background, arguing with some other Jew.

A period with no further arrests now began and lasted throughout August. Mossad attempted, with the assistance of an agent 'very skilled in bribery', to set up a fitting-out base at Bayonne in France but British interest caused the vessels concerned to move on to Bulgaria – Romania did not want more trouble with the British if the illegal immigrants were allowed to embark from their territory. The two ships, *Paducah* and *Northland*, were shadowed by various British warships from the time they arrived in the Mediterranean on 9 August and 3 September respectively until they entered the Dardanelles and went to the Bulgarian port of Burgas. At this stage the Soviets were interested in undermining their former Allies' policies wherever opportunity offered and it is not unlikely that they authorised Bulgaria and Romania to assist Mossad operations. Passengers brought to the *Paducah* and *Northland* were mainly Romanian but some originated in other parts of Eastern Europe, including Russia. One described the process by which they were brought across Europe, assembled at Bucharest and then moved on to Burgas, as organised with minute-to-minute precision. In order to provide sufficient force to intercept the two ships, the CinC reinforced the patrol with HM Ships *Cheviot*, *Childers* and *Haydon*.

The *Paducah* and the *Northland* emerged from the Dardanelles in company on 28 September and were shadowed by HMS *Chaplet* (Lieutenant-Commander C.G. Forsberg RN), and also HMS *Cheviot* until relieved by HMS *Haydon*, which, a passenger noted, hailed to enquire if medical assistance was needed. HMS *St Austell Bay* was sailed to provide additional boarding gear and remain to assist. At this stage the extent of naval operations covered the length and breadth of the Mediterranean. Apart from the patrol working close to the Palestine coast, HMS *Chivalrous* was shadowing the large suspect SS *Pan York* in the western Mediterranean heading east, whilst the despatch vessel HMS *Surprise*[62] (Commander N. Lanyon DSC RN) relieved the *Childers* in the task of shadowing another, the SS *Pan Crescent* from Venice to the Black Sea. An account of the activities of the two *Pan*s will follow.

D.1 took charge when the *Paducah* and *Northland* neared Palestine, allocating two destroyers and a frigate to cover the *Paducah* and three destroyers and a frigate to cover the *Northland* twenty miles to the south. The weather was ideal and the ships were duly arrested off Haifa and Jaffa respectively on 2 October, the Haganah having issued instructions that the presence of old people and children necessitated the avoidance of violence. Each of the two ships took evasive action but trailer pumps and boarding platforms proved effective and only onboard the *Northland* was there significant resistance, this resulted in four casualties, none serious, one being a member of the boarding party. The technique of countering use of boarding platforms by pushing them up with a long pole was becoming established onboard illegal vessels. As usual crewmembers concealed themselves amongst the passengers and onboard the *Northland* the bridge and engine-room were found to be deserted, with the wheel lashed and the engines running full ahead. The Paducah carried 1,347 and the Northland 2,560 immigrants. When the ships docked at Haifa, a noisy demonstration took place, and an attempt was made to persuade bystanders that a child who had died some days previous to arrival had been killed by tear gas. However, several passengers remarked on the lines of one who said to a British soldier: 'It's not against you, it's for the Press.'

An ex-Landing Craft Tank (LCT.256) named '*Despite All*' disguised as the *Ferida*, a regular and legitimate coastal trader, was arrested by HMS *Chequers* and HMS *Talybont* (Lieutenant-Commander N.J. Parker DSC RN) on 27 September carrying immigrants from Italy. Unfortunately, this relatively minor arrest was magnified into a major incident due to one immigrant being killed and two injured when a member of the boarding party was surrounded by five immigrants armed with crowbars and fired five rounds in self-defence. As the LCT came alongside in Haifa a quarrel broke out amongst the immigrants and the boarding party had to use their coshes to defend a young woman who sought their protection.

The CinC's foresight proved to be justified by intelligence that two larger and better-found ships than hitherto encountered were now about to be used for illegal immigration. These were the *Pan Crescent* and the *Pan York*, both of 1901 construction and formerly owned by the United Fruit Company but now said to be the property of the F&B Company of Panama, which had a connection with the now defunct Weston Trading Company. Each could carry an estimated load of 8,000 immigrants and whilst disembarkation of passengers from such large ships beached on the coast would be very difficult for the organisers, they might be relying on being taken by the Navy to Cyprus, now regarded as a satisfactory halfway house.

The movements of both ships were tracked assiduously. HMS *Chivalrous* (Lieutenant-Commander G.B. Barstow RN) patrolled the Straits of Gibraltar with aircraft co-operation and duly intercepted the *Pan York* shortly before midnight on 29 September. In the meantime the *Pan Crescent* lay at Venice where her agent was a known extreme Zionist and on 30 August she was damaged by an explosion which flooded her No. 2 Hold and caused her to bottom. The British Secret Intelligence Service was involved in main-land Europe in countering the flow of illegal immigrants; although Israeli sources alleged the explosives were placed by the expert diver Lieutenant-Commander 'Buster' Crabb, previously mentioned in this account as serving at Venice in 1946. He had however long since left and the explosive was not attached to her underwater surfaces. There are no other reports of refugee ships suffering damage of this kind and although the *Pan Crescent* went into dry dock, repairs did not take long.

Outside Venice a shadower, at first HMS *Magpie* (Lieutenant-Commander A.D.P. Campbell RN) lay in wait, and when on 25 September the *Pan Crescent* set off eastward, HMS *Childers* kept her company and signalled her details. The *Pan Crescent*'s high sides, 15-foot-long cargo derricks, capable of being secured horizontally as fending-off spars, and extensive steam pipes on the upper deck had, in the CinC's view, the potential to make her 'unboardable'. NOIC Trieste reported that there were plans for the immigrants to disembark in small boats and for the vessel to be sunk so she could not be used to remove them from Palestine; a launch would then take off her crew and land them at a pre-arranged place where provision existed for their return journey. HMS *Surprise* took over from the *Childers* until, as anticipated, the *Pan Crescent* entered the Dardanelles and went through to the Black Sea, her presence there causing the CinC to station a cruiser in the Eastern Mediterranean to await a reappearance. This task fell first to HMS *Mauritius* (Captain Lord Ashbourne DSO RN), which came from Trieste, where she had been stationed as a precautionary mea-sure during the troubles concerning the transfer of territory from Italy to Yugoslavia.

The *Pan York* did not go to North Africa but to Marseilles, where she fuelled and, despite British suspicions being made known to the authorities, was permitted to load food, not a readily obtainable commodity in those days of shortages but described as of American origin and far in excess of the needs of those onboard. She then sailed again in the same direction as the *Pan Crescent*; *Chivalrous* continuing to shadow her until the task passed to HM Ships *Volage*, (Lieutenant-Commander A.P. Northey RN), *Bigbury Bay* and *Surprise* in turn, until on 14 October, the *Pan York* entered the Dardanelles. Both *Pans* were now taken in hand at Constanza and there were frequent reports of large numbers of bunks being installed.

The CinC requested every possible measure to prevent the *Pans* leaving the Black Sea loaded with immigrants and suggested that the Turkish authorities be persuaded to intervene. The Illegal Immigration Committee agreed that the *Pan Crescent* might come into the category of 'unboardable ships' and that Ministers should be aware of this situation. Efforts were already being made to persuade the Turkish Government not to allow passage through the Straits by vessels carrying illegal immigrants. However, Turkey's relations with the Soviet Union were going through a difficult and dangerous time and the Minister of Foreign Affairs did not want to be charged by the Russians with failure to observe the Montreux Convention. As had been the case during the War, the Turks were also unwilling to do anything which might result in large numbers of Jewish immigrants being left on their hands. Naval surveillance in the Black Sea was not feasible since a warship could not pass through the Bosphorus for this task; consideration was, however, given to the use of a Red Ensign vessel such as a yacht or one of the Transports. For the time being one frigate was kept at four hours notice at Lemnos whilst the cruiser and the other frigate cruised in the area as required by the British ambassador in Athens. The British Minister at Bucharest suggested a naval vessel visit Black Sea ports and the CinC was prepared to send HMS *Pelican*, noting that the notification time required under the Montreux Convention for the Turkish straits was not an insurmountable problem and the warship might discourage embarkation of illegal immigrants by being present at the port where they were forecast to embark. This course of action was not pursued.

Concurrently, the High Commissioner expressed concern that some seven other ships carrying 4,000 or more illegal immigrants were forecast to arrive in the November. The prospect of the camps at Cyprus becoming swamped caused consideration to be given to refoulement for the *Pans*' passengers. But due to the uncooperative attitude of the Romanian and Bulgarian Governments refoulement to Black Sea ports was still seen to be impracticable.

In the meantime the two ships at Constanza were deserted by twenty Italians, two of whom were interviewed by the CID. They reported that numerous Americans were aboard, one being the Master of *Pan Crescent*; most did no work and if boarded by a destroyer their orders were to mingle with the passengers. The CoS Committee now sought the assistance of the BBC to provide publicity against preparatory activities for Jewish illegal immigration vessels in the Black Sea: the BBC agreed to do their best to discourage crews of ships like the *Pans*, who were already having trouble retaining their people, from sailing to Palestine.

On 15 November a vessel of a totally different nature, the 300-ton auxiliary schooner *Kadima*, was reported by an aircraft and then intercepted by HMS *Venus* (Lieutenant-Commander C.T.D. Williams RN). The following day she stopped three-quarters of a mile outside territorial waters and requested assistance. A boarding party went across and found 794 illegal immigrants who had embarked in Italy. Refoulement was considered but not pursued. On the same day a known suspect, the small motor vessel, the *Albertina*, alias. '*Aliyah*' or '*Immigration*', was found stranded and deserted off Nahariya. It was evident she had successfully landed her passengers, then estimated to number 150, a figure which was subtracted from the monthly quota. The *Albertina* proved to be the former *Pietro*, which made two passages in the autumn of 1945 before the start of patrols, and probably other voyages, possibly up to six in all, retrieving crew members from ships before they entered the area where interception became likely. On this occasion, an error of judgement brought her activities to an end.

PART IV:

PALESTINE PATROL AND NAVAL OPERATIONS, 1947–48: THE FINAL PERIOD

18

International Developments
and their Effects

The special committee appointed by the United Nations rendered its report on 1 September 1947. This recommended that the mandate be terminated and that Palestine be partitioned between the Arabs and Jews, but as an economic union. British administration was to continue for two years after which the separate Arab and Jewish states would be fully independent. A further recommendation was that 150,000 Jewish immigrants should be admitted immediately. Since this solution was not acceptable to either the Arabs or the Jews, HM Government declared that it was not prepared to impose it by force of arms and would make an early withdrawal. On 11 November the UN General Assembly agreed that the mandate should end on 15 May 1948 with the British withdrawing their administration and forces by 1 August. The final UN vote was taken on 29 November and the prospect of a reasonably early establishment of the Jewish state led to a noticeable lessening of hostility and resistance by illegal immigrants. It helped that on 11 November the United Nations General Assembly agreed (33 votes to 1) Resolution 2, calling on member states 'not to accord aid and protection to individuals or organisations which are engaged in promoting or operating illegal immigration, or activities designed to promote illegal immigration'. The resolution went on to call for the early return of 'repatriable' refugees. Britain, the Arab states and indeed America supported the resolution, whilst the Soviet 'bloc', bent on undermining the British position in the Middle East, was amongst 12 nations which abstained.

The change of policy in America went further, General Marshall was not at all content with the support being given to illegal immigration, and he spoke to senior American citizens in touch with the Jewish Agency in terms which brooked no argument. Another indication of the extent to which the tide had turned was given by a Danish salvage ship which declined to assist when chartered by Ginesta, the Marseilles agents, to bring in a suspect vessel broken down and proceeding under sail off Italy.

REACTION TO THE UN PROPOSAL

The Zionist leaders accepted partition as agreed by UNO for it at last endorsed the creation of a Jewish state, but the Arabs, both within and without Palestine, angrily rejected it. As the Syrian delegate to the UN warned, 'Arabs and Muslims throughout the world will obstruct it, and all Asia with its thousand million people will oppose it.' Arab reaction within Palestine was violent, the first attacks on the Jewish community beginning on 30 November. Further afield, Naval forces east of the Mediterranean had to be called in to deal with Arab reaction to news of the partition. In Aden a strike by Arabs started on 2 December and led on to looting and burning in the Jewish quarter of Crater the following afternoon. Despite the use of troops the situation there continued to deteriorate and the Governor requested naval assistance. The destroyers HMS *Cockade* (Lieutenant-Commander J.B. Cox RN) and HMS *Contest* (Lieutenant-Commander J.C. Cartwright RN) entered the port at midnight 3 December and sent armed landing parties ashore. These were mainly responsible for preventing further outbreaks of violence and for producing some order out of the chaos. Nine hours later the survey ship HMS *Challenger* (Captain R.N. Southern RN) arrived and landed another party. Casualties to date were 24 Arabs, 2 Indians and 75 Jews dead with many more injured.

Two companies of infantry arrived by air on 5 December and the situation continued to improve, but the naval landing parties remained ashore. Whilst demonstrating the versatility and flexibility of naval forces, the uprising showed the need for the British to remain even-handed as regards the separate interests of Arabs and Jews. The Middle East Army and RAF Commanders had reasons for not reinforcing the Governor further and he declined to allow the warships to depart until reliefs were provided from the East Indies Fleet.

FURTHER ATTEMPTS

Meanwhile an unidentified caïque, later found to be *Maria Annick*, penetrated to Tel Aviv on the night 3/4 December, and she landed some 167 passengers. In the afternoon of 22 December HMS *Verulam* intercepted a suspect thought to be named *Giovanni Maria*. She had embarked 50–100 immigrants off the Algerian coast on the night of 6 November but police had arrived and turned back 300–500 more. The task of shadowing was turned over to HMS *Chivalrous* (Lieutenant-Commander G.B. Barstow RN) who remained in company until the vessel entered territorial waters on 28 December and was arrested without opposition.

On the same day, an aircraft sighted a different suspicious vessel classified as 'doubtful' and HMS *Chequers*, which was on routine patrol, was sent to intercept. Commodore Palestine expected her quarry to be the 200-ton Turkish auxiliary sailing vessel *Tua Karago*. This proved correct and although at first only four people could be seen in her wheelhouse, a little more than one hour later her decks were crowded. A spokesman called over that as there were many women and children onboard and that their leaders had instructed them not to offer resistance. HMS *Volage* and the sloop HMS *Mermaid* arrived as reinforcements. At 0805 the *Karagu*, alias '*Lo Tafchidunu*', stopped when ordered and no resistance was offered to boarders, although one boarder broke his leg when he jumped on board. Her engines could not be restarted, whether this was due to sabotage could not be established, so *Mermaid* took the vessel in tow to Haifa. An unusual feature of this arrest was that two cameramen were found onboard, one in the uniform of an American war correspondent, together with a film actor and actress. They had visas and were making a film to include incidents during the voyage.

19

The *Pan*s Operation

Romania, where the *Pan*s lay, contained 450,000 Jews, the largest surviving Jewish community in Europe, and the Communist Party, currently engaged in eliminating other political parties, wished to see them out of the country. It did not augur well that the head of the American Joint Distribution Council was known to have met the organiser of illegal immigration from Romania and a very eminent representative of the Jewish Agency in Bucharest on 10 December. Their agenda had been reported to be ways and means of despatching the greatest possible number of immigrants as soon as possible. On 20 December the British diplomatic representative in Romania reported that the departure of the *Pan*s, with illegal immigrants embarked, was imminent. This news caused the Palestine authorities to start air searches.

Two days later the *Pan Crescent* sailed, although believed to be without passengers. HMS *Whitsand Bay* was sent to patrol outside the Dardanelles whilst HMS *Cardigan Bay* (F.5) stayed at short notice at Mudros. The CinC planned to increase the patrol off the Dardanelles to two frigates as soon as one or both *Pan*s were reported loaded and sail an additional cruiser accompanied by two destroyers from Malta to assist. On Christmas Eve, the Secret Intelligence Service reported 14,000 illegals en route through Romania to Varna in Bulgaria. This news was confirmed on Christmas Day by diplomatic staff in Bucharest who reported eight trains transporting 11,000 would-be emigrants, many of whom were nominated by the Soviet authorities. A Jewish source quotes as an example of bribes paid to Governments by Mossad the charge of $US50–60 made for every foreign Jew passing through the port of Burgas, with $US100 for every Bulgarian national. The influence of the United States Secretary of State continued to be exerted against further illegal immigration and the heads of the Jewish Agency in the USA were warned of the possible consequences of the *Pan*s attempting to complete their voyage. This led the Agency to send instructions that the ships were not to sail. Mossad nevertheless decided to go ahead anyway. Those on the spot believed that with the immigrants moving to the ports and without any money it was not feasible to call a halt. But steps were taken to inform the British that the two ships would be diverted.

On 27 December both the *Pans* departed from Burgas with passengers embarked and anchored off the Turkish control point in the Bosphorus. Passage of the two vessels through the straits has been said by an Israeli source to be one of the many occasions on which bribes were paid to individuals, in this case to senior Turkish police and Army officers, thus reviving a practice rife in old Ottoman days. The *Pans* were seen to be crowded with passengers, estimated to number 15,000, and Turkish Health Officials reported their morale to be high. But at 1350 on the same day the Jewish Agency informed the High Commissioner that the move was not in accordance with their arrangements and it was also learnt that the ships would be directed by the Agency to go to Famagusta. In the meantime CS.1 (now Rear-Admiral Symonds-Tayler DSC) in HMS *Mauritius* sailed from Poros to join the frigates patrolling south of the Dardanelles.

Closer to Palestine, HMS *Chivalrous* and HMS *Volage* intercepted an illegal immigrant vessel which they shadowed whilst she made her way Eastward under engine and full sail, with 'Haganah Ship 29th November 1947' painted on her wheelhouse. HMS *Chevron* joined during the afternoon of 28 December forty-one miles west-south-west of Cape Carmel and addressed those on deck in English and German. These remarks were received in silence but the illegal vessel altered course in the direction requested. The *29th November 1947*'s progress through the water then became more erratic until she requested a tow on grounds of engine failure. As the vessel was outside territorial waters the *Chevron* requested a signed affidavit, but the engine was evidently repaired as progress was resumed until she stopped shortly after crossing the 3-mile limit. *Chevron* went alongside and although her boarding party were not opposed, there was as usual no one except a doctor who would admit to being in authority or control and no co-operation. With Police Launch ML.1126 in company, the *29th November* was towed to Haifa.

INTERCEPTION OF THE *PANS*

At 0500 on 29 December 1947, the day following the arrest of the *29th November*, the two *Pans* emerged from the Dardanelles Narrows and set off southwards in company in the teeth of a gale. Both patrolling frigates duly met them, with CS.1 in *Mauritius* joining before dark. The *Pan York*, which was clearly in charge of her consort, gave CS.1 her destination as Haifa, but her sister-*Pan* remained silent. Other warships were on their way, with the aim of forming two boarding groups. The CinC considered a cruiser should be available to deal with each *Pan* and the light cruiser HMS *Phoebe* (Captain G.C. Colville OBE RN) joined CS.1 on 30 December.

Prospects were not improved by the Governor of Cyprus signalling that so many immigrants could not possibly be accepted on the island, due to there being insufficient troops to guard them. The CinC immediately offered naval assistance with ferrying reinforcements and troops from 6th Airborne Division in Palestine were despatched during the afternoon in a transport escorted by HMS *Chevron*. The CinC considered Cyprus to be a feasible destination and directed CS.1 to urge the *Pan*s to go direct to Famagusta. During the same afternoon Commodore Palestine passed to CS.1 the news, phrased as 'a reliable report', that the ships had sailed against the wishes of the Jewish Agency and that the Agency was believed to be giving instructions by wireless that if so requested, or ordered, by the Royal Navy they should go to Cyprus. Commodore Palestine added that the Agency expected these instructions to be followed, but he stressed the need to handle the matter very delicately and demonstrate a strong show of force.

D.1 in *Chequers* with *Chivalrous* and *Volage* was now steaming north to join CS.1 and at the same time conducting a sweep for another suspicious vessel. Nothing was seen and his ships joined up with the *Mauritius* early on the forenoon of 31 December, a fortuitous moment for a show of force, since CS.1 was about to negotiate by radio with the spokesman onboard the *Pan York*. This discussion proceeded on amicable lines, the spokesman, probably the overall commander Yossi Harel, formerly in charge of the *President Warfield*, acknowledging that the Agency had directed the ships to go to Cyprus or as directed by the Navy. But they would not do so voluntarily, only if a Naval Boarding Party, which would not be resisted, was placed onboard to take them there. Further, the immigrants must be allowed to retain their baggage. All these conditions were agreed. The spokesman also sought that there be no discrimination against the crews, legal or otherwise and regardless of nationality. CS.1 was able to give a personal guarantee as regards the boarding parties, including that they would not carry any weapons or wear helmets or play any part in identifying crews. The spokesman made it clear that undertakings given by a British admiral could be relied upon. At 1450 on New Year's Eve the two ships stopped for *Mauritius* and *Phoebe* each to send over boarding parties of two officers and 30 men to the *Pans*.[63] The boarders were received with the greatest friendliness, certificates were obtained that each ship had been boarded and the circumstances, and course was then set for Famagusta. In the *Pan York* the Master was found to have no authority to make decisions and there was a nucleus crew backed up by passengers, whilst the Master of the *Pan Crescent* never appeared, for reasons then unknown. Later it was said that this was due to objections to the Haganah taking charge. In his place the boarders dealt with two men, one, named 'Ike', affable but incognito, who was thought to be Navigator and is now known previously to have been the Master of the *Warfield*. In the *Pan Crescent* eighty-five percent of the passengers appeared to be Bulgarian and the remainder were Bessarabian or Polish Jews fleeing the Russians, all being desperate to leave Eastern Europe, where they were not accepted, before Russia prevented this. The passengers were well organised and firmly controlled, with arrangements for school lessons for the 500 orphans present, regular meals and a set routine for all onboard the *Pan York*, which included cleaning ship daily at 0830. There were about 40 doctors and 100 trained nurses in *Pan York* with a well-fitted sick bay.

A good deal of signalling now took place between naval authorities concerning the legalities, first of arrest on the high seas and second of authority for detaining the ships when they reached Cyprus. The CinC was already seeking clarification of legal aspects from the Admiralty but time constraints caused him to send advance instructions to CS.1 that the signed statements obtained were to confirm requests to be boarded and willingness to go to Cyprus. The Admiralty responded to much the same effect and added that both ships had become stateless, their Panamanian registration having been withdrawn by early November. The convoy – two cruisers, two destroyers, two frigates and both *Pan*s – arrived off Famagusta on New Year's Day. There they were joined by the *Chevron* and the *Pan*s anchored. Owing to the local authorities' fears that sabotage or other mishap might block the only commercial port in Cyprus the Resident Naval Officer had been unable to obtain an alongside berth and it was planned for Z-lighters to start unloading the ships immediately. CS.1 obtained an undertaking from the spokesman in *Pan York* that there would be no sabotage and after a two-hour argument with those ashore in Cyprus it was agreed that the *Pan*s could berth alongside one at a time. This was as well, since on 2 January the weather forced the use of Z-lighters to cease. The immigrants organised their disembarkation, which continued for several days, very efficiently and so troops in and near the ships remained unarmed. The *Pan*s were found to contain 15,169 immigrants and also 81 crew members, which on this occasion did not conceal themselves.

Due to the close watch kept on the *Pan*s and the groundwork laid by the US State Department and others, culminating in the tact exercised by CS.1, the interception phase of the operation had passed off without difficulties of the kind which so often attended arrests. This was as well since the boarding parties found both ships well prepared to resist, had they chosen to do so. The *Pan*s were high-sided vessels, without the upper works that made the *Warfield* vulnerable both to boarding and to damage, and their derricks were Admiralty Net Defence booms,[64] which could be lowered and swung outboard with their heads joined by a fore and aft wire. All the passengers had gas masks and the plan was to put all non-combatants below and then fight off boarders by means of coshes; there were 2,000 of these onboard *Pan York*, as well as other weapons, but not firearms. In these conditions, the chances of boarding parties gaining control without deaths on both sides would have been slim. CS.1 might have been placed in a situation of the kind envisaged by the CinC, making it necessary to hold off and steer the *Pans* to a destination where the passengers could be arrested when they attempted to land. The overall Haganah commander has been criticised by some involved on his own side for agreeing to diversion and his response has been that he was concerned at the risks to the lives of his passengers if he did not do so. He knew that a stay in Cyprus would not rule out, but only delay, safe arrival in the Promised Land.

Things having turned out as they had, there was now the problem of detaining the two empty ships and also the legal difficulties associated with arrest and detention. The Government decided against the doubtful legality of seizure on the high seas and in favour of arranging local legislation enabling it to hold both ships. In response the Master of *Pan York*, acting on behalf of his owners, lodged a protest against the Navy's actions. CS.1 took part in these negotiations, which included obtaining from the Attorney-General assurances that the crews had not committed any offence for which they were liable to prosecution, and then departed leaving D.1 in charge. By 9 January all the passengers and their baggage were ashore but even then a naval guardship had to remain to ensure their crews did not remove the ships. Apart from this tedious task, which continued for many weeks, she was also periodically required to supply both *Pans* with fuel. By now the camps in Cyprus contained 30,668 immigrants, against a capacity of 34,000, and one of the possibilities, discussed at great length, was that the *Pans* be used to transfer them to Palestine when the mandate ended.

20

The Final Arrests

Towards the end of the *Pans* operation, a vessel, thought to be No. 293 on the list of suspects and presumably the ship sought earlier by D.1's force, was reported aground off Naharia, north of Acre. *Chevron* was sent to investigate. She had landed about 500 immigrants on the Palestine coast at midday. This vessel is now known to have been the *Archimedes*, which had embarked 537 illegal immigrants at Bari and may not have been included in the Intelligence schedules of arrivals. She had crept down the Lebanese coast and beached herself just after passing the border with Palestine. A boarding party found her empty and abandoned; the police later rounded some of her erstwhile passengers up.

Although the Admiralty had for long opposed authorisation for attempts to divert inbound illegal immigrant vessels to Cyprus, the *Pans* operation had demonstrated that this course of action was feasible. Refoulement, the actions of General Marshall and expectation that the end of the mandate would mean only a short period of detention all contributed to greater willingness to see out a wait there. Revised orders instructed the Palestine Force that in future when an illegal vessel was intercepted, attempts were to be made to persuade her to go direct to Cyprus and, failing that, to steer for Haifa. Assistance outside territorial waters might only be provided if applied for in writing and in a properly attested, thumb-printed document. In every case the vessel was to be boarded on entering territorial waters. Another activity had now to be countered; on land the Arabs were starting gunrunning in preparation for fighting the Jews when the British departed.

The 29 November 1947 United Nations Resolution called for the evacuation of a port on the Palestine coast by 1 February 1948 and for it then to be available for immigration. But the Cabinet decided this would cause such conflict between Arabs and Jews that it could not be done before the mandate ended. Thereafter the British would have quitted all the harbours on the coast except Haifa, which was needed as an enclave for the evacuation due to be completed later. The work of the Patrol therefore continued through the last months of the mandate and as the Palestine Police was one of the first organisations to be disbanded, the Navy took a larger responsibility for the defence of the port facilities of Haifa. Nor could reliance be placed on the Haifa port tugs handling arrested, or indeed any, ships and one or other of the Mediterranean Fleet's two Fleet Tugs (HMT *Brigand* and HMT *Marauder*) had to be at Haifa for most of the time until the mandate ended.

The security situation ashore became increasingly difficult and Royal Marines were sent to cope. 40 Commando Royal Marines (Lieutenant-Colonel R.D. Houghton MC RM) was the first unit to arrive and took over security duties in the port on 3 February, experiencing inter-community violence from the first day. Although the Jewish Agency deplored attacks on the British,[65] who were so soon to leave, the more extreme elements could not be restrained and the situation between Jew and Arab deteriorated, leading to the Royal Marines suffering casualties. At first 40 Commando's camp was sited between the Arab and Jewish quarter, with gunfire being exchanged nightly between the two, but later they moved into the immediate port area and controlled traffic, patrolled the stores and sheds and even assisted with underwater searches of ships.

Unlike the previous year, traffic in illegal immigrants did not abate during the winter, although there was no serious resistance to any arrests. On 31 January HMS *Childers* investigated a suspect two-masted sailing vessel detected by air reconnaissance some 70 miles north-north-west of Cape Carmel and bearing the name '*Sylvia Starita*'. No more people were on deck than might be expected with a vessel of this type, but two days previously Commodore Palestine's had signalled a warning that a clear upper deck might not be sufficient evidence of innocence. After three hours on the scene, the destroyer made another close approach, giving blasts on her siren and calling again by loudhailer. At this stage the tarpaulin over the hold was seen to have been partially rolled back, and after a pause the immigrants, evidently realising that *Childers* had not been fooled, poured up on deck and displayed a notice confirming the vessel as a Haganah ship named '*Heroes of Ezion*'. *Childers* called again by loud-hailer and explained, in English, German and, through the good offices of her Maltese NAAFI Canteen Manager's Italian, that the immigrants' best policy was to go straight to Famagusta, but if they chose to go to Haifa then they would be arrested at the 3-mile limit. After about an hour a response was signalled by torch that the immigrants were determined to go to Haifa, needed no assistance and would allow the vessel to be boarded at the limit.

When territorial waters were eventually reached, the *Starita* was stopped and *Childers* went alongside to transfer boarders led by Lieutenants Gill and Stein, both veterans of the *Warfield* boarding. The *Chaplet*, which had joined to assist the *Childers*, held off. No opposition was encountered and measures to suppress opposition, such as tear gas and hoses, were not needed. The passengers were quiet and co-operative and course was set for Haifa.

ERA Ravenscroft, another veteran of the *Warfield*, and two stokers found the Engine Room had been vacated, leaving the engine running. Before reaching the entrance, Lieutenant Gill prudently conducted manoeuvring checks and air bottles were found to be too empty to put the diesel engine into reverse, so the journey was completed under tow by HM Tug *Marauder*.

Aircraft reports brought HMS *Cheviot* into contact with the wooden motor vessel *Cicilio* on 10 February, she was found to have her decks crowded with passengers and agreed to go to Haifa. HMS *Chaplet* joined during the evening. *Cheviot* had to employ a good deal of coaxing and endure a certain amount of prevarication before the *Cicilio* entered territorial waters and obeyed instructions to stop the following morning. As usual there was no sign of a Master but the passengers actively assisted the boarders. HMS *Chaplet* put onboard a Palestine Police Officer and the tug *Marauder* then towed the *Cicilio* to Haifa where, as had been the case with *Starita*, she was berthed alongside HMS *Phoebe* with a Royal Marine guard.

The *Cicilio* was followed by the *Abdul Hamid*, first detected on 19 February by air reconnaissance. This vessel was a two-masted schooner and she was intercepted under sail and engine by HMS *Childers* some 25 miles north-north-west of Beirut. She appeared a little uncertain as to her position, which was not surprising since the weather of the last few days had not permitted astro-navigation, and so a course to steer was provided and this was followed during the night. The immigrants onboard the *Abdul Hamid* becoming noticeably more cheerful when Haifa came in sight the following morning. By this time HMS *Bigbury Bay* had joined, followed by a police launch. After entering territorial waters, *Childers* and *Bigbury Bay* transferred boarders led again by Lieutenants Gill and Stein RN. There was no opposition. ERA Ravenscroft found the engine still running; there had been no sabotage and after a brief pause for control and manoeuvring checks the arrested vessel reached the harbour entrance under her own power. She was again berthed on HMS *Phoebe* whose Medical Officer took over the care of the sick. A few passengers had minor injuries due to clambering into a small boat which, despite warnings, remained turned out with the warships came alongside. A Jewish doctor was onboard and numerous passengers were found to be suffering from spending 20 days at sea in vile conditions. Lieutenant Gill's report noted ignorance amongst passengers of the dangers of crowding to the ship's side or being in lifeboats when HM Ships came alongside and action followed to provide verbal warnings on future occasions.

GUN RUNNING

At one stage soon after the war, Jews in the British zone of Germany obtained a licence for fishing in the North Sea, and the British authorities then found them not landing much fish but running arms to a Displaced Persons camp. The AJDC, the CORT and Vaad Hatzla had long been suspected of assisting in gun-running and once the decision of the end of the mandate was made known, Jewish representatives set about purchasing arms by legal means, although the intention to bring them in by clandestine means was implicit. Meanwhile the Arabs were suspected of bringing in arms from Syria and the Lebanon and in January the current list of suspect vessels included a vessel suspected of carrying arms for Arab personnel. It was foreseen that illegal immigrant vessels might also take part in that activity and the Patrol was cautioned against exposing boarding parties to possible small arms fire. The Foreign Office, the Colonial Office and the Admiralty put it to the Lord Chancellor that his earlier conclusions on Palestine's right of self-defence would justify the arrest of gunrunners on the high seas. His response went no further than that arrest was possible, but he would wish to be consulted again before action was authorised. He added, somewhat gratuitously, that the situation would be different after the mandate ended. Fortunately, an international authority was now available to resolve the problem of arrest on the high seas and the UN made the supply of arms to either side an international offence, which all countries were justified in preventing whether afloat on the high seas or ashore.

The justification for fears that the transition from the mandate would not be a peaceable one was demonstrated when, in March, HMS *St Austell* Bay found the American ship *Flying Angel* at anchor off Tel-Aviv disembarking half-tracked vehicles. Thirteen out of 50 vehicles consigned to Haifa had already been cleared by junior Customs officials and removed inland. But the Palestine Government forbade further unloading and ordered the ship to withdraw from Palestine waters. She was escorted to Port Said, where she entered the Suez Canal. 40 Commando now became engaged in preventing illegal arms being unloaded at Haifa and attempts to obtain British weapons, including many by plausible Jewish males disguised in British uniforms. This duty was recalled in a Royal Marine ditty sung for some years after the campaign in Palestine.

THE LEGAL ISSUES

Shortly after the Flying Angel incident D.1 expressed his frustration with the current rules for arrests. He had noticed that international law allowed arrest on the high seas on grounds of self-defence and quoted two cases where insurgents had been prevented from completing voyages to countries where they intended to support rebellions. His paper hit the nail exactly on the head when arguing that international law was largely a matter of case law and failure to take measures of self-preservation could lead to lack of decided law. Unbeknown to D.1 this was exactly the course of action which the Admiralty favoured earlier. It had, however, been ruled out by the Prime Minister directing that British interests would not be served by trespassing on what little international law there was, not to mention incompatibility with the line taken concerning the Corfu Channel incident. The situation could not be changed. M. Branch judged that the British position on international maritime law should not become too widely known, partially, perhaps, because the Three Mile Limit was not being strictly observed. Indeed, M. Branch was doing its best to keep quiet the fact that the *Warfield* boardings had taken place in International Waters, it was a very sensitive matter politically. So the formal response went no further than restating the principle that in peacetime ships could only be stopped or searched on the High Seas if they were intending to breach international law. D.1's action in raising the matter shows he was not being kept adequately informed. The response may have underestimated the need to take much tried senior commanders into the Admiralty's confidence, explain matters more comprehensively and thus provide a better means of maintaining morale and a sense of purpose amongst their men.

Just at this point the legality of an arrest came before the Judicial Committee of the Privy Council[66] as an appeal by the owner of the *Asya*, intercepted at a very early stage of the patrol, versus Attorney General Palestine. The former alleged that the arrest had been made outside territorial waters but judgement went against him. The Privy Council held that the Mandatory Power was carrying out a common policy the execution of which had been entrusted to it by other powers (originally the Principal Allied Powers Post First World War) and that it was confronted with 'an unlawful invasion of its territory'. Further the Privy Council noted that *Asya* displayed no flag.

Wishing to clarify the situation for future occasions, the Admiralty informally enquired whether the Lord Chancellor now modified his earlier opinion. Not surprisingly the same obstacle was raised as blocked every earlier proposal of this kind – some form of international tribunal such as the International Court of Justice could only give the last word. In any case M. Branch concluded that on the whole the country had more to lose than gain in seeking a revival of formerly enjoyed maritime rights, another possibility which D.1 had advanced.

When forwarding D.1's paper, Flag Officer (Destroyers) had suggested an analysis of the legal situation should be promulgated to the Navy. For the reasons already shown, M. Branch opposed anything of that kind and instead proposed a lecture on the subject at the Royal Naval College Greenwich. At VCNS's direction an analysis was put in hand, but with no urgency, and it took twelve months before a single typed copy of the results was circulated to a few members of the Naval Staff. By then the operation was dead and buried and VCNS did not take a further hand to stop this aspect of 'lessons learnt' going to ground and ensure appearance in a more accessible or permanent form.

After a further twelve months a member of M. Branch, neither a lawyer nor an 'operator', delivered a lengthy talk on maritime international law to the RN Staff Course at Greenwich. Although the course had access to classified material, M. Branch may have seen the presence of students from overseas as necessitating continued caution. Only one paragraph of the script dealt with seaborne illegal immigration into Palestine. This ignored all but one aspect, blandly stating that it was an offence only against municipal law and for that reason arrests could be made only inside Palestine's territorial waters. The 'self-defence' possibility, the effect of the overriding political requirement stated by the Prime Minister, shutting off recourse to the International Court, and the unfortunate coincidence with the Corfu Channel case were all left unmentioned. These were exactly the kind of wider considerations which staff courses exist to make known to students being prepared for management tasks and leadership at the higher levels of their service. Further, municipal law had not covered the situation quite as fully as the lecture implied. It had been the authority under which, at the request of the Palestine Government, the Patrol was able to make arrests, but the legal officials had proved unable to obtain the conviction of those onboard prosecuted for offences against it. Also the Privy Council justified confiscation of a ship on other grounds, which applied inside or outside territorial waters. Thus for one reason or another touch was lost with the many legal 'lessons learnt' and their effect at a time when developments in international relations and institutions increasingly affecting the way in which the Navy did its business.[67]

ARRESTS

On 1 March, HMS *Venus* intercepted the schooner *Rondina 2*. The next arrival, the *Esmeralda*, sailed from Italy, picking up more passengers at Monte Cristo, some being from North Africa. She was reported on Easter Sunday (28 March) by a reconnaissance aircraft 63 miles west of Cape Carmel. HMS *Verulam* reached her target at 1400 and found her flying the Italian flag and displaying the name '*Pepino Savona*' newly painted on a board. Five men thought to be crew members were seen on deck, studiously ignoring the approaching destroyer, but questions put in Italian led to a claim that the ship was bound from Genoa to Tel Aviv with a cargo of empty barrels and pearls. Nevertheless, faces and fingers could be seen through holes in the foremost hatch cover and soon swarms of illegal immigrants burst out on deck and made a dash for the heads, having evidently been cooped up below from the time the aircraft appeared.

The *Verulam* dropped back for shadowing until the illegal vessel's Master called for the destroyer to close again for further consultation. As she came up abreast, the *Esmeralda* put her wheel over and struck the warship a glancing blow, damaging two frames and doing some other minor damage. HMS *Virago* (Lieutenant-Commander I.N.D. Cox RN) and HMS *Venus* joined before darkness fell. With the barometer falling rapidly and the wind increasing to Force 5–6 from the southwest, it soon became clear that the *Esmeralda*'s spokesman was trying every trick to get her taken in tow or boarded on the high seas, despite the vessel being in increasing danger due to rolling scuppers under and with hatches to her holds uncovered. When territorial waters were entered at 0339 the order was given to board her. The *Esmeralda* resisted by violent manoeuvring but fetched up with both ships alongside. The *Verulam*'s boarders had a nasty drop of 10–20 feet as the ships rose and fell in a heavy swell but were all onboard by 0343. *Virago* moved her boarding party down to her Iron Deck and it was across some three minutes after *Verulam*'s party. Although on the previous evening the immigrants appeared ready for a fight, no resistance was encountered and *Verulam* put this down to severe buffeting by the seas and seasickness. The two destroyers drew clear and, the *Esmeralda*'s engine having been sabotaged, *Venus* had her in tow for Haifa by 0430, a very smart piece of work in the prevailing weather conditions.

At 1235 on 12 April an aircraft reported a vessel answering to the description of the *Vivara* suspect listed by Intelligence. By 1503 HMS *Virago* intercepted her thirty-nine miles west of Cape Carmel, and found the vessel to be carrying illegal immigrants and showing the name '*Rina*' but closely resembling the *Vivara*. Singing was at first the only response to messages by loud-hailer but after 30 minutes an English-speaking spokesman announced that there were 810 passengers aboard and the vessel would stop to allow boarding on entering territorial waters. HMS *Pelican* (Captain F.2) embarked Palestine Police representatives and then joined the *Virago*, as did HMS *Verulam*. In the meantime the immigrants sang happily, giving the impression of 'Charabanc trippers' rather than bellicose immigrants. The *Verulam* refrained from issuing warnings, anticipating that the *Rina* might stop or sabotage her engine outside territorial waters, with all the legal complications that might cause. Once inside territorial waters at 2120 the destroyers were ordered to board and, as prearranged, the *Verulam* instructed the *Rina* to stop. She did not immediately do so and *Virago* went alongside her starboard quarter, six men boarded before the two vessels parted company. A few minutes later both destroyers were alongside and the boarders were in control. There were no casualties.

Virago passed her towing wire, moved ahead and had the *Rina* under tow by 2130. Charts showed the vessel had been to Naples and then made her way from the Aegean via Pathos, she was evidently making for Haifa. There appeared to be no doctor amongst the immigrants, two women had given birth and one more baby was on the way. The cruiser HMS *Newcastle*

(Captain S.H. Paton CBE RN) had been recalled from a visit to Tripoli (Lebanon) to help tranship immigrants and the transport *Empire Rival* berthed on her later in the day. *Rina* was placed alongside the *Newcastle* at 2315 and by 0055 immigrants totalling 822 and their baggage had been taken off, searched, sprayed with DDT insecticide and placed onboard *Empire Rival*, which sailed at 0125. Amongst the immigrants were 67 children, including a 3 day old baby. Female searchers failed to arrive and their task had to be undertaken by four selected Chief Petty Officers who were reported to have undertaken this duty successfully and 'with dignity', most of those concerned reappearing 'wreathed in smiles'.

Captain F.2 praised the *Verulam* and *Virago* for a smartly carried-out boarding operation and good ship handling. He had heard of no illegal vessel so easy to deal with, earlier he had been led to believe that propaganda and softening up were essential preliminaries to boarding, but on this occasion the immigrants were cheerful and under such good control that he decided it would do more harm than good.

The situation ashore in Haifa was by now reaching a crescendo and on 22 April Jewish forces mortared the Arab quarter, from whence thousands of refugees were seeking to leave by sea, being attacked as they did so despite protection by 40 Commando RM. 45 Commando R.M. (Lieutenant-Colonel E.C.E. Palmer DSO RM) had to be flown in as reinforcements on 1 and 2 May and on 3 May 42 Commando (Lieutenant-Colonel I.H. Riches DSO RM) arrived by sea, having embarked and sailed from Malta in the LST HMS *Messina* (Lieutenant-Commander T.E. Edwards RN) four hours after being ordered to move. 42 Commando landed at Haifa and then went to Jerusalem and searched vehicles for arms and ammunition, using rocks from the ruins of King Herod's palace to weight 40-gallon drums employed as road blocks. British positions were between the Arabs and the Jews and each night the two sides engaged each other with small arms at increasing intensity the closer the end of the mandate became. When British forces left Jerusalem, 42 Commando moved to Haifa.

HMS *Chevron* returned on 22 April in time to see boats streaming up the coast filled with escaping Arabs. Two days later she arrested the *San Michele*, a modern Italian motor ship, at the three-mile limit and towed her to Cyprus. HMS *Newcastle* was back at Haifa on 24 April for the transhipment of 798 illegal immigrants to the *Empire Rival*. The immigrant ship was put alongside the *Newcastle* at 2255 with the passengers singing, they remained in good humour and the transport sailed at 0030. Food onboard came from UNRRA supplies, some tins were marked 'Best wishes from friends in America', and the passengers were noted as being 'very fit and of a good disposition'.

HMS *Pelican* towed in to Haifa the *Tadorne* carrying 558 very dirty immigrants on 27 April. Once again HMS *Newcastle* had arrived to conduct the transshipment. By now the Arab crew of the port tug had fled and the replacement Jewish crew sabotaged her when a Naval guard arrived onboard for berthing *Tadorne*. This did not result in any delay, since the officer in charge of tug guard simply used an MFV and two of the *Newcastle*'s power boats instead. *Tadorne* was put alongside the Newcastle at 0637 and the transports *Empire Comfort* and *Empire Rival* followed. The last illegal immigrant was off the *Newcastle* by 0939 and the transports sailed for Famagusta. On this occasion a hard core of male and female Jews of 'disreputable' appearance attempted to persuade their compatriots to resist and eventually some of these had to be forced off the *Tadorne* by a boarding party.

HMS *Chieftain* intercepted the *Borea* carrying 243 immigrants on 12 May. *Borea* declined a suggestion that she remain outside territorial waters for 48 hours and would then be free to do as she please. Instead, and unaccountably, her Master opted for diversion, so that on the day that the mandate ended, her passengers were on their way to Cyprus.

21

The Withdrawal

The British Mandate came formally to an end on 15 May 1948. The broad pendant of Commodore Palestine was struck and His Excellency the High Commissioner departed in the cruiser HMS *Euryalus* (Captain C.C. Harvey RN). He was escorted out of Palestine waters by the aircraft-carrier HMS *Ocean* (Vice-Admiral Sir Thomas Troubridge KCB DSO (Flag Officer (Air) and Second-in-Command Mediterranean Station)), commanded by Captain E.M.C. Abel-Smith RN, together with HM Ships *Chevron*, *Childers*, *Volage*, *Pelican* and *Widemouth Bay*. British Army forces then withdrew into the Haifa enclave preparatory to a final departure. By this time the Jews had declared the creation of the state of Israel and the encircling Arab states launched the war they forecast to President Truman almost three years earlier.

In the Haifa area the Israelis had by now eliminated Arab opposition and this made the situation easier for the Royal Marines, who sometimes established a quite good liaison with the Haganah, many of whom had served in the British Army and were by now in undisputed control outside the Haifa enclave. A very large quantity of military equipment was being withdrawn though the port and the main problem became the security of these stores and the Commando's own weapons. Into this difficult scene suddenly intruded the *Pan York* and *Pan Crescent*, whose oil supplies the British authorities had deliberately restricted so they could not voyage from Cyprus to Haifa prior to the final British departure. By painstakingly straining their stock through sludge in their tanks the two ships succeeded in mustering sufficient fuel for the voyage.

At the end of June, the remaining British troops, including both RM Commandos, embarked in four transports, six Landing Ships (Tank), Z-Lighters and a Hospital Ship. The operation was commanded by Vice-Admiral Troubridge flying his flag in the aircraft-carrier HMS *Triumph*. *Triumph*, with 800 and 827 Naval Air Squadrons embarked, arrived at Haifa early on the morning of 29 June, in company with *Volage*, to provide air support. The aircraft-carrier held four Seafire fighter aircraft, each armed with four Rocket Projectiles, at 30 minutes notice for launch whilst RAF aircraft searched for two British army tanks, whose 4/7 Dragoon Guards drivers had been suborned into driving through barbed wire near the airport into Israeli hands. FO(Air) Mediterranean noted that 'those in the know estimated their ill-gotten gains as £5,000 per tank, paid in any desired currency into any bank in the world',[68] others have given a higher estimate. Nothing was seen and so at 0630 the following morning *Triumph* renewed the search, but the objects of their attention had clearly been concealed under cover.

At 1240 on 30 June the General Officer Commanding (Lieutenant-General G.H.A. MacMillan CB CBE DSO MC) and the Air Officer Commanding (Air Commodore W.L. Dawson CBE) stepped into the GOC's launch and departed from Palestine. HMS *Phoebe*, in which they took passage, fired a salute whilst *Triumph*'s aircraft conducted a flypast. There was no relaxation in the security situation in the port of Haifa where fighting between Arabs and Jews continued. A naval doctor was called to the aid of an Arab hit by a sniper on the outskirts of the dock area. Whilst doing so he was wounded by the sniper, who was then dealt with by the Royal Marines. 40 Commando guarded a perimeter which decreased in size as the last remaining British elements departed, withdrawing yard by yard until the final mortar base plate position was on the ramp of the LST HMS *Striker*. Embarkation being complete the force, escorted by two destroyers and one frigate, departed. The CinC stationed a destroyer off the Levant outside territorial waters for some further days in case of developments necessitating naval intervention, including cover for the transportation of the inhabitants of the Cyprus camps to Israel.

22

Summary and Conclusions

THE 1936–39 ARAB REVOLT

Lack of troops and conflicting priorities made it difficult for the War Office to reinforce Palestine at the onset of the two main outbreaks of violence during the 1936–39 Arab revolt. Cruisers and capital ships could reach a scene of action ashore quickly and carry out a very wide range of activities ashore for lengthy periods. (The same could be said of the destroyers at Aden a decade later.) Imperial policing was one of the roles for which the Mediterranean Fleet existed and, in addition to Royal Marine detachments in the larger warships, the Navy maintained a Landing Party in each ship of destroyer or sloop size and upwards, trained to provide military assistance to the civil power ashore. The ships stationed at Haifa 1936–38 were successful in their tasks there and yet remained available, dependent on priorities, both for current operations caused by the Spanish Civil War and also the major naval conflict then possible in consequence of the Abyssinian crisis. There is no better example of the flexibility and utility of naval forces than at Palestine in this era. The requirement to maintain Landing Parties in surface warships ended in the late 1980s and tasks necessitating forces of that kind are now undertaken on a grander scale by amphibious warfare vessels with an embarked force. These are biased to that role and their capability for purely naval warfare is necessarily more limited.

CONCEPT OF OPERATIONS, 1945–48

Interceptions by the Navy were normally the final stage of several layers of interdependent countermeasures.

Intelligence. Comparison of the very comprehensive and detailed summaries circulated by the Cabinet (Official) Illegal Immigration Committee with subsequent events demonstrate that considerable success was achieved in

168

identifying, marking and reporting suspect vessels. This allowed time for efforts by diplomatic means, sometimes successful, to prevent embarkation of immigrants and departure for Palestine. Nevertheless the satisfaction expressed by those in Whitehall concerning the gathering of intelligence was not always felt to quite the same extent by those conducting operations. Good intelligence was particularly necessary to ensure the principle of economy of effort could be observed and air searches tailored to real needs.

Reconnaissance. It was very rare that a ship arrived off the coast without her movements already being tracked and a vessel from the patrol being homed on by an RAF aircraft. Sweeps in the early days by fighter aircraft provided good coverage of large areas but the pilots were handicapped by the navigational limitations which always affect single seat crews. Warwick aircraft were able to cope in this respect, could search further out and track suspects for longer periods, which they did to great effect.

Warships. The patrol provided ships of sufficient capability, power and endurance to keep an effective watch for long periods off a lengthy coast; respond to intelligence reports or air detections or make detections for themselves; and then ensure vessels carrying illegal immigrants were brought into Haifa. The minesweepers were probably the ships which suffered the most strain. Apart from lack of manpower for boarding, rigging tows and keeping the ships going, they were relatively slow ships, although their reciprocating propulsion machinery enabled quick manoeuvring. The turbine-engined sloops were more strongly manned but not easy to take alongside an elusive illegal vessel, being slow to accelerate and lacking stern power, much the same could be said of the frigates. The destroyers (including the 'Hunts') with their speed and power provided the backbone of the Patrol. The Palestine Force was fortunate in that the ships were equipped with well-tried, robust machinery, although the minesweepers sometimes suffered from being overdue for refit. A destroyer Captain who commanded both 'V' and 'Ch'-class destroyers, the latter during the patrol, considered (in 1997) the loss of the slightly higher maximum speed in those modern destroyers was more than made up for by outstanding reliability. Great praise is due to engine room crews for maintaining high levels of serviceability for lengthy periods many hundreds of miles from dockyard support.

COMMAND, CONTROL AND COMMUNICATIONS (C3)

The presence of a Flag Officer with an operational staff and a cruiser on the spot were essential to the Palestine Patrol getting away to an efficient start in 1945. The former provided moment to moment control and the right level of representation to ensure not only that the Navy met the Palestine Government's requirements but also to co-ordinate naval arrangements with those of the other services, the Palestine Government, the Palestine Police and the CinC at Malta. This task could not be undertaken by FOLEM, who was tied to Egypt by the work of renegotiating the Anglo-Egyptian Treaty and other tasks in his extensive area.

The cruiser ensured the availability and sufficiency of effective, well run naval communications, which could not otherwise have been provided so promptly. HMS *Superb*'s experience and the problems, which later beset the communications station set up ashore, demonstrated the extent to which comprehensive facilities and adequate experienced signals staffs were necessary. A type of ship less well equipped in these respects, or one only periodically available through undertaking patrols herself, could never have coped with SNO(A)'s communications load.

Events soon demonstrated the need for arrangements whereby the air and naval searches were more efficiently co-ordinated. With shortage of Maritime Reconnaissance aircraft making the use of other categories necessary, AOC Palestine could scarcely be expected to pass operational control of his maritime operations to SNO(A). Strangely there is no evidence of an RAF Liaison Officer being attached to SNO(A) and that would have helped. Until the task became lengthy the setting up of a small Maritime HQ ashore, collocated with the First Division HQ at Mount Carmel, was not, in terms of expense and manpower, sufficiently justified. With JHQ Jerusalem already operating, CS.1 chose instead to add an RN liaison officer to the Army, Royal Air Force and other staffs already there. The Navy thereby benefited from the expertise of an existing organisation which also greatly assisted in the provision of intelligence and information from the Government of Palestine. Later on, the provision of a Naval communications element at the First Division Headquarters meant the cruiser's communications facilities could be dispensed with. This was as well since apart from being needed elsewhere on the Mediterranean Station, she was a highly attractive target for sabotage. But the difficulties which were immediately experienced, highlighted during two arrests, show that for at least some time this new arrangement was less efficient, due to requirements for resources, in particular supervision and maintenance, being under estimated or not allowed. Use of a cruiser for transhipments also proved necessary from time to time and particularly in the last phase of the operation when the Jews were taking over control of Haifa.

After the cruiser departed, Captains (D) soon met the difficulty, which so often affected that post, of being saddled with scarcely compatible functions – senior naval officer ashore and afloat, commanding their Flotilla and also their own Destroyer Leader. Events demonstrated that the senior naval officer exercising tactical control needed to be permanently at Haifa and could not be intermittently in less good touch at sea. The introduction of Commodore Palestine became essential and by the time the post was instituted this rank was the right level for dealing with other commanders and authorities. An alternative might have been to bring each resident Captain (D) ashore in turn, to act in the Senior Naval capacity. However, major operations such as the *Warfield* necessitated the presence of a suitably senior and experienced officer, preferably one who knew his team of men and ships, in command at sea.

SECURITY

The Second World War had seen the start of attempts by swimmers and divers to attach explosives to ships in harbour or at anchor and attacks made by Haganah on Police craft and evidence gained from intelligence demonstrated the threat to warships at Haifa. Rigorous precautions were necessary and with the many sentries needed and constant interruptions by deterrent explosive charges, a night at Haifa was always an arduous experience. Fortunately the resident cruiser could be dispensed with by the time the risks outweighed her usefulness. The ultimate countermeasure would have been for the patrol to remain constantly underway, but at a time before replenishment at sea became readily available the additional consumption of oil fuel would have caused difficulties. Precautions had also to be taken in Cyprus and, as has been mentioned, a transport was indeed attacked and damaged whilst at Famagusta. Years later the Master of the *Warfield* told the former Commanding Officer of *Childers* that the ambition of the Palyam had been to sink a destroyer in Haifa harbour. Events during the Palestine Patrol revitalised the attention given self-protection against underwater attack in harbour. In particular, Buster Crabb's efforts enabled ships' own teams to conduct underwater searches to protect their ship's bottom. 'Shallow Water Diving', as it became known, proved so useful in this and other ways that his work led to it being adopted for use throughout the Navy.

For the Navy there was nothing similar to the deception practised by Jews serving with the British Army in France, Italy and Greece. Nevertheless those activities, each in its own way, illustrate the need for security precautions against service personnel becoming subverted, particularly by 'causes', and also measures to retain their support. Where troops are present, there are also supplies of arms, food and other stores and the presence of occupying British forces, including a Palestinian element, in Italy and Greece made holdings vulnerable to theft and other forms of misdirection.

LEGAL REGIME

Whether or not employing firearms, illegal entry by large numbers of foreigners with the intention of occupying territory could well be held to be an invasion. A self-governing country could have claimed a right of self-defence under the United Nations Charter but, under the mandate, the position of Palestine was less clear-cut in this respect. Lack of legal precedent, i.e. of case law, swayed policy at a time when international law was becoming increasingly dominant. The Corfu Channel incident also had a malign influence since the British had to remain above reproach whilst calling for Albania to be brought to justice. Despite the appreciation during the recent war of the need to keep sailors well informed there was little appreciation of a need to explain matters better within the Navy.

REFOULEMENT

Refoulement was no sudden reaction to the *President Warfield* but had its genesis in the likelihood of accommodation for illegal immigrants in Cyprus being filled to overflowing and the need to check embarkation and voyages from Italy. The Mediterranean Fleet was reinforced in plenty of time to provide the escorts necessary for vessels returning illegal immigrants. However, the success of refoulement was dependent on the ability to disembark immigrants once they had been taken back whence they came. There needed to be agreement that returned immigrants would be accepted back and that force could be used to put them ashore. In the case of the *Warfield* passengers the Ambassador had given warnings to the effect that the second condition would not be met. The odium attracted by the episode was another, although not conclusive, factor in refoulement not being tried a second time. Refoulement to Italy was briefly considered but also felt to be impracticable. In any case after the *Warfield*, obstacles to the embarkation of illegal immigrants in France and Italy became more effective. This caused the larger illegal immigrant vessels to be diverted to Bulgaria and Romania to embark their passengers and there was not the slightest possibility of those nations agreeing to accept returned immigrants.

Refoulement needed a greater degree of support not only from nations directly involved but also those whose public voiced views from the sidelines. Nevertheless the firm action taken with the *Warfield* passengers and the possibility of further refoulement seem to have played a part in causing the Jewish Agency to discourage violent opposition thereafter. Diversion to Cyprus became seen as a more satisfactory compromise. The British, for their part, succeeded in housing the numbers involved without, as might have been expected, allegations of operating 'concentration camps'.

In any case as 1947 gave way to 1948 other developments made the necessity for refoulement less and less pressing.

NAVAL PUBLIC RELATIONS

The press were always responsive to events in Haifa but in the whole period covered by this account on only about three occasions were press representatives present onboard an arrested illegal vessel. A British Press representative was present onboard a warship during the *Lochita* arrest and wrote a responsible and supportive article which appeared on the front page of his newspaper. The *Daily Telegraph* naval correspondent also offered to write an article describing the difficulties being encountered by the Navy. But the attention of the Press was in any case more taken up by the murderous activities of Jewish terrorists ashore, not to mention the many other crises which followed the end of the war. (In today's circumstances this aspect would be very different, with a more critical media demanding presence onboard warships and hiring aircraft to observe from overhead.) Even so the activities of the patrol were increasingly brought to the notice of the public. Although when arrest was resisted and violent methods had to be used, the first blows were always struck by the immigrants, friends and relations of the naval personnel involved were amongst those who queried whether the Navy should be involved in preventing persecuted Jews reaching their homeland. This activity had inevitable overtones of the recent activities of Nazi organisations. For many years to come there will in some quarters be enduring bitterness and adverse, often misleading, comment. Nevertheless, the Navy's competence and humanity meant that the Service escaped criticism on the scale that might have been reached.

RN PERSONNEL

This narrative cannot convey all the demands and dangers of boarding operations, the effects of weather and dark, the tempo and need to seize fleeting opportunities. Despite the difficulties and risks of clambering on to evasive vessels under way, then meeting well equipped opposition and sometimes ending up in the sea, the only naval fatalities were through inadvertent discharge of a firearm in 1939 and the capsize of a boat in 1947, neither a direct result of opposition by crew or immigrants. Each of those incidents illustrates the normal hazards of naval activities, even before opposition is encountered. The training provided in the 1946–48 period at the RM Training Centre, Ghain Tuffieha was essential to safe and successful opposed boarding operations. Throughout the operation, lasting two and a half years, a very high order of efficiency, resourcefulness, discipline and seamanship was demonstrated by ships companies composed of regulars, time expired regulars held back by the war, reservists, Hostilities Only and National Service personnel. This was despite all the turbulence caused by demobilisation of individuals and reductions in manning being in full swing. The majority had been through an arduous war and in 1945 the Commander-in-Chief Mediterranean Fleet had expressed the hope that it would now be possible to show them the better side of naval life. A Senior Rate serving in a destroyer he regarded as exceptionally well led, recalled morale as low and only maintained by the diversions organised when away from Palestine.

In consequence of the recent war the patrol was, in the main, manned by very experienced officers. This particularly applied to the Commanding Officers, a large proportion of whom had served for long periods in destroyers, and the Commander-in-Chief also insisted that those appointed as his ship Captains should be experienced ship handlers. In this they excelled and despite the hazards caused by the lack of stability in a great many illegal immigration vessels and their evasive manoeuvres, no interception or arrest ever led to a collision which resulted in one capsizing or sinking or being damaged to an extent which caused loss of life or serious injuries.

Only the toughest and fittest Jews survived the concentration camps. If the effects of this element seemed unreasonable and untrustworthy, it was because they had learnt guile and the brutalisation to which they had been subjected made them determined to overcome what seemed to be unreasonable opposition to travel to a safer homeland. Despite their knowledge of what the Jews had suffered from Hitler, members of ships' companies might be expected to be antagonised by immigrants who showed them so much hostility and whose compatriots ashore were killing and kidnapping British servicemen. Nevertheless, contemporary accounts show that whilst contemptuous of the squalor, members of Boarding Parties remained fair minded, were not given to excessive force, and once opposition ceased did what they could to ease the lot of the immigrants, provide first aid and make friends. During 50th anniversary reunions of illegal vessel crews in Israel in 1997, the Royal Navy's unique forbearance was acknowledged and praised.

THE NAVY'S TASKS

Palestine's geographic position and the presence of Arab nations on all her land borders meant seaborne immigration became by far the most practicable route for reaching the Promised Land. The naval counter encompassed a great many linked operational functions. Some arrests were made by single ships, others by several ships working together. In the case of the *Warfield* and the *Pan*s a considerable force was employed. A significant proportion of the Navy was involved for a lengthy period yet there were no disasters and few failures and the Service emerges with great credit. For no one is this more true than the individual members of boarding parties, whose part was summarised by the CinC Mediterranean Fleet in the autumn of 1947:

> The success of the boarding operation is largely dependent on the ability of the boarding party in getting over in a large body at the first moment of impact; subsequently it depends on their courage, resourcefulness and good temper in the face of a determined and provocative opposition. ... their behaviour and forbearance in the face of heavy odds won the day in all these operations.

Notes

1. Historical background largely from N. Bentwich *Palestine* (Ernest Benn, London, 1946) page 64. This balanced work, written in the 1930s, avoids the prejudices of later accounts.
2. The word 'Zionism' was probably first used by one Nathan Birbaum in articles written in the 1880s. Theodor Herzl adopted the idea in his book *Der Judenstaat* published in Vienna in 1896.
3. H.A.L. Fisher *A History of Europe* (Edward Arnold, London, 1936). Lloyd George invited Fisher, a distinguished university historian, to join his Cabinet as President of the Board of Education 1916–1922. He opposed the Mandate.
4. The Balfour Declaration was written into the British Mandate, despite the strong objections of the Arabs.
5. The Wailing Wall is sacred to the Jews as part of the Temple and to the Arabs as the Western face of the platform of the Dome of the Rock, from which Mahomet is believed to have ascended to Paradise. The situation remains very sensitive, as illustrated by serious disturbances in 1996, and more recently.
6. White Paper issued May 1930.
7. Text of signal 2045/5/10/34 (i.e. a signal sent at 2045 GMT on 5 October 1934) from Admiralty to Commander-in-Chief, Mediterranean Fleet (Sir W.W. Fisher):

> Palestine Government have asked whether one of HM Ships could be detached to patrol the coast north and south of Haifa in order to discourage organised attempts at illegal immigration. Admiralty are not prepared to agree to a ship being specially detailed, but arrangements should be made for ships visiting Haifa to keep, on their way to and from ports, a special lookout for suspicious vessels and if fuel and other circumstances permit, to make a short detour along the coast for this purpose. The movements of any suspicious vessels should be reported to the Palestine authorities, the detailed arrangements being made locally. No other action should be taken. The responsibility of stoppage or seizure if vessels are within territorial waters rests with the Palestinian authorities.

8. The term 'sloop' dates from the age of sail but was adopted in the First World War for vessels built for mine-sweeping and anti-submarine operations. Post-war sloops were given increasingly heavily gun armaments but they remained smaller and slower than contemporary destroyers, besides not being equipped with torpedo tubes. In time of peace they were very useful for independent operations in remote parts of the Empire.
9. J.H. Godfrey papers in Naval Historical Branch (Naval Staff Directorate).
10. So called because they wanted a revision of the Mandate and the absorption of the territory East of the Jordan into Palestine.

11. The organisation known as Mossad since the establishment of the State of Israel is not connected with the Mossad of earlier times.
12. Denezhko claimed a 7,000-ton steamer; on the previous day he had sunk a Turkish schooner which he claimed as a 'tanker' and before his patrol ended he was to claim two more 'tankers', which appear to have been totally imaginary. J. Rohwer, *Allied Submarine Attacks of WWII, European Theatre of Operations* (Greenhill Books, London, 1997).
13. Lord Moyne was a man of many talents and a great friend of Winston Churchill. He left the House of Commons before the war but was called back into wartime government by Churchill, serving first as Secretary of State for the Colonies. The post of Minister Resident in the Near and Middle East had been found necessary to provide sufficiently senior political representation in those theatres of war. The Stern Gang had been rejuvenated by the arrival of Mr Menachim Begin. Moyne's murder appalled the Zionist leadership. Churchill had done much for the Jews when Colonial Secretary in 1921 and he was continuing to lend support despite a host of very pressing tasks.
14. President Truman's letter dated 24 July 1945, to Prime Minister Churchill. By the time of delivery Mr Attlee was in office and attending the Potsdam Conference at which Truman was also present. Attlee. responded promptly on 31 July 1945 and a later (31 August 1945) letter from Truman confirms they had discussed the subject in the margins of the conference. The number of Jews in the United States is estimated at 250,000 in 1870. By 1936 it rose to 4.5 million. The Jewish vote was, and remains, very significant in the calculations of US politicians, no more so than in the immediate aftermath to the Second World War. Although in the United Kingdom Jewish voters did not enjoy similar influence, a substantial proportion of Members of Parliament in 1945–1948 were Jewish. The Under-Secretary of State for Foreign Affairs 1945–51 has recorded the strength with which they pressed the Zionist cause and the difficulties this caused the Foreign Secretary (Mr E. Bevin).
15. CO 537 series.
16. The famous 'Military Branch'. A branch of the Admiralty secretariat serving as the intermediary between Ministers and the 'Naval Staff', the section of the Admiralty, which under the Chief of the Naval Staff handled plans, policy and operational matters. 'M. Branch', as it was known, advised on political and financial matters and liaised with other Government Departments. It was manned by the Admiralty branch of the Civil Service and predated the naval manned 'Naval Staff', being in origin the secretarial staff of the Lord High Admiral when that office was executed afloat. The functions of 'M. Branch' continued within the 'Navy Department' after the unification of the Service Ministries in 1964 but mainly passed to the central 'Defence Staff' when a further reorganisation took place in 1985.
17. For use by the Head of the Jardine Matheson company as a means of conveyance for visits to his firm's offices at Hong Kong and Treaty Ports on the China coast. Later the Duke of Westminster owned her.
18. The former Lieutenant-Commander Kenworthy MP who served in the Royal Navy until the end of the First World War, distinguishing himself as a founder member of the Naval Staff's Naval Plans Division. He became prominent in the House of Commons representing the Labour Party until 1931 and later inheriting a title. At this time he had a good deal to say in the House of Lords.
19. ADM1/18584
20. Three Cunninghams were concerned with Mediterranean and Palestine matters. This surname was shared by the First Sea Lord (Admiral of the Fleet Sir Andrew Cunningham who became Viscount Hyndhope), his brother the High

Commissioner (General Sir Alan Cunningham) and the unrelated Commander-in-Chief Mediterranean (Admiral Sir John Cunningham) who succeeded to the post of First Sea Lord in the autumn of 1946.

21. Tennant was no stranger to difficult tasks: in late May 1940 he had been dispatched to organise 'the Dunkirk end' of the evacuation of the BEF, a poisoned chalice which he had survived to return to command and survive the sinking of the *Repulse*. In 1944, commanding the Levant Station, he was in naval command at the Allied re-occupation of Athens, which was opposed only by the Greek Communists and during the summer of 1945 he had the difficult task of soothing both the French and Syrian authorities.

22. Whilst corresponding to the arrangements at the time the terms used were not then employed but are those in current use (see BR1806 *The Fundamentals of British Maritime Doctrine*) as they are more readily understandable.

23. 'Caïque' is simply the word in the Eastern Mediterranean for a boat. Craft so described were built generally of wood, being 100–180 feet long with, at this time, sail giving way to engine.

24. Field Marshal Lord Gort VC GCB CBE DSO and 2 Bars MVO MC was in the late stages of a terminal illness, to which he succumbed in 1946.

25. Lieutenant Wells-Cole qualified as a standard diver (ie hard helmet) and for shallow water during his long gunnery course.

26. On one occasion in the first half of 1946, a pro-Zionist MP (and later Cabinet Minister) was told by the Jewish Agency of their plans for an act of sabotage and he consulted Mr J. Strachey MP, Under-Secretary of State for Air and a member of the Defence Committee of the Cabinet. Strachey seriously questioned his Government's policy on Palestine and gave his agreement: bridges across the Jordan were blown up by the Haganah in June 1946 and although no one was killed the Army's communication routes were impeded.

27. The British man-in-the-street first learnt of the hitherto obscure very left-wing pro-Zionist Professor Laski following his call, during the 1945 election campaign, for a Labour Government, if elected, to submit its programme to the Party Executive Committee, as is the practice with Communist Parties. After the election it was made clear to him by Mr Attlee that he should not attempt any further interference.

28. Captain M. Richmond DSO OBE RN had been relieved as D.3 by Captain W.H. Selby DSC RN on 5 December 1945; the next five months of the *Saumarez's* life were to be very testing.

29. The choice of the names of two Panama ports, *Balboa* and *Colon*, for the ex-Flower Class corvettes obtained from Canada was evidently to help disguise them as Panamanian vessels.

30. ADM1/19615

31. In civilised accommodation with internationally approved standards of lifesaving equipment, neither of which applied in the vessels plying the illegal immigrant trade.

32. 71,000 between 1933 and 1945, according to Martin Gilbert, *Atlas of the Arab–Israeli Conflict* (Oxford University Press, New York 1994). This figure was exceeded only by the USA and USSR, with approximately 250,000 apiece.

33. The Fifteenth Cruiser Squadron had become the First Cruiser Squadron

34. This apparent discrepancy was subsequently found to be due to the phenomenon whereby a frame aerial taking bearings of an airborne trailing aerial gives the reading as the point where the projected line of trail of the aerial meets the ground.

35. Personal recollections of the late Captain P.S. Hicks-Beach OBE RN in 1997. He was concerned to keep the passengers interested. All that he had to say rings

true, besides being very able and excellent company in any circumstances, Hicks-Beach possessed tremendous style.

36. ADM1/19615
37. Large flat-topped low-powered lighters manned by Royal Army Service Corps crews and intended for ferrying troops during amphibious and inshore operations.
38. J. Williams *The Algerines* (J.F. Williams, 1995).
39. The *Athina*'s radio operator apparently hid his radio so the rescue parties could not find it. There is also some suggestion of a Haganah post on Sirina. Reports from the warships make no mention of any search and a senior member of the *Chevron* party could not recall the subject ever coming up.
40. ADM1/20630
41. An encounter recalled with pleasure by the erstwhile Master of the *Ulua* in 1997.
42 ADM1/20642
43. ADM1/20643
44 Ibid.
45 Personal recollections of Lieutenant-Commander E. Ravenscroft RN.
46. Sloops, 'Hunt'-class escort destroyers and corvettes were combined with frigates such as *Whitsand Bay* into a common 'frigate' type in 1947.
47. When acknowledging the situation with the sailing of the *Warfield*, M. Bidault remarked to Mr Duff Cooper that this was not a suitable raison d'etre for a ministerial crisis which would only bring down a government unlikely to last a more than few weeks anyway.
48. In a 1997 television programme concerning the voyage filmed and shown in Israel, a man claiming to have held the axe said: 'If he needed a chopping, he would get it'.
49. In May 1988 the *Sunday Times* magazine account of the arrest of the *President Warfield* contained the following:

> In a cloud of tear gas, British commandos fought their way onboard and took over the wheelhouse. The boarding party opened fire in all directions. Bodies piled up on deck. A 15-year-old orphan was killed outright and two American Jewish sailors died of their wounds.

50. The Palestine Police report listed three male immigrants dead (including Bernstein who died after reaching hospital). The 28 immigrants (10 males, 17 females and 1 child) in need of hospital treatment were sent to the Government Hospital at Haifa. Only 7 were found to have serious injuries and the remainder, accompanied by 34 relatives, were then sent to the Atlit clearance camp.
51. Those in the *Warfield*'s after steering compartment did in fact possess a compass.
52. Lieutenant Shallow soon left HMS *Childers* for flying training and after obtaining his pilot's wings was killed in an aircraft accident.
53. Former Vichy official, became Free French supporter and much later President of France.
54. The Colombian authorities are said to have dismissed their representative in Paris for his involvement.
55. ADM1/20684
56. Ibid.
57. Ibid.
58. Ibid.
59. *Ocean Vigour* : 622 men 544 women 246 children
Runnymede Park : 650 men 550 women 197 children
Empire Rival : 604 men 591 women 290 children

Some of the children were Hungarians whose parents had remained in Hungary and now made enquiries seeking their return. The men were kept in 'cages' and escorted when outside. Women and children were free to come and go onboard.

60. CO537
61. ADM1/20730
62. A 'Bay'-class frigate fitted out as a CinC's yacht which had the role of substitute flagship. She carried a reduced armament a twin 4-inch gun mounting and two 40mm Bofors Guns.
63. Since Royal Marines were borne only in cruisers and not the smaller ships, and the *Ajax*'s marines did not reach *President Warfield*, this is probably the only occasion any Royal Marine boarded an illegal immigration vessel during an interception or an arrest.
64. A wartime anti-torpedo device whose effectiveness was debatable, mainly because it reduced the speed of the ship so equipped.
65. And indeed on the Arab population – on 13 December, the Agency had denounced acts of reprisal and had restricted Haganah to defence of Jewish settlements.
66. The Judicial Committee acts as the Supreme Court for British territories which lack their own Supreme Courts, which was the case in Palestine.
67. Interestingly, during the uprisings which started in the 1950s, the French rulers of Algeria took firmer action against suspected gun runners. Naval vessels were empowered to intercept suspected vessels within 12 miles of the Algerian coast and take them in to be searched. These measures were announced openly. The author observed two destroyers intercepting a sizeable merchant ship in early December 1960 – from the bridge of HMS *Verulam*.
68. ADM1/21108. The tanks were Comets but lines which found their way into a Naval report took them to be the earlier Churchills and ran:

> Half a million for a Churchill
> Bring along the crew as well
> Haganah will make you Captains
> Better pay than IZL

ANNEXES AND APPENDICES

Annex A:

Illegal Immigrant Vessels

(**Note:** Appendices 1–4 do not include vessels unknown to the naval authorities at the time.)

APPENDIX 1: 1934–APRIL 1939

Date	Vessel Name	Sailed From	Number Embarked	Outcome
1934				
– –	VELOS	–	–	Landed
1937				
– Dec.	ARTEMISSA	Greece	120	Landed at Tantura
1938				
– Jun.	ARTEMISSA	Greece	386	Landed at Tantura
19 Oct.	ARTEMISSA	Italy	220	Landed at Tantura
– –	ELLI	Romania	244+	Landed at Natanya
18 Dec.	CHEPO	Romania	734	Landed
1939				
– Feb.	ARTEMISSA	Romania	237	Ship and 17 immigrants arrested
– –	KATINA	Romania	1250	Landing interrupted by warship after 600 reached shore
– –	ATRATO	Italy	386	Landed
23 Mar.	SANDU	Romania	269	Arrested and returned
– Apr.	KATINA	Romania	650	Landing interrupted
1 Apr.	ASTIR	Romania	724	Arrested and returned
– Apr.	AGHIOS NICOLAOS	Romania	750	Intercepted but may have returned later
11 Apr.	ASSIMI	Greece	369	Arrested and returned
– Apr.	Small schooner	–	176	Arrested
22 Apr.	AGHIA ZONI P	–	600	218 immigrants arrested

APPENDIX 2: PERIOD OF ROYAL NAVY PATROLS IN 1939

Date	Vessel Name	Sailed From	Number Embarked	Outcome	HM Ship
2 Jun.	LIESEL	Romania	906	Intercepted	PANGBOURNE
– Jun.	MARSIS		385	Intercepted	IMPERIAL
1 Jul.	LAS PERLAS	Romania	370	Intercepted	IVANHOE
7 Jul.	ex-ASSIMI	Greece	248	Arrested on landing	-
28 Jul.	COLORADO	Romania	–	Intercepted	IMPERIAL

APPENDIX 3: CESSATION OF ROYAL NAVY PATROLS, 1939–40

Date	Vessel Name	Sailed From	Number Embarked	Outcome
1939				
19 Aug.	AGHIOS NICOLAOS	Romania	800	Landed
23 Aug.	PARITA	Romania	800	Landed and arrested
– Aug.	DORA	Holland	500	Landed
1 Sep.	TIGER HILL	Romania	1500	Landed and arrested
19 Sep.	NOEMIJULA	Romania	1136	Entered Haifa harbour
– –	RUDMITCHAR	Bulgaria	3–400	Three voyages bringing 3–400 First voyage 297 found drifting in open boats.
1940				
8 Jan.	RUDMITCHAR	–	800	Landed
17 Jan.	HILDA		729	Intercepted by Contraband Service
– Jan.	DELPA II	–	224	Not known
9 Feb.	SAKARYA	Turkey	2612	Arrested by Boarding Party
20 Nov.	PACIFIC MILOS	Danube	1888	Arrested and transferred to PATRIA for deportation to Mauritius
21 Nov.	ATLANTIC	–	1771	Held with PATRIA survivors
– –	DARIEN	Romania	878	Detained at Atlit Camp until 1942

APPENDIX 4: VESSELS FROM BULGARIA AND ROMANIA TO TURKEY, 1944

Date	Name	Departure	Number Embarked	Outcome
– Mar.	DARIEN B	Romania	800	Landed
– Mar.	ILCAH A	Romania	410	Landed
– Apr.	MARITZA A	Romania	266	Landed
– May	MARITZA B	Romania	318	Landed
– Jul.	KAZBEK	–	517	Landed
– Aug.	MORENA	–	309	Landed
5 Aug.	MEFCURA	–	394	Sunk – 5 saved
– Aug.	BULBUL	–	410	Landed with 5 saved from MEFCURA
– Nov.	SALHEDDIN	–	547	Landed
– Dec.	TOUROS	–	958	Landed

APPENDIX 5: 1945 PRIOR TO START OF ROYAL NAVY PATROLS

Date	Vessel Name	Hebrew Name	Description	Sailed From	Number Embarked	Outcome
28 Aug.	SIRIUS	DALIN	Fishing Vessel (FV) 170 tons	Italy	35	Landed at Caesarea
4 Sep.	NETTUNO A	NATAN A	50 tons	Italy	79	Landed at Caesarea
9 Sep.	GABRIELA	–	50 tons	Greece	40	Landed at Caesarea
19 Sep.	PIETRO A	–	150 tons	Italy	168	Landed at Shefayim
1 Oct.	NETTUNO B	NATAN B	50 tons	–	73	Landed at Shefayim
26 Oct.	PIETRO B	–	150 tons	Italy	174	Landed at Shefayim

APPENDIX 6: DURING PERIOD OF ROYAL NAVY PATROLS, 1945–48

Date	Vessel Name	Hebrew Name	Description	Sailed From	Number Embarked	Outcome	Warship
1945							
23 Nov.	DIMITRIOS	BEREL KATZENELSON	Motor vessel (MV) 170 tons	Greece	221	20 arrested	PEACOCK
25 Dec.	MARIE	HANNAH SZENESH	Steel trawler 250 tons	Italy	254	Not intercepted	–
1946							
7 Jan.	RONDINA	ENZO SERENI	Wooden MV 550 tons	Italy	908	Intercepted	TALYBONT
25/26 Mar.	KISMET ADALIA	WINGATE	Sail and motor built 1899 144 tons	Italy	248	Intercepted	CHEVRON
27 Mar.	ASYA	TEL HAI	Turkish vessel 430 tons	France	748	Intercepted	CHEQUERS
13 May	SMYRNI	MAX NORDAU	Motor caique 761 tons	Romania	1662	Intercepted	JERVIS
18 May	FEDE	DOV HOS	Motor schooner 600 tons	Italy	1041	Intercepted	CHARITY
	and FENICE	E . GOLOMB	Motor schooner 298 tons	Italy			
7 Jun.	AGHIOS ANDREAS	HAVIVA REIK	Motor caique 140 tons	Greece	464	Intercepted	SAUMAREZ
25 Jun.	COLON (ex-BEAUHARNOIS)	JOSIAH WEDGWOOD	Improved FLOWER Class corvette 970 tons	Italy	1278	Intercepted	VENUS
1 Jul.	AKBEL	BIRIA	Old Turkish wooden caique 284 tons	Belgium	1001	Intercepted	VIRAGO

Date	Ship name	Hebrew name	Description	Flag	Tonnage	Action	Intercepting vessel
29 Jul.	BALBOA (ex NORSYD)	HAGANAH	Improved FLOWER Class corvette 970 tons	Yugoslavia	2760	Intercepted	VENUS
31 Jul.	HOCHELAGA	HACHAJAL-HATVRI YAGUR	Steamer built 1900 628 tons	Holland	497	Boarded	SAUMAREZ
11 Aug.	SAGOLEM		Turkish aux MV 255 tons	France	758	Intercepted	BRISSENDEN
12 Aug.	ARIC SAIAM	HENRIETTE SZOLD	Turkish caique	?	535	Intercepted	VENUS
12 Aug.	AVANTI	KATRIEL YAFFE	Brigantine 550 tons	Italy	615	Intercepted	VOLAGE
14 Aug.	SAN SISSIMO	KAF GIMEL YORDEI HASIRA	Coaster jury rig. 300 tons	Italy	784	Intercepted	TALYBONT
16 Aug.	ISLE-DE-LA-ROSE	AMIRAM SHOCHET (IDEROS)	Aux schooner 150 tons	Italy	183	Landed	–
2 Sep.	FEDE II	ARBA HIRUYOT	ex-FEDE	Italy	997	Intercepted	CHILDERS
21 Sep.	ADRIANA or ARIELLA	PALMACH	Wooden motor barquentine 300 tons	Italy	605	Intercepted	ROWENA
18 Oct.	ALMA (ex FENICE)	BRACHA FULD	Steel schooner 298 tons	Italy	816	Intercepted	CHEQUERS
30 Oct.	SAN DIMITRIO	LATRUN	Steamer built 1871. 733 tons	France	1279	Intercepted	CHIVALROUS
24 Nov.	LOCHITA	KNESSSET ISRAEL	Steamer built 1889. 1870 tons	Yugoslavia	3914	Intercepted	HAYDON
9 Dec.	ATHINA	RAFIAH	MV built 1898 273 tons	Yugoslavia	815	Sank	–

Contd

187

1947							
8 Feb.	MERICA	LA NEGEV	Wooden aux barquentine built 1875, 292 tons	France	664	Intercepted	CHIEFTAIN
16 Feb.	SAN MIGUEL	HAMA'APIL HA'ALMONI	Steam ship built 1876, 472 tons	France	913	Intercepted	WELFARE St AUSTELL BAY
27 Feb.	ULUA	HAIM ARLOSOROFF	Ex-US Coastguard cutter, 898 tons	Sweden and Italy	1416	Intercepted	CHIEFTAIN
8 Mar.	ABRIL	BEN HECHT	Built as steam yacht, 753 tons	France	601	Intercepted	CHIEFTAIN
12 Mar.	SUSANNAH	SHABTAI LUSINSKY	Aux schooner 400 tons	Italy	838	No interception	–
29 Mar.	SAN PHILLIPO	MOLEDET	Steamer, 71 yrs old, 749 tons	Italy	1577	Intercepted	CHARITY
13 Apr.	GUARDIAN	THEODOR HERZL	Steamer built 1907, 1768 tons	France	2623	Intercepted	St BRIDE'S BAY
23 Apr.	GALATA	SHEAR YUSHJV	Turkish coastal steamer.	Italy	773	Intercepted	CHEVIOT
16 May	TRADE WINDS	HATIKVAH	50 year old former US revenue cutter, 500 tons	Italy	1420	Intercepted	VENUS
23 May	ORIETTA (or AGHA) ORIENTE)	LOCHAME-HAGETAOTH	3 masted schooner, 400 tons	Italy	1459	Intercepted	BRISSENDEN

Contd

Date	Name	Former Name	Type	Destination	Tons	Status	Interceptor
29 May	ANAL	YEHUDA HALEVI	Former Shetland Is steamer. 253 tons	Algeria and Sicily	399	Intercepted	TALYBONT
18 Jul.	PRESIDENT WARFIELD	EXODUS 1947	Chesapeake steamer	France	1814	Intercepted	–
27 Jul.	BRUNHA	YOD DALET HALALEI GESHER HAZIV	3 masted schooner	France	684	Intercepted	ESPIEGLE
28 Jul.	LUCIANO M	SHIVAT ZION	Auxiliary caique	Algeria	398	Intercepted	CHIVALROUS WIDEMOUTH BAY PROVIDENCE
27 Sep.	FERIDA	AF-AL-PE-CHEN	USN Mk II LCT 9 (LCT 256)	Italy	446	Intercepted	TALYBONT
2 Oct.	PADUCAH	GEULAH	Cross Channel steamer 915 tons	Bulgaria	1385	Intercepted	CHAPLET CHEVIOT
2 Oct.	NORTHLAND	MEDINAT HAJEHUDIM	US Coastguard cutter. 1273 tons	Bulgaria	2664	As above	–
15 Nov.	RAFFELUCE	KADIMA	Auxiliary schooner 300 tons	Italy	794	Intercepted	VENUS
16 Nov.	ALBERTINA	ALIYAH	Motor caique. 100–150 tons	France	187	No interception	–
4 Dec.	MARIA ANNICK (or MARIE)	HAPORTZIM	Auxiliary schooner 50 tons	France	167	No interception	–

Contd

Date	Ship	Hebrew name	Type	Country	Tons	Status	Interceptor
22 Dec.	MARIA GIOVANNI	KAF TET BENOVEMBER	3 masted aux schooner	France	677	Intercepted	VERULAM
22 Dec.	KARAGO	LO TAFCHIDUNU	Schooner	Italy	881	Intercepted	CHEQUERS
29 Dec.	ARCHIMEDES	UNITED NATIONS	Aux schooner.	Italy	537	No interception	-
1948							
1 Jan.	PAN CRESCENT and PAN YORK	ATZMAUTH KIBBUTZ GALYOT	Banana ships, Both 4570 tons	Bulgaria	7557 / 7612	Intercepted	WHITSAND BAY / CARDIGAN BAY
31 Jan.	SYLVIA STARITA	LAMED HEI GIBOREI KFAR ETZION	Auxiliary schooner.	Italy	280	Intercepted	CHILDERS
10 Feb.	CICILIO	YERUSHALAIM HANETZURA	MV 678 tons	Italy	678	Intercepted	CHEVIOT
19 Feb.	ABDUL HAMID	KOMEMIUT	Aux. schooner 293 tons	France	704	Intercepted	CHILDERS
1 Mar.	RONDINA 2	BONIM-VELOCHAMIM	Schooner	Yugoslavia	982	Intercepted	VENUS
28 Mar.	ESMERALDA	YEHIAM	Aux. schooner 650 tons	Italy	773	Intercepted	VERULAM
12 Apr.	VIVARA	TIRAT ZVI	-	Italy	810	Intercepted	VIRAGO
24 Apr.	SAN MICHELE	MISHMAR HAEMEK	-	France	785	Intercepted	CHEVRON
26 Apr.	TADORNE	NACHSHON CASTEL	French trawler	France	528	Intercepted	PELICAN
13 May	BOREA	LANITZACHON	-	-	243	Intercepted	CHIEFTAIN

Notes:

1. Colonial Office report dated 25 Nov. 47 gives the following details:
   a. 39 ships arrived of which 35 arrested prior to beaching.
   b. 11 ships forfeited, with 1 appeal dismissed by Privy Council and 8 outstanding.
   c. 24 cases where application for forfeiture in progress or under consideration.
   d. 1 ship sold by Palestine Government and 1 returned to owners.

Annex B:

Illegal Immigrant Ships' Names

APPENDIX 1: NAMES OF ILLEGAL IMMIGRANT VESSELS:
PERIOD OF NAVAL PATROLS, 1945–48

Name	Former and other name(s)	Hebrew name
ABDUL HAMID	SETTE FRATELLI	KOMEMIUT
ABRIL	ARTHEUS, ARGOSY	BEN HECHT
ADRIANA	ARIELLA	PALMACH
AGHIOS ANDREAS	–	HAVIVA REIK
AKBEL	–	BIRIAH
ALBERTINA	PIETRO	ALIYAH
ANAL	EARL OF ZETLAND	YEHUDA HALEVY
ARCHIMEDES	–	UMOT MEUCHADOT
ARIC SAIAM	ARIETE SALOM	HENRIETTE SZOLD
ASYA	–	TEL-HAI
ATHINA	–	RAFIAH
AVANTI	MARIA SERRA	KATRIEL YAFFE
BALBOA	NORSYD	HAGANAH
BOREA	TUGLIA CRISTINA	LANITZACHOR
BRUNHA	–	YOD DALET HALALEI GESHER HAZIV
CICILIO	CICINO VIAREGGIA ABBRUZIANA	YERUSHALAJIM HANETZVIA
COLON	BEAUHARNOIS	JOSIAH WEDGWOOD
DIMITRIOS	–	BEREL KATZENELSON
ESMERALDA	PEPPINO	YEHIAM
FEDE	CUDIO/OWEN SOUND	DOV HOS
FEDE II	–	ARBA HIRUYOT
FENICE	PHOENICIA	ELIAHU GOLOMB
FENICE II	–	BRACHA FULD
FERIDA	LCT 256	AF-AL-PI-CHEN
FRANCO	MERICA	LANEGEV
GALATA	GIAN PAOLO/AMILIA	SHEAR YASHUV
GUARDIAN	–	THEODOR HERZL
HOCHELAGA	–	HACHAJAL HA'IVRI

IDEROS	ISLE-DE-LA-ROSE	AMIRAM SHOCHET
KISMET ADALIA	NORIS ex VILA	WINGATE
LOCHITA	ANNA	KNESSET ISRAEL
LUCIANO M	–	SHIVAT ZION
MARIE	ANDARTA/AMORTA	HANNAH SZENISH
MARIA ANNICK	W.V. MARIE	HAPORTZIM
MARIA CHRISTINA	KARUGA	LO TAFCHIDUNU
MARIA GIOVANNI	–	KAF TET BENOVEMBER
MERICA	FRANCO	LANEGEV
NORTHLAND	–	MEDINAT HAJEHUDIM
ORIETTA	AGHA ORIENTE	LOCHAME HAGETAOT
OWEN SOUND	–	CADIO
PADUCAH	BIARRITZ	MORENVO/GEULAH
PAN CRESCENT	EL VALLE/CHAVER	ATZMAUTH/HA ACOT
PAN YORK	EL DIA	KIBBUTZ GALUJOT
PRESIDENT WARFIELD	–	EXODUS 1947
RAFFAELLUCCIA	ELIE	KADIMAH
RONDINA OF SAVONA	–	ENZO SERENI
RONDINA II	–	BONIM VELOCHAMIM
SAGOLEM	–	YAGUR
SAN BASILIO	–	See Note 1
SAN DEMETRIO	SODRA SVERIGE	LATRUN
SAN EUSEBIO	–	See Note 1
SAN PHILLIPO	EGIL/PATRIA/MOLEDET	SAMUEL GUSTAV HERMELIN
SAN MICHELE	SALVADOR	MISHMAR HAEMEQ
SAN MIGUEL	RUNEBERG/CHERUT	HAMA'PIL HA'ALMONI
SAN PHILLIPO	SAN FELIPE/EGIL/NESHER	MOLEDET
SAN PISERO	SAN SISSIMO	KAF GIMEL YORDEI HASIRA
SAN SPYRIDON	–	See Note 1
SIRIUS	SAN MARCO/ALBERTINA	DALIN
SMIRNI	SMYRNA/ISMIRNI/IZMIR	MAX NORDAU
SUSANNAH	ROSA	SHABTAI LUZINSKY
SYLVIA STARITA	–	LAMED HEI GIBOREI KFAR ETZION
TADORNE	–	NACSHON-CASTEL
TRADE WINDS	GRESHAM	HATIKVAH
ULUA	UNALAGA, ULUA	HAIM ARLOSSOROF
VIVARA	RINA	TIRAT ZVI
VRISSI	LADY VAGRANT	See Note 2

Notes:

1. Procured in Sweden but did not leave the Baltic.
2. Sank at Genoa in April 1947. Said to be due to an explosion and British underwater sabotage suspected locally.
3. Cover names allocated by Mossad are not all included above.

APPENDIX 2: HEBREW NAMES GIVEN TO VESSELS

Hebrew name	Meaning/translation
AF-AL-PI-CHEN	Despite All
ALIYAH	Immigration
ATHZMAUT	Independence
AMIRAM SHOCHET	One of 'The 23' lost 1941
ARBA HERUYOTH	Four Freedoms
ARBAASREI GIBOREI	14 Heroes of Aziv. Killed at Aziv in June 1946.
BEN HECHT	US playwright, Zionist and Revisionist supporter.
BERL KATZENELSON	Jewish socialist leader.
BIRIA	Jewish settlement, resisted British dislodgement.
BONIM VE'LOCHAMIM	Builders and fighters
BRACHA FULD	Female killed during Haganah operation in support of attempted landing.
HAIM ARLOSOROFF	Jewish Palestinian leader murdered by unknown assassins in 1933.
DALIN	Code name for E GOLOMB
DOV HOS	Labour leader killed in motor accident
ELIAHU GOLOMB	Founder of Haganah
ENZO SERENI	Labour leader and SOE parachutist executed by Germans.
GEULA	Redemption
GIBOREI ETZION	Heroes of Etzion. 35 Haganah members killed and mutilated by Arabs in ambush near Etzion.
HA PORTZIM	Blockade Runner (OR) Break Through
HACHAJAL HA'VIVRI	The Hebrew Fighter
HAMA'APIL HA'ALMONI	Unknown Refugee
HAKEDOSHA	The Holiness
HAGANAH	Jewish Defence Force
HANNAH SZENESH	Poet and SOE Palestinian parachutist executed by Germans.
HAPORTSIM	Break Through
HATIKVAH	Hope: Title of Jewish national hymn.
HAVIVA REIK	SOE Palestinian parachutist executed by Germans in Czechslovakia.
HENRIETTA SZOLD	Zionist and philanthropist (1860–1945)
JOSIAH WEDGWOOD	British Member of Parliament and Zionist sympathiser.
KADIMAH	Forward
KAF GIMEL YORDEI	'Twenty-three'. Jewish commando unit lost with British Army officer during war.
KAF TET BENOVEMBER	29th November. Date of UN resolution.
KATRIEL YAFFE	Commander onboard SS TIGER HILL. Killed in SOE operation 1941.
KIBBUTZ GALUYOT	Ingathering of Exiles
KNESSET ISRAEL	Jewish Community.
KOMEMIUT	Independence
LANEGEV	To the Negev
LAMED HEI GIBOREI KFAR ETZION	35 Heroes of Etzion

LANITZORCHON	To Victory
LATRUN	British internment camp.
LOCHAME HAGETAOT	The Fighters of the Ghetto
LO TAFCHIDUNU	Unafraid or You Shall Not Frighten Us
MAX NORDAU	Zionist Leader.
MEDINAT HAYEHUDAH	Jewish State
MERED HAGETADOT	Fighters of the Ghetto
MISHAL HAEMEQ	Kibbutz, repulsed Arab attack 1948.
MOLEDET	Patria (Homeland)
NACSHON-CASTEL	Operation to relieve Jerusalem 1948.
NEPTUNO	Neptune
PALMACH	Haganah Strike Force (Army).
RAFIAH	Internment camp.
SHABTAI LUZINSKI	Jewish Worker in Italy died in motor accident.
SHE'AR YASHUV	The Remainder Shall Return
SHIVAT ZION	Return to Zion
TEL HAI	Jewish settlement in Galilee, held off Arab attacks 1920.
TIRAI ZVI	A valiant Jewish settlement.
THEODOR HERZL	Father of political Zionism.
UMOT MEUCHADOT	United Nations.
WINGATE	British soldier (Chindit leader) and Zionist sympathiser when in Palestine 1938.
YAGUR	Settlement used as Palmach arms depot and destroyed by Police.
YEHIAM	Settlement repulsed Arabs 1948.
YEHUDA HALEVI	Distinguished Spanish Jew 12th-century poet and founder of modern Hebrew language.
YERUSHALAYIM HANETZURA	Jerusalem Besieged
YOD DALET HALALEI GESHER HAZIV	Casualties of Haganah operation 17 June 1946

Annex C:

Palyam Marine Sabotage Operations, 1945–47

2 Nov. 45   Three Police Launches at Haifa and Jaffa.
18 Aug. 46   HMT *Empire Heywood* at Haifa.
22 Aug. 46   HMT *Empire Rival* at Haifa.
13 Feb. 47   Two Royal Army Service Corps and a fishery Protection Launch at Haifa.
3 Apr. 47   HMT *Ocean Vigour* at Cyprus.
4 Apr. 47   HMT *Empire Rival* en route Egypt.
19 Jul. 47   HMT *Empire Lifeguard* at Haifa.

Annex D:

The Balfour Declaration

Foreign Office

November 2nd 1917

Dear Lord Rothschild,

I have much pleasure in conveying to you, on behalf of His Majesty's Government, the following declaration of sympathy with Jewish Zionist aspirations which has been submitted to and approved by, the Cabinet.

'His Majesty's Government view with favour the establishment in Palestine of a national home for the Jewish people, and will use their best endeavours to facilitate the achievement of this object, it being clearly understood that nothing shall be done which may prejudice the civil and religious rights of existing non-Jewish communities in Palestine, or the rights and political status enjoyed by Jews in any other country.'

'I should be grateful if you would bring this declaration to the knowledge of the Zionist federation.'

(signed)

Yours

Arthur James Balfour

(*Source:* Copied from photograph obtained from British Library)

Note:
1. Wording drafted by Lord Milner. (USofS Colonies – HofC debate 21 July 1937.)

Annex E:

Transfer of Harbour Defence Motor Launches to the Palestine Police 1946: A Tardy Process

Harbour Defence Motor Launches (HDMLs) were 72-foot twin-diesel-engined craft, rather smaller than the contemporary 120 foot Fairmile Motor Launches used for so many purposes in and after the Second World War. Originally equipped for anti-submarine purposes with sonar sets and depth charges, they also carried 20mm Oerlikon guns and machine guns. HDMLs were later renamed Seaward Defence Motor Launches and continued in service in the Royal Navy and elsewhere for many years, including the Hong Kong Flotilla (1949–1958) and hydrographic survey tasks.

FOLEM endorsed the Palestine Police's request (1 Feb.), noting that the HDMLs present in his area were already fully occupied in Greek waters and the Dodecanese, indeed one engaged on minesweeping tasks had been mined only recently. The application went on to the CinC who under cover of letter dated 23 February forwarded it to the Secretary of the Admiralty, suggesting alternatives for finding hulls from within his own command. A month passed before the section of the civilian secretariat dealing with operational matters, Military Branch, sought the views of the Colonial Office, who replied on 16 April strongly supporting the submission.

Nothing having been heard by the end of May, the CinC signalled (CinC Med 312006B May 45) requesting a reply, only to hear that the matter was receiving attention and a further signal would be made. It seems other branches within the Admiralty were still being consulted since on 24 July the Head of MF(L) noted that there was no objection and that the cost of an HDML was £14,000 exclusive of armament and stores. Since the craft were not to be sold as warships, but for civilian purposes, he felt that Treasury sanction was not necessary. By this time the Colonial Office had evidently been in touch with the Palestine Government, who threw a spanner in the works by asking that two of the larger Fairmile B Class Motor Launches be supplied instead of one of the HDMLs. In the meantime M Branch II signalled CinC Med that the preferred course was a straightforward sale and requested he establish whether the Palestine Government would be willing to purchase the boats. In the meantime two HDMLs with Gardner engines already on the station were to be earmarked and guidance on their value was sought.

On 16 September CinC Med reported that the Palestine Government were considering the proposal and that the value of each of his well used HDMLs was approximately £6,000. This signal crossed with a letter from FOLEM passing on a request for the B Class MLs. The CinC Med noted that their Lease Lend engines had to be returned to the United States of America but sent the request on to the Admiralty. Ten days later the High Commissioner for Palestine, who had taken in the message about engines for B Class MLs, telegraphed the Secretary of State for Colonies requesting three rather than two HDMLs. FOLEM was evidently in the picture and on 13 October signalled that the Palestine Government sought a total of three HDMLs, armed with a 40mm Bofors gun forward and a 20mm Oerlikon aft. M Branch now decided the Treasury did after all need to be consulted. On 3 November this was done, seeking agreement for a transfer to the Palestine Government free of charge, citing the war service and consequent poor state of Police launches they were replacing. The original cost of an HDML was given as £16,500, inclusive of armament, but those available were each worth £6,000.

At much the same time the Deputy First Sea Lord enquired at the daily meeting regarding progress with providing HDMLs for the Palestine Police. M Branch's representative responded that the Palestine Government was pressing for supply to be without cost and then confused HDMLs with another type of small craft and added, erroneously, that the HDMLs had Lend-Lease engines which must be returned. On the same day the High Commissioner (F.M. Viscount Gort) reported to the Colonial Office the loss of three Police launches by sabotage and requested an early decision on HDMLs. A Colonial Office note to the Admiralty, marked 'IMMEDIATE', brought about the desired effect and the Admiralty signalled approval for transfer of three HDMLs. This was to be without prejudice to eventual terms of transfer, which were still under consideration. CinC Med then ordered that HDMLs 1145, 1246 and 1277 be transferred to the Palestine Government as soon as they could be made ready. Captain Coastal Forces Mediterranean despatched HMMLs 1145 and 1246 and both craft were turned over to the Palestine Police at Haifa on 4 January 1946, one year after the original request and concurrent with the final departure from the Dodecanese of FOLEM's HDMLs which could not be spared from there earlier.

This was by no means the end of the tale. HMML 1277 had not been employed recently and so had been lying idle with little or no maintenance being done. Thus she left for Palestine after her sisters, on 26 January 1946, and was found by the Marine Division of the Palestine Police to be in need of extensive repairs and overhaul. (The defects have a note of reality since rudder blades required replating and the author experienced a detached rudder blade plate in a similar craft in 1956.) Since the Palestine Government were by then understood to be contracting with the Middle East disposal mission for Fairmile Launches, NOIC Haifa sought approval to defer transfer of 1277. Eventually, she was replaced by a sister-ship, HMML 1126.

By now the Treasury had responded to M Branch and that 'gifts' amounting to more than £12,000 could not be sanctioned. M Branch then wrote to the Colonial Office seeking the Palestine Government's long term intentions. On 20 May the Colonial Office telegraphed the Palestine Government enquiring if the craft would be retained permanently. But by the end of the summer the High Commissioner had decided the craft's low speed made them unsuitable for permanent acquisition. The Colonial Office then wrote to the Admiralty that more suitable craft were being sought and quoting a precedent for the loan continuing for the time being.

The High Commissioner had evidently taken expert counsel and on 7 September enquired if any of the 'Gay Corsair'-class Motor Gunboats (MGBs) were available, if not something else of that kind. The Colonial Office took up his cause and sought M Branch assistance for the Admiralty to make available fast diesel engined Motor Gun Boats (MGB). Three of the former Gay Corsair Fairmile F Class remained (MGBs 2003–5 but by then bearing Norwegian names). They were lying at Itchenor in an excellent state and about to be marketed at some £8,000 each. But circulation of the proposal within the Admiralty revealed that their Paxman Ricardo engines had an unfortunate history of unreliability and a life of only 700 running hours, also there were few spare parts. Nevertheless the Colonial Office requested something better be found, either then or in two or three years time. But the price for the HDMLs now came down to £3,000 each.

The next move was a visit to the Vice Chief of the Naval Staff (28 November) by the Head of the Palestine Police, who was having difficulty with the Colonial Office handling his needs effectively. Before any further correspondence via that conduit he wished to explore the loan of six craft capable of 16 knots with three days endurance and six harbour patrol craft, either Motor Fishing Vessels (MFV)s or HDMLs. On the following day the Naval Staff reported that B Class MLs met the specification and that six could be found from the 14 about to be put into reserve at Malta. There were ample spares. CinC Mediterranean also had 55 MFVs, not including 26 harbour craft at Malta, and could spare six, to be replaced from the UK. The Head of the Palestine Police was evidently already in touch with the CinC, who provided details of maintenance requirements, which led the Inspector General to conclude that maintenance of MLs would be beyond his resources. The same message was passed back to VCNS. The Inspector General had also heard that his Government had now agreed to purchase the HDMLs currently on loan. The same message was passed to VCNS.

At much the same time CinC Med informed M Branch that a considerable number of spare parts were being requested by the Palestinian Police and confirmation was then sought from the Colonial Office that their cost would be refunded. The outcome is not recorded but Head of MF(L) signalled on 2 April 48, not two months before the mandate ended, that payment for three HDMLs had been received on 23 December 47.

Annex F:

The Arab Reaction in Aden
to the United Nations Organisation's
Proposals for Partitioning Palestine

In December 1946 Naval forces outside and to the East of the Mediterranean were called on to assist with Arab reaction to news of the partition directed by the United Nations. At Aden a three day strike of Arabs started on 2 December and by the first evening led on to looting and burning in the Jewish quarter of the town of Crater. Troops were sent in and calmed the situation, but, by the following afternoon, it was out of control again. The situation continued to deteriorate despite all available troops, including Aden Protectorate Levies (native troops), being called out. Two destroyers, HMS *Cockade* (Lieutenant-Commander J. Cox RN) and HMS *Contest* (Lieutenant-Commander J.C. Cartwright RN) were in the vicinity, on passage for England with crews mainly composed of men due for discharge on grounds of age or service following the end of the war. The Governor requested assistance by these two ships and they arrived at Aden at midnight the same day (3 December).

Each destroyer immediately sent ashore an armed landing party composed of 1 officer and 40 men. *Contest*'s party was employed supporting Levies preventing trouble spreading to Steamer Point (the port area) where the physical presence of the warships and use of their searchlights at night helped maintain calm. The second landing party, from *Cockade*, travelled to Crater under the control of Acting Commander H.N.A. Richardson DSO DSC RN, who had arrived four days earlier to relieve the Resident Naval Officer (Commander J.G. Brodie RNVR). One-third of the Jewish Quarter of Crater had already been destroyed. The sailors backed up Levies and a small contingent of RAF NCOs in trying to enforce a curfew and dealing with numerous looters and snipers. They succeeded in this task and until the afternoon of the following day were mainly responsible for preventing further outbreaks of violence and producing some order out of the chaos.

HMS *Challenger* (Survey Ship) (Captain R.N. Southern RN) arrived 9 hours after the destroyers. Later in the day *Contest* sent two officers and

60 men to relieve the Crater party, whilst *Cockade* and *Challenger* augmented the Steamer Point contingent with 1 officer and 40 men and 1 officer and 25 men respectively. By dusk the situation in Crater was under fair control and attempts to set fire to Jewish property during the night were frustrated by Naval pickets, police and Levies. But the Levies had proved unreliable when called on to use firearms against their fellow Arabs and their ammunition had to be removed. (Captain Southern later commented regarding 'a soldier's constitutional right to join in any looting' but this was after additional allegations when British reinforcements arrived.)

The following forenoon (5 Dec), two companies of the North Staffordshire Regiment arrived by air from the Canal Zone and went to Crater. The Levies were withdrawn to their barracks whilst the Navy continued to patrol the Jewish Quarter and man barricades there. Old fires had broken out again and during the night there was sporadic sniping and occasional attempts to fire Jewish buildings. A total of 15 officers and 270 troops had arrived from the Middle East and the ships had landed 205 officers and men. By 6 December the ability of sailors manning barricades to establish friendly relations with both Arabs and Jews had achieved noticeably beneficial results. Casualties to date were 24 Arabs, 2 Indians and 75 Jews dead, with many more injured.

The situation then slowly improved but the naval landing parties remained ashore. No further Army reinforcements arrived and CinC Middle East Land Forces resisted pressure from the Chiefs of Staff to provide any. He felt the Navy should provide cruisers. In any case AOCinC Middle East lacked transport aircraft for moving more troops. (Head of Military Branch, Admiralty subsequently noted this was not how such matters should be conducted). In the meantime CinC East Indies signalled a date on which the destroyers were to depart, having the Admiralty's agreement not to divert his cruisers from events in which they were already engaged. However, the Governor intervened, wishing to retain *Contest* and *Cockade*. He demonstrated a mastery of both Colonial Regulations and King's Regulations and Admiralty Instructions by drawing Captain Southern's attention to articles which necessitated the Senior Naval Officer deferring to the wishes of the local Colonial administrator. The CinC then gave in and sent HMS *Manxman* (Captain L.F. Durnford-Slater RN)(Fast Minelayer) and HMS *Gambia* (Cruiser) (Captain A.J. Baker-Creswell DSO RN) (Cruiser) to arrive on 15 and 16 December respectively. The warships already present remained until 14 December, when *Challenger* departed to continue surveying tasks, and 15 December, when the destroyers sailed to arrive back in their home ports on Boxing Day (33). One Army company arrived as reinforcements on 17 December.

On board *Contest* and *Cockade* considerable tooth-sucking resulted from the BBC giving prominence to the arrival of the Army without any reference to the Navy. It turned out that neither the Chief of Naval Information (CNI) nor his Army opposite number had issued any information and the BBC were relying on a report from a Reuter correspondent. On 22 December CNI issued a statement that the two destroyers would be back on Boxing Day, having missed Christmas in their home ports due to the part they played at Aden. But by then the BBC and press were no longer interested.

Events at Aden demonstrate the consequences of decisions concerning Palestine for other areas under British rule, not to mention the whole Arab world

Sources

PUBLIC RECORD OFFICE FILES

1. ADM1:

14671	Recruitment of Palestinians (1941–1943)
18521	M.09777 Future of Admiralty Establishments and Naval Requirements in Levant, EM, Red Sea and Suez Canal Areas after the War.
18542	M.010248 CinC Med – Peacetime Policy of the Med Fleet
18560	Naval Command in the Mediterranean
18584	FOLEM ROP Aug 45
19358	FOLEM 169/00184/8 date 30 Jan 46 – RONDINE
19377	M.688 FOLEM Rope Oct 45
19401	M0974 FOLEM RoP Dec 45
19402	M983 D3 RoP Nov 45
19422	M1115 15thCS RoP Dec 45.
19433	M.01180 15th CS RoP Feb 46.
19501	M1761 Sale of HDMLS to Palestine
19508	M.1826 15thCS RoP Jan 46
19518	M.01991 AGIOS IOANNIS
19532	Interceptions May–Aug 46
19559	MO2401 CinC Med RoP Jan–Mar 46.
19560	M02403 Med Stn RoPs Jun 46.
19563	M02419 Med Cmd RoP Mar 46
19566	M02425 Med Stn RoP Jan 1946
19567	MO2426 Med Stn RoP Apr 46
19582	MO2603 GOFFE
19615	CinC Med RoP Aug–Sep46:
19757	BALBOA
19565	SAGOL
19566	Med Stn RoP Jan 46:

19572	VENUS arrest
19855	HMT DEVONSHIRE and Grand Mufti
19856	Summary of Jewish Immigration into Palestine by sea
19591	ARIELLA
20589	SAN DIMITRIO
20595	ATHINA Rescue
20598	LOHITA
20621	Med Stn RoPs Aug 46–Jan 47.
20630	DC (RAD) ROP Feb 47
20642	SAN FELIPO
20643	GUARDIAN
20661	ANAL
20671	CINCMEDFLT ROP Feb 47
20677	CinC Med No 2288 Med 47/001415/6/16 date 30 Aug 47
20684	Return of illegal immigrants to France.
20685	PRESIDENT WARFIELD.
20694	LUCIANO
20730	RoP RAD Med Apr 47
20761	Suspect 208 ex-BRUHA
20777	ex-SIRINA Behaviour on passage
20778	HofC statement
20789	Palestine Illegal Immigration Policy post *Warfield*
20793	PANS
20917	Note to PM pre WARFIELD
21087	PANs Dec 47/Jan 48
21089	Anti-Jewish Disturbances in Aden 1947
21091	LO TAFHIDUNA
21092	'29 NOVEMBER 1947'
21094	HAMID
21095	CICILIO
21102	SYLVIA STARITA
21103	ESMERALDA
21106	Maritime International Law: Diversion and Detention of Vessels on the High Seas.
21108	VIVARA

2. CO 537:

1705	Palestine Immigration
1706	Immigration into Palestine
1711–1714	Action Against Jewish Organisations
1720–1721	Ditto
1793–1801	Palestine Immigration
1802–1804	Measures taken to counteract illegal immigration

1812–1813	Illegal Immigration
2367–2369	Palestine Immigration
2371–2383	Measures taken to counteract illegal immigration
2384–2389	Illegal Immigration
2393	Illegal Immigration
2396–2402	Illegal Immigration
2404	Illegal Immigration

3. FO 371:

61802   Palestine – Immigration

4. HMS NEWCASTLE

OP/5811 dated 15 April 1948
OP/5852 dated 25 April 1948
OP/5854 dated 27 April 1948

BOOKS

The Algerines, Jack Williams. J.F. Williams, 1995.
BR 513 – Syria, Geographical Handbook Series – Naval Intelligence Division. Revised edition 1943.
BR 514 – Palestine and Transjordan, Geographical Handbook Series – Naval Intelligence Division. Revised edition 1943.
The Big Gun Monitors, I. Buxton. World Ship Society – Trident Press, 1978.
The British in Palestine, B. Wasserstein. Royal Historical Society, 1978.
By Sea and Land, R. Neillands. Weidenfeld and Nicolson, 1987.
CB 03165, *The Campaign Against Massed Illegal Jewish Immigration into Palestine – Nov. 45–Aug. 47*, 1948.
The Chariot of Israel: Britain, America and the State of Israel, Lord Harold Wilson. Weidenfeld and Nicolson, 1981.
Clandestine Immigration into Palestine: 1938–1942 and The Post-War Years, articles by P.H. Silverstone.
The Egyptian Expedition, J.H. Rose Ch. XIX in *The Cambridge Modern History*, Vol. VIII, Cambridge University Press, 1904.
Exodus 1946, D.G. Holly. Little, Brown, 1969. Revised edition US Naval Institute Press, 1995.
Exodus Calling, N. Degani. Ministry of Defence Publishing House, Israel, rev. edn, 1997.
The Friends, N. West. Butler and Tanner, 1984.

Ha'Haganah, ed. M. Naor, Ministry of Defence Publishing House, Israel and IDF Museum, 1987.

A History of Europe, H.A.L. Fisher. Edward Arnold, 1936.

A History of Zionism, W. Laqueur. Weidenfeld and Nicolson, 1972.

Illegal Immigration into Palestine, unpublished Naval Historical Branch note by Captain Macintyre, 1966.

Interception and Boarding of Illegal Jewish Immigration Ships, synopsis by Lieutenant-Commander (later Rear-Admiral) D.A. Dunbar-Nasmith, DSC.

John Strachey, H. Thomas. Eyre Methuen, 1973.

Mehemet Ali, W. Alison Phillips. Ch. in *The Cambridge Modern History*, Vol. X. Cambridge University Press, 1908.

Memoires, L.A.F. de Bourrienne. 1829–31.

Memoirs: The Memoirs of Field Marshal Lord Montgomery, Lord B.N. Montgomery. Collins, 1958.

The Origins and Evolution of the Palestine Problem, Part 1: The United Nations. New York, 1978.

Palestine and The Great Powers, M.J. Cohen. Princeton University Press, 1982.

Peace and War: A Soldier's Life, Lt-Gen. Sir Frederick Morgan, KCB. Hodder and Stoughton, 1961.

Psychological Warfare and Propaganda: Irgun Documents, ed. E. Tavin and Y. Alexander. Scholarly Resources Inc., 1982.

Publish It Not: The Middle East Cover-up, (Lord) C. Mayhew and M. Adams, Longman, 1975.

Running the Palestine Blockade: The Last Voyage of Paducah, Capt. R.W. Patzert. US Naval Institute Press, 1994.

Second Exodus: The Full Story of Jewish Illegal Immigration to Palestine 1945–1948, Ze'ev Venia Hadari. Vallentine Mitchell, 1991.

War Diary Naval, 9 June–11 July 1941.

Wavell: Scholar and Soldier, Vol. I, J. Connell. Collins, 1964.

Yarrows, 1865–1977. Yarrow and Co., 1977.

ARTICLES, THESES AND OTHER SOURCES

'Arab Revolt of 1936', Y. Bauer. *New Outlook*, 1966.

'British Strategy and The Palestine Question, 1936–39', M.J. Cohen, *Journal of Contemporary History*, Oct. 1972.

'Cadastral Mapping of Palestine, 1858–1928', D. Gavish and R. Kark, *Geographical Journal*, Vol. 159, Pt 1, Mar. 1993.

'Details of Jewish Illegal Ships', F. Liebreich, 1997, unpublished dissertation.

'From Cooperation to Resistance: The *Haganah* 1938–46', Y. Bauer, *Middle Eastern Studies*, 1966.

Godfrey Papers, unpublished papers of late Admiral J.H. Godfrey, CB.

'Interception and Boarding of Illegal Jewish Immigration Ships', synopsis by Lieutenant-Commander (later Rear-Admiral) D.A. Dunbar-Nasmith, DSC.

'L and M Class Fleet Destroyers', M.J. Dyer.

'Palestine: Britain's Crown of Thorns', Christopher Sykes. BBC 'British Empire' Series 1972.

The Paris Salon, Christie's New York catalogue, 11 Feb. 97.

'Moyne Assassination, Nov. 44: A Political Analysis', M.J. Cohen, *Middle Eastern Studies*, Oct. 1979.

'Palyam', Yehuda Ben-Tzur, 1998.

'The Revolt of 1936', B. Kalkas, in *The Transformation of Palestine*, ed. I. Abu-Lugzod, 1971.

Index

Note: entries followed by *ill.* appear in the plate section. Sub-entries are arranged in chronological order.